16.39

D0728944

IN *the* EMBRACE
of the
ALLIGATOR
fictions from Cuba

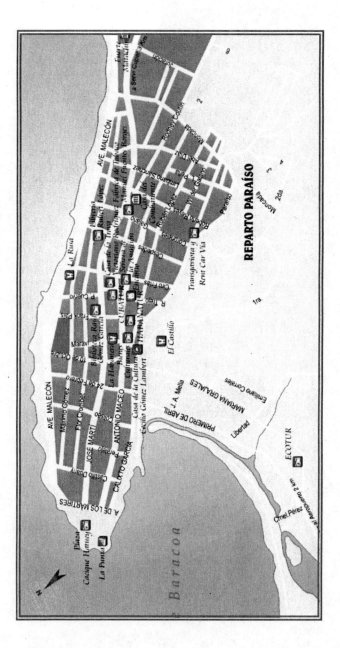

IN *the* EMBRACE *of the* ALLIGATOR

fictions from Cuba

❧

AMANDA HALE

thistledown press

© Amanda Hale, 2011
All rights reserved

No part of this publication may be reproduced or transmitted in any form or by any means, graphic, electronic or mechanical, including photocopying, recording, or any information storage and retrieval system, without permission in writing from the publisher or a licence from The Canadian Copyright Licensing Agency (Access Copyright). For an Access Copyright licence, visit www.accesscopyright.ca or call toll free to 1-800-893-5777.

Thistledown Press Ltd.
118 - 20th Street West
Saskatoon, Saskatchewan, S7M 0W6
www.thistledownpress.com

Library and Archives Canada Cataloguing in Publication

Hale, Amanda
In the embrace of the alligator / Amanda Hale.
Short stories.
ISBN 978-1-897235-87-4

I. Title.
PS8565.A4313I67 2011   C813'.6   C2011-901712-1

Cover photograph *Plaza San Juan Dios by Night* by Jan-Olof Olsson
Cover and book design by Jackie Forrie
Printed and bound in Canada

APR 05 2012

 Canada Council
for the Arts

Conseil des Arts
du Canada

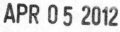 SASKATCHEWAN
ARTS BOARD

 Canadian
Heritage

Patrimoine
canadien

Thistledown Press gratefully acknowledges the financial assistance of the Canada Council for the Arts, the Saskatchewan Arts Board, and the Government of Canada through the Canada Book Fund for its publishing program.

IN *the* EMBRACE
of the
ALLIGATOR
fictions from Cuba

For my Cuban friends, with enduring gratitude for their warm-hearted hospitality, for their generosity of spirit, and for their extraordinary talent of inclusion.

Contents

11   First Steps, Last Steps

29   El Caballo de Rosamund

45   Señora Amable Ponce

53   La Colonial

66   Salón de Belleza

78   Creative Non-Fiction

92   Her New Red Dress

102   What's So Special?

110   The Death of Pedro Iván

127   The Barbacoa

132   La Terraza

136   Palace of the Princess

145   Mirian Zelda Dreams

152   Erminda's House

164 *Rio Miel*

180 *The Same Mouth*

199 *Between the Sheets*

204 *Witnesses*

210 *Lorenzo's Museum*

216 *The Prisoner*

218 *Faux Pas*

230 *Hard Guavas*

234 *Calle Enramada*

240 *Ololo*

246 *Caridad and the Magic Maleta*

251 *The Whales were Trying to Tell Us*

265 *Epilogue — Day of the Tsunami*

Onaldo slept and dreamed of El Caimán, the grand alligator that was Cuba and which had slept for centuries, half submerged, its jaw in Oriente, its tail in el norte, and its eyes slits behind which the force of nature dreamed. In Onaldo's dream he saw the creature's eyes open and they were gold and red like molten metal swirling in a vortex which drew him in. He was not afraid. He felt safe in the embrace of his island . . .

First Steps, Last Steps

February 2007, Havana

HE LAY SLUMPED IN THE CORNER, BARELY visible as I entered and opened the shutters to let the sun pour in, warming him. I looked at him for a long time as he lay there, his face impassive, and tried to imagine how he might be and how I might tend and strengthen him. His legs were twisted, as though they'd been torqued and broken, his feet wrapped in burlap with cardboard soles and twine to hold them firm. I'd done the left one, Leila the right, our hands twisting and binding. It was Sunday, our day off, but I couldn't stay away, so I'd left her sleeping and walked alone through Central Havana, savouring the brief freshness of the early morning streets, still wet from the water trucks that had scoured the day's filth into the night.

The suitcase was open, lid leaning against the wall, fragments of cloth escaping in wisps like Christopher's cigarette smoke. Only two weeks since we'd arrived with the case full of materials — scissors and surgical gloves, chicken wire, cheese-cloth, glue, fabric, and rice paper from Toronto's Chinatown. I mixed a batch of glue, tore strips of rice paper and added a layer to the hands hanging on long threads from the ceiling. The tapered fingers seemed to reach, as Christopher's fingers had when I'd placed tulips in his dead hands, their stems long and thin like our bodies, full of sap. We'd surrounded him with flowers — lilies and daffodils, iris and hyacinth. I still felt the smooth firmness of his flesh on my lips, dense as marble, and I was lifted out of myself by the memory of my brother's beauty. A sudden movement jolted me as though Christopher had come to life, my head twisting, expecting to see our *cimarrón* rise from his corner stumbling on boneless legs, his arms flailing. But he lay motionless, waiting for me, watching.

I tore wide strips of paper and crossed to his sunlit corner. A fountain splashed in the courtyard below and birds were hopping and scratching amidst the tough worm-like roots of palm trees. A loamy smell mixed in the warm air with the aroma of coffee from the restaurant across the street. Soon the flower sellers would come, trundling their barrows of lilies and sunflowers, laden for another clear blue day with a cruise ship in port and the promise of Havana Vieja's streets crowded with tourists. I dipped the paper in a mixture of white glue and water and wrapped his neck, cradling him in my arms. Would he survive? He was silent and submissive to the care of my hands — hands that had so recently held my brother's hand, covered by my sisters' and mother's hands - the game we'd played as children that always ended in a scramble of clapping and laughter as all our hands flew into the air.

His body seemed to shift as I laid his neck gently on the floor in a patch of sun. I felt the increasing heat and that prickly sensation that takes hold of the body, summoning its sensations, trapping us inside the discomfort of our sweating skin as the day intensifies. Just then the familiar cacophony of Los Zanqueros started up in the distance, overlaid with the monotonous beat of *Chan Chan* from the café opposite — *Cuando Juanita y Chan Chan en el mar cernían arena* . . . I leaned from the balcony and watched the stilt-walkers advancing up the narrow street, tourists appearing from nowhere, clustering, snapping their digital cameras at the tall figures dressed in carnival colours. A woman cradled her baby as she danced on hoofed stilts and a handsome boy trumpeted into the blue sky as my man slept in the sun, gathering strength against a future that threatened and beckoned, daring him to stand again.

Leila and I lodged at Cíntia Rodriguez' *casa particular* in a high-ceilinged room that opened onto a central courtyard with a small fountain in the centre, almost hidden by cascading plants. Water drizzled from the mouth of a stone dolphin and we listened at night to the trickling water making a river of our whispered words as we talked about our *cimarrón* and planned for the next day. Then I'd lie awake wondering what lay beyond Havana. When I slept finally I dreamed of him and how he would look when he was whole. We were woken each morning by the sound of scales from the piano teacher's apartment upstairs. She had a variety of students — beginners who stumbled their way over the keys, and more advanced players who had mastered Chopin, Mozart, Bach and Beethoven. Cíntia hated them all and complained as her cook, Caridad, served breakfast, beaming and wringing her hands with pleasure as she watched us eat. Caridad's hands were like boneless white doves. "*¿Esta bien? ¿Quiere más?*" she'd ask, raising her thinly pencilled brows.

During the next week our man darkened and grew. We attached his hands, breath-inflated surgical gloves with elongated papier-mâché fingers, and stained them with strong tea brought from Canada. Into his left palm Leila painted a circle of blue crossed with a line of earth, and a tiny tree branching out along his fingers, roots grasping the cluster of veins at his wrist.

His strong neck enabled him to stand erect finally, suspended from the same lines that had held his hands. We swaddled him with a layer of transparent plastic, leaving a trail which appeared in a photograph as a luminous path defining his way, then sewed shirt and trousers onto this plastic skin and painted a red tree on his back branching into the chest — its roots blood vessels to irrigate nascent lungs. With a mixture of ochre and umber I darkened his pallor while Leila ridged gluey cheesecloth across his skull and scumbled it blue-black. I moulded ears close to the head, gave him sight, smell, touch and taste, while with wire and paper Leila made a heart and opened his chest and anchored it there, red veins trailing in defiance of gravity, feeding like wild orchids on the thick air of the Havana afternoon.

Next morning Leila stopped short as she entered the gallery, almost tripping me in my urgency to see him. Our *cimarrón* was alive. He commanded the long colonial gallery with a gesture of defiance, his body twisted for a final glance at what he left behind as he ran for freedom — a dog made of ribbed banana leaves slashed with bright red, small piles of earth, bone, salt and sugar, tiny glass vessels of blood and water surrounding a woman reclining in the courtyard of the Casa Blanca. His feet carried him forward, locked in that moment, an African slave escaping to the mountains, only to return in the night to sabotage the sugar mill machinery.

"I'm shocked each time I see him," Leila said at midday. "I can't stop thinking he's real."

I was crouched by the empty suitcase, (it still smelled smoky like Chris's apartment), and when I looked up I saw Chris walking across the linoleum floor of the hospital caféteria, his long legs wobbly, pants hanging loose. How he'd turned, grinning with the effort of it, holding us captive as we'd watched him make his slow way.

"Come on, let's get you back to the ward."

Sarah and Julia on either side of him. His feet shuffling. He would have fallen had not my sisters held him, his fragility cushioned by the steadiness of their generous bodies.

The bus was cold. I put my jacket on and settled into a window seat, but still the frigid, over-conditioned air shivered through me as I watched people on the other side of the glass move slowly through the sweltering heat. We pulled out of Havana, my first trip outside the capital, on a twenty-one hour journey to Baracoa. My plan was to start there and work my way back via Santiago, Holguín, Trinidad, Cienfuegos, Santa Clara . . . but part of me was still in the gallery, crouched in the corner, watching our *cimarrón* for signs of life.

At our opening the viewers had circled him, staring intently, and I had watched them, wondering if they too felt his magnetism and promise. We had arranged a performance by two dancers — a pale, dark-haired girl who'd stood behind our languid woman lounging in her rattan chair while a mulatto boy with a bundle of dreadlocks had circled and emerged from the *cimarrón*, leaving him like a long shadow. They had danced the history of blood mixing in small vessels, earth and bone scattering as they'd dashed each other to the floor. She'd drawn his story, a long red cord, from his silent mouth, then she'd wound her body with it, circling and spiralling until she was bound to him forever. And he had picked her up like a white bird trailing feathers and carried her from that room whose walls were covered with four generations of colonial mural fragments — stepping out of history into a future called Cuba.

The first stop was in Matanzas — a word which means slaughters — named for the drowning of thirty Spanish soldiers crossing a river to attack an aboriginal camp on the far shore.

The native fishermen whose help they'd enlisted had flipped the boats and the heavily armored Spanish had drowned. It was a dinner break but I wasn't hungry. When everyone piled back on the bus and we started up again my mind drifted. I knew that the largest colonial sugar plantations had been in Matanzas and I imagined my *cimarrón* chained in the hull of a roiling ship not knowing where he was going, to a small island where his blood would change the history of the world, mixing with Spanish, Taíno, Chinese, European . . . I watched endless acres of sugar cane rustling, shimmering green-gold in the evening light, and saw him running through the tall cane, a blur of limbs racing for freedom, the red dog chasing him, my hands swollen with his gesture and with the animal that pursued him as I rode south, hunched inside my jacket, still in love with our rebel. I didn't know then that I was called. I entered that night of darkness and hunger like a sleepwalker.

Baracoa

His room was on the first floor of a flat-topped building on Calle Coronel Cardoza. Each afternoon as he walked home from work he passed a mural celebrating Fidel, Che, Camilo, Jose Martí, Antonio Maceo . . . all the revolutionary heroes, fading now in the fierce afternoon sun. His doorway was a giant maw with a broken-toothed sidewalk where the stones had heaved and settled all crooked.

Onaldo climbed the steep uneven stairs, his shoulders hunched as he reached the dark hallway with its damp concrete floor and the communal toilet next to a bucket of standing water by a cavernous sink. In his room was a narrow bed, a wardrobe, a chair, a small table. Framed photographs of the landlady's grandparents stood on top of the wardrobe where his shirts hung — green, gold, checkered blue — all from the *tienda de ropa reciclada.* He hit a switch and the fan whirred to life, pushing humid air around the room. No power cuts today — a blessing.

Onaldo sat at the table and began his work. He was soon absorbed, sorting through a sheaf of papers, making notations with a red pen gripped between his fingers, lop-armed spectacles perched on his fleshy nose. Once he'd found the room and made his decision everything had changed. He'd begun to write again. Everything seemed possible. On his days off he would crowd into the back of a *camioneta,* joining the crush of people who stood like cattle, bumping through dusty streets into the countryside where the air was cooler. He would visit with the *campesinos,* listen to their stories, kneel before their altars. Esmeralda had a ginger lily growing near the entrance to her one-room house and the fragrance of the white flower filled the dark interior. She was ninety-one years old, knew all about herbs and remedies, and her altar to Osain, the one-eyed, one-legged, one-armed healer, dominated the room and drew Onaldo to his knees. He saw Esmeralda now, her wrinkled face, her knob-knuckled hands, and heard her high quavering voice as he wrote in his firm hand, the letters sloping and rounded like his body.

He leaned into the wall, rocking on the legs of his chair as he sifted in his mind through the roots of Baracoa — the history of his people enslaved, shipped from Africa, worked to death on sugar plantations, their bodies fallen to earth, angels of bone and salt, sweat separating, absorbed by the earth, feeding the plants that would heal their progeny. As he rocked Onaldo heard a voice, faint but insistent. He couldn't understand the words, but they had an urgency that stirred him. In his head a television blinked coloured images into the room where Migdalia sat, legs curled under her, watching the *novela* . . . twenty years ending in separate lives lived behind the curtained doorways of two separate bedrooms, Yarisel in a cot beside him . . . *"Abuelo, Abuelo, leeme un cuento."* He picked her up, but it wasn't his granddaughter he held. It was Izabel, three years old, child of his first marriage. This was how he saw her still, the daughter he'd lost to the streets. She hadn't told them she was a *jinetera*, a jockey girl riding tourists for money. Carmen, with a mother's intuition, had guessed . . . the new clothes, expensive jewellery, makeup and nail polish . . . Izabel had married a Canadian tourist and escaped to Montréal. The marriage hadn't lasted, but there was a granddaughter in Montréal.

"If I had convertible currency I would go there, to the north, and find her. I would bring my granddaughter home."

His chair landed squarely on four legs, splintering Migdalia, Izabel, Carmen, wiping the screen blank. He brushed his hand against the stubble of his cheek and shook his head, glancing at his watch. He was hungry, but it was early yet. He hunched over the table again and began writing, his red pen pressing into the pale underside of his long fingers as they reached back into the history of Baracoa and beyond, to Africa.

Minerva put a plate of pork and gravy in front of him with a mound of rice and beans and a sideplate of fried plantain. *"Buen provecho."* Onaldo smiled as he picked up a fork and lowered his face to the business of eating. Since the move he'd been eating at Minerva and Rolando's house. There were no cooking facilities in the building on Coronel Cardoza, so he gave his *libreta* to Minerva and she collected his food rations at *la bodega* and cooked for him. Some days he ate in the street, sandwiches and *refrescos* at roadside stalls. Everything had a temporary feeling since the move, as though he were waiting, marking time, his heart beating uselessly in anticipation of something he couldn't even guess at, and that indeed might never happen. When he'd left Carmen and moved in with Migdalia it had been temporary, yet here he was twenty years later, still waiting. In Cuba we wait, he thought. For decades I've been waiting for something to change. And now what am I waiting for — music at my funeral? When his plate was empty Onaldo asked for more. Sometimes he'd eat two full plates at Minerva's table and would still want more, like a teenager. His body had no faith in the next meal, as though that time, that 'Special Period,' had robbed him of his capacity for satisfaction, leaving him with a gnawing emptiness, as though his hunger could never be satisfied. After his second plate he sat a while with Rolando who was sucking his teeth and prodding at them with a matchstick. They rehashed the day, Rolando complaining about the neighbour's pigs that had broken through the fence and trampled his vegetable plot, rooting for the tender carrots he'd looked forward to harvesting. After a while Onaldo excused himself, intending to return to Coronel Cardoza and work on his manuscript. But he found himself lingering on the main street, seeking the company of strangers, waiting for something, that voice again in the back of his head, stronger now, insistent.

I found a *casa particular* with a small but passable room, and a winding staircase onto the roof with a breathtaking view over the town. After a meal of chicken and rice, served by the vigilant landlady, I lay on the bed, dragged down to a depth where there was no light and no memory. I'd slept fitfully on the bus, waking through the night cold and hungry, and had dreamed of Christopher, the mystery of his difficult life still unfolding. I had discovered more about him since his passing than in all those years of being his youngest sister. There had been something repulsive to me about him despite his dark good looks, something that made me tense when we'd share the obligatory family kiss. Speeding through the Cuban night in a refrigerated bus, I had awoken with a new awareness of my brother, something inexplicable, as though he had spoken to me from whatever realm he now dwelt in, and my habitual pockets of caution were cleansed with what I can only describe as love — something bright and burning which freed me from fear. In his final weeks we had begun to heal our rift, becoming like children again with our two sisters. But now I realized that it had been only a beginning and that my brother was revealing himself to me in a way I had never imagined him. He was dashing, rakish, almost seductive. They say we only dream about ourselves, but when we allow the dead to inhabit us and live through us where do the distinctions begin?

I was completely disoriented when I woke, not recognizing the strange little room, which was really no more than a narrow walkway around the double bed. It was nine-thirty. The sky was dark and a golden moon hung suspended like a cardboard cutout in a school play. I splashed my face, brushed my teeth, and ran my fingers through my hair, which was thick with heat and humidity.

The light of television screens flickered from open doorways along the narrow street of Diez de Octubre, strobe-lighting my uneven path. Above me the moon, still unbelievable. The drumbeat of dance music vibrated in the air, growing louder as I reached the main street and saw light spilling onto the street from a crowded bar. I glanced in and almost immediately a woman's voice called my name. "Karina!" An arm reached out to grab me. It was my friend, Anna, from Montréal. She'd been in Havana with us and had left early, supposedly bound for Isla de Juventud. I hadn't expected to see her in Baracoa. She pulled me inside and shouted in my ear as we watched the folkloric dancers leap and whirl to the rhythm of the drums, Changó pacing back and forth, menacing us with his flashing eyes and his thunderbolt stick.

When the show was over and the musicians began selling CDs I became aware of someone watching me. I turned and saw a man with a steady gaze leaning into the wall in the corner. He smiled at me and I smiled back, elated still with the passion of the dancers. Then he pushed away from the wall and began to move slowly towards me, his long limbs loose as though he were in slow motion, that smile illuminating his face, and for a moment I had a flash of our *cimarrón* breaking free, coming to life. Then he was beside me, his hand on my arm, and he spoke in Spanish, his voice deep and dark, enfolding me. I could hear Anna and her German friend, Rosamund chattering in the background, but everything had changed. The world was a liquid place, the street outside a river with water swirling around our ankles as we stepped into it after what seemed like hours of talking in the crowded bar where no one existed but the two of us within a press of bodies. Moonlight bathed his face, bleaching one side, running in rivulets down his neck. I wanted to raise my hand to that neck, to touch it and remember it, but I simply watched his mouth, his startling pink tongue and strong white teeth pushing his lips forward, a river of words pouring out, carrying me.

An ancient church loomed before us like crumbling bone in the moonlight as we walked towards Parque Central.

"I'll take you to the Casa de la Trova," he said, clasping my hand in his.

Onaldo's uncle had been a famous singer, he told me, *un trovador popular,* and his portrait hung there at La Trova. Music flared from the open doors, consuming the night air like a fire. I stared up at the portrait on the far wall looking for a resemblance as the dancers jostled against me, hips swinging, feet tripping deftly, arms flying high above their whirling bodies. I took my place within the circle of his arms.

"Did your mother teach you to dance?"

"Everyone dances in Cuba. It's like breathing. We danced in the house, on the street, at school, everywhere. My father played the trumpet. He wanted me to play, his only son. But I have no talent for music. I'm a writer. That is what I do."

I took the thread of his story and wound my body with it as he moved me around the dancefloor. I stopped translating and felt his life bloom inside me, felt the dance in myself, emerging from the final shuffling of my brother, the stiff-legged stumbling of our mother as we'd made our way to the lakeshore to cast his ashes on the water. I danced for them, the first and last steps, the circle of my life closing on this certainty.

We lay on his narrow bed in the dark room, cracks of light splitting the shutters. The rain fell in torrents and he held me close as he told me his dream. He said he'd dreamed of Izabel, his daughter, of holding her, and had been surprised to wake with me in his arms, a white woman from another country. He caressed my face with his white palms and gazed at me, unbelieving. For two days and nights we were inseparable, drinking each other in with an unquenchable thirst. I couldn't stop smiling. Then, on the third night, as I lay on his bed, my hands cupped around his patient face, recognition fired my fingers and smouldered through my body, lighting me like a beacon in the storm that swept us, drenched, onto the shore.

"We're living in a bubble," I said. "What will happen when it bursts? I wish you could come with me to Santiago."

"I'll come," he said, smiling. Simple as that. And I saw how we could leave together, expand our world, the next step.

The switchback of La Farola, the road leading away from Baracoa, winds through mountainous jungle, west towards Guantánamo and Santiago de Cuba. I drifted, my head on Onaldo's shoulder, new sounds curling in my mouth, reshaping my tongue — *amante mío, dulcemente, suavemente, papaya, la lengua de almohada* — words and phrases fluttering like bright birds trapped — *rodeado de sonrisas, asombro, siento tan placer, burbuja, beneplácito, bienestar, anidar en tus brazos* . . . Both of us writers, we shared words, the sensuality and music of the sounds, the way the tongue and lips and teeth caress each other in the slippery making of our words. I had to keep looking at Onaldo, I couldn't help it, I couldn't believe in his miraculous existence unless I could see him. I was in a haze of constant desire, standing in a room filled with light from long, long ago. He held me in his arms through the five-hour journey, and we wove into each other, burrowing and nestling against the future. Time was short. We were held by our desire, a web cradling us over a canyon of disbelief. In my backpack was a plane ticket to Havana.

He read to me in our hotel room. His brown chest was naked, and he held a sweating beer in his hand as he leafed through the pages of his manuscript, eager as a lover. I sat on the arm of his chair and leaned over his shoulder to read the words, not yet trusting my ear, and saw a riot of marginal notations in red, insertions and densely worked text, all handwritten over the original blue writing. I closed my eyes and backtracked through my life to the hideout under the kitchen table, a small child listening for the sense of things in that strange place so far from the soul's home, and I began to understand the story behind the words, the record of Onaldo's life in Baracoa, his journeys into the countryside to unearth the long-buried lives of Africans sold into slavery, bringing with them to another world their own gods and goddesses. I felt the collective grace of their lives, their endurance and survival, and the uncomfortable complicity of my own, an outsider. But when I coupled with him all my knowledge fell away and I was free.

He took me to Milnovecientos, a restaurant with a huge framed testimonial in the lobby, in the bold hand of Fidel Castro. This was thrilling to me, excited as I then was about the Revolution. Leila and I had painted a mural depicting the triumphs of the Revolution before we created our installation on the painful colonial history that preceded it.

"This is where we came for the wedding supper," he said as we took our seats on the terrace upstairs, "With Izabel and Michel, before she married him and went to Montréal."

We ordered prawns, rice, salad, and cold glasses of beer. A group of musicians played in the corner of the terrace and the trumpeter, an old man with dark skin and soulful eyes, came to our table and played *Dos gardenias para ti,* his trumpet muted and sweet. Onaldo's eyes glistened and I didn't know if it was the memory of his father that moved him or of his lost daughter and the grandchild he'd never seen. Death and absence are twins.

Later I watched him sleep with his head thrown back in a gesture of abandonment. He looked like a boy despite his fifty-seven years, his face resting on my silk blouse, brown arms curved, hands loose against the whiteness of the sheet, legs slightly bent as though he were running in eternal pursuit of something. I lay down beside him, pressing my breasts and belly into his back, and wrapped one arm across his body, the other cradling his curly head.

La Iglesia de la Caridad del Cobre is at the top of a long winding hill, and as we climbed I felt we were moving step by step into a world of credibility.

"Montréal is close to Toronto," I heard myself say. "I can take you there. We'll find your daughter."

Our hands entwined, the blinding sun, the sweetness of our skin touching. And the smell of warm wax and yearning as we entered the sudden darkness of the vaulted church. The Virgin of Charity wore a golden dress.

"She is Ochún," Onaldo said, "Our Santería orisha, a goddess with human qualities who governs love."

He told me how she'd been rescued from the ocean by three sailors in a storm, how the wooden figure had been bone dry when drawn from the water, how the sea was instantly becalmed. I stepped forward close to the railing and looked up into the face of the little doll, invested with so many desires, and I prayed for our love to endure. Then I threw in a coin for Caridad, the cook in Havana.

"You must go to the church of the Virgen de la Caridad del Cobre and make this offering for me," she'd said, pressing a coin into my palm as I was setting out. "It is near Santiago de Cuba and it is our holiest sanctuary. I am named for her."

The next morning we were woken early by a call from the receptionist. I dressed quickly and folded my nightgown into my pack while Onaldo showered. As we left I took a last glance at the room I would remember forever. A taxi was waiting for us outside on Calle Enramada and we clung to each other in the back during the all-too-short ride to Antonio Maceo airport. After I'd checked in we sat drinking coffee in silence, sharing a ham and cheese sandwich that tasted like sawdust.

We went outside to say goodbye. I watched the palms against the gathering blueness of the sky. Strange how pale and soft the early mornings are after the blooming of the night sky with its riot of stars — how the sky intensifies gradually from the moment of dawn, building towards that piercing midday blue. I could hardly bear to look at him then. I held him blindly, my face against the thin cotton of his shirt. I thought for a moment that I might break down and cry, but I didn't. I suffered the silence with him and let him go, our lips bruised, stained with parting.

I walked through the glass doors into the airport without looking back, passed through security and entered the waiting lounge. Then I went to the window and watched Onaldo. He stood on the sidewalk, his small bag of belongings clutched in his hand. I knew exactly what was inside — his toothbrush, a yellow shirt, spare socks and underwear, his rubber thong sandals — *chancletas* — wrapped in newspaper, and a bottle of *Voltaje* cologne. I remembered my brother's belongings handed to me in a green garbage bag, in the hospital after his death — his toothbrush, paint-splattered spectacles, address book, bank book, a fountain pen, and the large brown shoes that finally broke my heart and sent me headlong down the Toronto sidewalk, sobbing and gasping for breath like the runner I'd been as a child, running away from the family lodged inside me.

Onaldo seemed lost, walking one way, then another, looking around as though searching for something. I knew that he was going to stop in Guantánamo to see his mother and sister on the journey back. Perhaps he was considering the best way to get to the bus station. We hadn't discussed anything immediate, only my return to Havana and the idea of a journey to Montréal. He would have to apply for a passport and visa. I would need to make inquiries about the procedures for sponsoring him. It was new territory for us both. I couldn't quite believe in the fulfilment of our fantasy, but it was enough to sustain me on that lonely flight to Havana.

Havana

THE *CIMARRÓN* LOOKED SOMEHOW DIFFERENT, AS THOUGH all the viewers had drained him of his energy. I cut the threads and held him in my arms, an inanimate collage of cheesecloth, wire, burlap and glue. The gallery director wanted to keep him as a talisman so I carried him to the office and sat him on a chair in the corner. Anamaría, the curator, fished a battered hat out of a cupboard and placed it on his head at a rakish angle.

"We must give him a cigar and a glass of rum," she said, tossing her cloud of coppery hair, something of the movie star about her. With silver rings on every finger and even on her thumbs, she took a bottle from the cupboard and poured a shot, placing the glass at his side. We laughed at him, slumped like a drunken sentinel, and I remembered how Christopher's head had drooped as we rode up in the elevator, all the pride gone out of him as he surrendered to us, and how a pale blue vein had pulsed under his drooping eyelid, the one damaged by a forceps birth.

We'd made our *cimarrón*, Leila and I, only to lose him as he changed form and gained his true life. I saw myself dancing with him, a trail of light defining the path of our stumbling steps in those early days when his hands still hung disembodied from two threads. I remembered the dancers at our opening, the red cord that joined them, leading me to Baracoa, to the Casa de la Trova where Onaldo had danced me in a circle of certainty that life is never what we have been led to believe and can always confound us. We must solve the puzzle without knowing what it is . . . *la paradoja de la vida, maleta, cimarrón, padecemiento.*

I left our man slumped in his corner, and walked out onto the street with Anamaría, the life he had given me burning brightly as the music continued, over and over ... *Cuando Juanita y Chan Chan en el mar cernían arena, como sacudía el jibe a Chan Chan le daba pena* ...

El Caballo de Rosamund

WHEN ROSAMUND ARRIVED IN BARACOA SHE WAS immediately surrounded by young men offering bici-taxi services, (even though, as she later learned, it was illegal for bici-taxis to take foreign clients). She felt elated after the bus ride along La Farola, the highway built after the Revolution, with its spectacular vistas appearing round each corner as the bus curved and climbed through mountainous, thickly treed terrain.

Rosamund had prepared well for her journey, reading about Cuba and selecting Baracoa for its delightful description of geo-cultural richness. *A coastal enclave held by a system of rivers flowing to the Atlantic Ocean, bordered to the north and west by jungle. A pocket of cultural difference within Cuba, the music, food, and linguistic particularity bearing an Afro-Caribbean flavour.*

She selected a cyclist — a tall curly haired mulatto named Henry, which he pronounced, she noted, with a guttural H, more like a J — and asked him for accommodations in the centre of town. Henry grinned and hunched over, pedalling hard to transport Rosamund and her luggage, which included a flute and several books on linguistics as well as a fair-sized German-Spanish dictionary. They arrived at a colonial building on the main street within view of Parque Central and the historic Catholic church which, he told her, had been built by Columbus, and where Hernando Cortés had been married.

Rosamund surveyed her spacious high-ceilinged room, unpacked, ate a hearty lunch on the flower-trellised patio, and ventured out.

She drew much attention with her halting gait. Some stared while others came forward to help, but Rosamund smiled and thanked them in her very proper Spanish, complete with a lisp acquired in Barcelona, and indicated her metal cane with its circular arm support. In this way she arrived at Parque Central and sat a while — time enough for a quick appraisal while she herself was appraised by the locals lounging there.

On either side of the park was an array of restaurants and bars, principally La Trova, the musical heart of Baracoa, where three bands rotated so that the average tourist, alighting for three or four days, received an impression of infinite variety. The Catholic church dominated the town centre and Rosamund was soon drawn to enter it. She had a generous body with swelling breasts and rounded, somewhat misshapen hips, her arms well-muscled from pulling herself forward, her right hand a little twisted from the constant gripping of her cane. But what the woman begging at the entrance to the church noticed was Rosamund's periwinkle eyes, the softness of her peppery hair, the ready smile that graced her face and announced her as one who had surrendered to her condition. Predictably, Rosamund stopped to place a coin in the woman's hand.

She did not pray. She stood in the centre of the church and looked around her at the religious images, at the altar cascading with coral-coloured *isora* flowers, at the cross which was said to have come from Spain with Columbus and which had been taken to Santiago de Cuba for the recent visit by the Pope. *El*

Papa — strange that he should have the same name as a potato, thought Rosamund, for such was the tenor of her linguistic musings. Besides which she had that very morning ordered *papas fritas* with fish for her dinner, the *dueña* of her *casa* being insistent that Rosamund select the menu in advance. La Señora knew that she would lose her foreigner to the fierce competition on the street if she did not secure her custom at breakfast time.

At nine in the evening, after dinner and a nap, Rosamund ventured again onto the street and began her slow course towards La Trova. She wore a new dress of crisp white cotton, embroidered across her breasts and over her lap. From her ears dangled tiny white birds embedded in clusters of pearls. Her eyes were shadowed in soft blue with a subtle touch of mascara on the lashes.

Before she reached La Trova a man stepped in front of her and offered his arm. He said something in rapid Spanish and while she was trying to decipher his words he pulled out a chair from a sidewalk table and gestured for her to sit. Rosamund protested, but allowed herself to be seated, glancing at the people crowded around small tables, drinking from rum bottles and '*tukola*' cans.

"Please, Señorita," the man said, "Let me buy you a drink."

"But I want to go to La Trova."

"The music at La Trova will start later. The night is young. Ángel," he said, offering his hand.

Rosamund stared up into his face. It was difficult to determine his age — forty, perhaps thirty-five, or even thirty — a smooth, boyish face. His eyes, behind John Lennon glasses, were dark brown, his skin olive — more Spanish than African, she thought, although every Cuban seemed to be a mixture.

"My papá was a famous musician here in Baracoa. You'll see his photo in La Trova ... El Cayambo."

She wiped the corner of her mouth with the hand she had used to grasp his. It smelled of lemon mixed with something sharp and pungent, like a half-forgotten spice. Her mother had painted her fingers with bitter aloes at night to prevent the child from biting her nails, but Rosamund had dipped them in the water glass then continued her gnawing.

"And you? Are you a musician?" she asked, and when Ángel nodded she exclaimed, "Ah, I too am a musician. I play flute and cello, and I'm learning to play the mandolin." She was about to tell him of her passion for Renaissance music, especially the Spanish music of travel and adventure which she played weekly with her chamber quartet at home in Frankfurt, but while she was formulating her sentence he broke in.

"I write songs, but I have no guitar. My father's guitar, my inheritance, is in El Museo Matachín."

As Rosamund exclaimed at the injustice of the appropriated guitar, at the same time expressing a desire to visit the museum, Ángel excused himself, returning moments later with two plastic cups of rum.

"*Salud, amor y dinero,*" he said, winking at her and nudging her glass with his. He downed his drink in one gulp while Rosamund sipped hers hesitantly. She swallowed and made a face as the bitter white rum burned her throat.

"*Muy fuerte*" — very strong.

"Ah, in La Trova you will drink a mojito — *más suave*" — milder. Ángel grinned at her, then his brow furrowed slightly as he spoke hesitantly, "Forgive me for asking, but ... did you have an accident?"

"No." Rosamund laughed and sipped again at her rum, beginning to relax. "I had polio as a child. After many operations

I was able to walk again." She grasped the reassuring metal of her cane. "But I must always have the help of . . . " she searched for the word " . . . this."

"*El bastón.*"

"*Sí, mi bastón.*"

Ángel smiled. "You are brave to travel alone to Cuba."

"I love to travel," Rosamund said with a flourish. "I have explored many cultures and languages. I speak French, Italian and English, and I'm learning Greek and Turkish."

"But why Cuba? To practise your Spanish? You speak very well."

"Ah, thank you. But no, the truth is that I decided to visit Cuba when Fidel Castro became ill last year, because I am afraid that the Cuban Revolution may die with him."

He shook his index finger back and forth vigorously. "Our Revolution will never die. In Cuba we celebrate every anniversary of the Revolution, every battle, every triumph. Fidel will not die."

"But he is an old man, and very sick . . . "

"*El Comandante* is getting better. You can read his *Reflecciones* every day in *Granma*. Soon he will appear on television announcing his return to power. You will see."

Rosamund shrugged and smiled at the young man's passion as he continued to speak. She hoped he was right, though she felt somewhat sceptical. No matter. It seemed the most natural thing in the world to be discussing politics in Spanish with a handsome Cuban in white linen trousers. As the warmth of the rum loosened her tongue, Rosamund had the sensation of multilingualism, a sensation not unlike riding on the back of a horse — her old childhood dream returning now. Her fantasy had begun during those years in a series of body casts, and it had sustained her, galloping across the world on her very own horse, inseparable from her body — a black stallion named *Negrito*.

"*El Negrito.*" She confided her dream to Ángel, sipping hesitantly as he handed her another glass of rum.

"In *el campo* there are many horses," he said. "I will find one for you."

Rosamund's shoulders rose as she clasped her hands with joy and gave Ángel a radiant smile.

Next day, stepping out into the hot sun, Rosamund encountered a Canadian woman sitting in the park with her backpack. She was looking for a place to stay, she said, but had very little money and needed to share a room. Rosamund liked Anna immediately and invited her to share her room, which had two big beds.

"And I invite you also to share my meals, Anna. There's far too much food for me," she said. "Anyway, I need to lose some weight. And you are thin. You must eat."

Anna was pursued by Adonis, a bici-taxi boy she'd met in the park. He came in the late afternoon to take Anna and Rosamund to Finca Duaba, a cacao plantation a few kilometres east of the town. Rosamund was merry as ever, especially when she saw horses on the street pulling wagons full of *campesinos*. They were sad specimens with jutting ribs compared to the more spirited animals they passed grazing in the fields, but every horse reminded Rosamund of her childhood dream and of Ángel's promise.

"Ángel is going to find a horse for me to ride," she told Anna, and there was a proud luxuriance in her demeanour as in one who feels admired.

Rosamund couldn't dance — it was too painfully awkward for her — but Ángel didn't seem to mind. On their second date he helped her up the steps of La Trova and they sat up front listening to *la musica tradicional,* watching the salsa dancers whirl like dervishes. Rosamund marvelled at the expertise of their casino turns, and as she watched, her blue eyes crinkling with pleasure, she imagined herself astride her *caballo.* No wonder they call Fidel *El Caballo,* she thought. He has carried the Cubans forward and given them freedom.

"Now that Fidel is in bad health surely he must retire and hand over power to his brother," she had remarked to her landlady at lunch, but the woman had simply glanced up and shrugged, then resumed clearing the table.

"I'm going to borrow a friend's motorbike," Ángel said, leaning into Rosamund's shoulder, speaking into her ear above the beat of the music. "Tomorrow we will go to *el campo* to look at a horse."

Rosamund hardly slept that night. Listening to Anna's steady breathing in the darkness, a marvellous idea came to her. She could *buy* a horse! What better than to keep a horse in Baracoa and visit each year to ride him. She woke early and was first in line at the bank to change her money. At 11 AM she was sitting on the patio waiting for Ángel. She waited and waited. When lunchtime came she picked at her mound of rice and chewed on a grisly piece of pork, wishing Anna were there to help her. They had discussed over breakfast Rosamund's feeling of breathless suspension in Cuba, "Nowhere more palpable than here," she had said. "Despite its isolation, Baracoa has a strong pulse, easily taken in such a small town."

"Adonis says the majority of the population live in the countryside. He's offered to take us to his brother's place tomorrow. D'you want to come?"

"I have my own trip to *el campo* today . . . with Ángel," she had said.

"Oh yes, I forgot. Well, I must go. I'm meeting Adonis at the beach at noon, and I have to check my e-mail first." Anna had rushed off in her usual flurry of energy.

Rosamund lay down for a siesta after lunch, but every creak and rustle of the old house caused her to catch her breath, listening, waiting.

Finally in the evening she went out and made her way down the now familiar route to La Trova. There was no sign of Ángel, but it was impossible to be alone in Baracoa. She was invited to join a group of Cubans she'd met the previous night, and she asked them if they'd seen Ángel.

"Ángel? I don't know. Haven't seen him all day," Víctor said.

"I saw him in La Punta," Conchita said, "in the afternoon. But he didn't say nothing."

"He lives in La Punta, no?" Rosamund asked. It was a small neighbourhood just east of the centre, a mere five-minute walk from Rosamund's *casa*.

"*Sí,* with his mamá, and his brother."

She felt foolish — a middle-aged woman chasing a young man. But it wasn't Ángel she wanted, it was *El Negrito* of her dreams. She tried to explain, but Víctor laughed and teased her, "Ah, *el caballo!* Ángel is your *caballo!*"

Rosamund drank too much and had to be accompanied home at 2 AM when La Trova, Rumbo, and La Terraza had all closed, and Parque Central was empty save a few couples listing against each other and an old man curled up on a bench snoring. The church towered over him, a waxing orange moon rising behind it.

The soft green mountains filled Rosamund with longing as Adonis turned off the main road at Jamal and pedalled hard along a bumpy dirt road, avoiding deep ruts made during the rainy season. Anna was snapping photos of the mountains, the swaying palms, leaning across to capture a bougainvillea and rose-encrusted *casita*. Despite her thick head from last night's mojitos it was clear to Rosamund from the way that Adonis kept turning to grin at Anna that they had become lovers. There was a sweet solicitousness to the boy's gestures and Anna had lost her edge. Rosamund would have been jealous had she not been on the lookout for her horse. I don't need Ángel, she thought defiantly, I am an independent woman.

They came to a halt finally in front of a tall cactus fence divided by a pathway of red earth which led to a thatch-roofed *casita*. Adonis mopped his sweating brow and neck with a greyish cloth, then offered his hand to Rosamund. He helped her up the dirt steps and introduced her to his brother, Ramón. She accepted the chair that was offered in the *sala* and settled herself while the lady of the house brought her a tiny cup of hot sweet coffee. Adonis and Anna had vanished so she found herself chatting with Ramón and it wasn't long before they came to the topic of *caballos*. With sparkling eyes and a coquettish air she asked Ramón about the possibility of purchasing a horse.

"*Los animales pertenecen al Estado,*" he replied — The animals belong to the state.

"This cannot be true," Rosamund protested. "Surely I can buy a horse if there is one for sale?"

Ramón shook his finger at her, his face without expression, then he offered his hand and led her down the corridor, through the kitchen where his wife was preparing lunch, and out to the back yard, shaded by banana palms.

"*Mira,*" — look, he said, pointing through a coconut grove to a clearing where two horses grazed, one a dull brown, the other black.

"*Negrito!*" Rosamund clasped her hands and stared at her dream horse, at his swishing tail, at the twitching and quivering of his strong neck and haunches. "Can I ride him?"

Ramón gestured for her to wait while he sauntered over to the lean-to and pulled a dusty saddle off its hook. She stood shifting impatiently from foot to foot, her pulse quickening, while Ramón sauntered through the tall coco trees, saddled up her *Negrito* and led him into the yard. Rosamund could barely breathe as he picked her up and lifted her onto the docile animal. High in the saddle she searched with her weak legs for the stirrups, but there were none. Ramón laughed and handed her the reins, then he led the horse slowly out of the yard and into the clearing. The brown horse raised its head, whinnied to *Negrito,* and continued foraging. Rosamund tilted her face to a perfectly blue sky. Ah, what better than this? she thought. *Mi Negrito Cubano!* Her legs dangled against his ribs as the horse ambled forward, picking up speed when she dug her heels in and clenched his mane, inhaling the sweet pungent smell of him. Rosamund felt an unequalled sense of freedom. Although she was not galloping, nor could she, she was moving more rapidly than she could ever have hoped for. To sit astride a living creature, at one with his body, moving forward effort-lessly — what could match this?

When her ride was over and she had limped back to the *sala* she offered 300 pesos to Ramón for his *Negrito.*

"*¡No, no!*" he exclaimed, "*No es posible, Señora.*"

Rosamund tried to explain, thinking that he had perhaps misunderstood her about the money, thought it was payment for the ride, but Ramón simply stared at her, then he laughed and shrugged, making a dismissive gesture with his hand. Just then Adonis and Anna reappeared with flushed cheeks and tousled hair, so Rosamund asked Adonis to intervene with Ramón, but the boy only confirmed what his brother had said. The horse is not for sale. Animals are owned by the state. And he told her that they would eat the lunch now that his sister-in-law had prepared for them.

After lunch Rosamund paid and asked for one more look at *Negrito,* cupping his whiskery muzzle in her hands, feeling the warmth of his breath and the velvety softness of his gentle mouth, wishing, wishing that he could be hers.

As Adonis pedalled them down the dirt road towards the *carretera* he kept turning to grin at Anna, reaching his hand back to fondle her sunburnt knee which was scraped with what looked to Rosamund like a burn from a straw-filled mattress bursting from use. But her thoughts soon turned to her own concerns. One more week in Baracoa then I must return to Havana for my flight home to Frankfurt. Only one week to find my *caballo.*

That night Ángel was waiting for her in Parque Central. His eyes filled as he apologized. He had to take off his glasses, and Rosamund offered her embroidered handkerchief.

"I am so sorry, Rosamunda, for missing our appointment yesterday, but my mamá had a crisis and I had to take her to the hospital. There was no time to advise you, because I had to rush to the hospital on my friend's motorbike. I sent you a message with my friend, Aníbal. Didn't he tell you?"

Ángel threw his hands in the air, exasperated as Rosamund shook her head.

"That idiot!" he said. "I couldn't come myself, because I had to wait all day in emergency with my mamá, then all evening at her bedside as they prepared her for tests and x-rays."

"What is wrong with your mamá?"

"I don't know yet, but she is very, very sick. She can't eat . . . she's in so much pain . . . "

He had to stop. Rosamund laid her hand on his arm. She understood illness, and she felt selfish and guilty for her impatience with Ángel.

"The conditions in the hospital are very bad," he said, "There are no clean bed sheets, the bathroom is shared by twenty people, and the food is not worth eating. No wonder my mamá has no appetite." He dropped his head and sobbed.

Rosamund twisted her fingers, her mouth working with unspoken words. "What can I do to help?" she asked.

"Forgive me for saying this, but I have no money. I gave it all to Aníbal for the motorbike yesterday to buy *gasolina* to take you to *el campo*. I need money to buy some chicken for my mamá."

"Ah!" Rosamund gasped and opened her purse.

"No, no, no! I am Cuban, I am proud, I cannot accept money from you."

Rosamund insisted, pressing twenty convertible pesos into his hand. "Is this enough?" she asked. "I can give you more."

Ángel hesitated, his face pained with the grief of the situation.

"What is it? Tell me," Rosamund coaxed.

"What would make my mamá more happy than anything would be to hear me play my father's guitar again."

"But this is not possible. Your father's guitar is in the museum."

"It's true, but there is a guitar very similar. It belongs to my friend. He wants to sell it to me, but I have no money."

"How much does he want?"

Ángel shrugged. "I don't know . . . 300 pesos?"

"It's very expensive," said Rosamund, pulling back. Three hundred pesos was the sum she associated with her *caballo*, never to be matched by a guitar.

"Maybe 250 . . . I don't know. When I play for her she'll get better, I know it. She will close her eyes and imagine that it is my papá playing."

"Will you play for me too?"

"Yes, of course I will, Rosamunda," he said, summoning a brave smile as he replaced his spectacles, looping the thin wire arms over his ears. His hair was cropped closely, giving the effect of an almost shaved head, very popular with Cuban men. He gazed into her eyes. "*Mi ángel Alemana*," he said — My German angel. Rosamund paused a moment, savouring his words, wanting to run her hand over his smooth head, then she dipped into her purse and counted out 300 pesos. "Try to get it for 250," she said.

She had not planned to let Ángel have his way with her. On the Saturday before her departure, she found herself, after two strong mojitos and a shot of straight rum, in his apartment. Of course his mother was not there — she was still in the hospital where she was reportedly recovering fast with daily music therapy.

"And where is your brother?" Rosamund asked.

"He's with Mamá at the hospital."

It was one of those situations which, looking back, Rosamund couldn't fathom. One minute she was standing by the table in their humble kitchen, then she had magically crossed through an archway into a room which held only a bed scattered with dirty clothing. She blamed herself for allowing it to happen. After a few feeble thrusts Ángel slumped on her, panting like a dog. Afterwards they took a bici-taxi and rode in silence to Parque Central, but before they reached the park Rosamund feigned tiredness and asked to be dropped off at her *casa*. Ángel helped her out of the taxi and stood by while she paid.

"When are you leaving?" he asked.

"In two days."

"I'm going to miss you. I love you, Rosamunda."

He tried to kiss her, but she turned her face so that his lips only brushed her cheek.

Anna was leaving too and they had planned to travel together on the bus to Santiago. From there Rosamund would fly to Havana. But there was one more night. As Anna climbed the hill to the El Ranchon disco to meet her Adonis, Rosamund deliberated before setting out once more for La Trova where Ángel was waiting for her at a table with a bottle of rum. She glared at him angrily, but when she saw all her friends gathered, waiting for her — Víctor, Conchita, Ángel's brother, Leo, all the *bailadoras* of La Trova — her face dissolved into a smile and she was filled with nostalgia and a warm sense of belonging. So that when Ángel leaned down to kiss her lips she was able to put the memory of his clumsy lovemaking behind her and tilt her face to receive his kiss. After all, it was her own fault; she'd had enough lovers of both genders to know better than to succumb to such a boy. The search for the perfect male lover was like her search for *El Negrito*, but somehow that quest was ingrained in her, in some innocent, unquestioning part of her where hope flamed unquenchable.

The bottle was almost empty by the time Ángel leaned across the table and took her hand in his.

"No," Rosamund said and pulled away.

"*Mira*, Rosamunda," he whispered, "I've found a *caballo* for you, a beautiful black stallion, *muy fuerte.*"

"It's not possible for me to buy a horse," she said. "They told me in *el campo* that animals belong to the state."

"No, no, Rosamunda," he moaned, shaking his head sadly, and then, slowly and carefully as though he were explaining something to a child, "Only the *vacas*. The cows belong to Fidel, because they are very important to give milk for the children."

"But I don't understand," she protested. "Ramón told me very clearly that horses are owned by the state and are not for sale."

"Not for sale to *extranjeros*, Rosamunda. Like houses, ownership of horses must be in the name of a Cuban," he gestured, pointing both hands into his chest. "*Mira*, this is the perfect *caballo*. Stay one more day and I will take you to see him."

"It's too late, Ángel," she said sadly. "What a pity this has come too late. It was my dream."

"No, no, it's not too late. I can buy the *caballo* for you and I will send you a photo. Trust me. You will see him and you will love him. Then you will come back to Baracoa next year to ride him."

"How much for this horse?"

"He is a very special horse. My friend wants 500 pesos for him . . ."

"*Mein Gott!*"

" . . . but I talked to him and he agreed to let me have him for only 450 pesos."

"This is too much. He must be a stud horse!"

"Yes, he is a stud horse," Ángel said enthusiastically, "We can make money from breeding him."

"But I don't have that much money."

"Maybe I can talk him down to 400, but there is the food too. Horses eat a lot."

"They eat grass."

"Yes, but they must have other food too, expensive food to make them strong."

Ángel leaned forward and grasped Rosamund's hands.

"*Mi caballito*," she murmured, whether to Ángel or to her dreamhorse, she was unsure. Rosamund's head swirled with a sense of freedom and well-being on the eve of her departure.

"Let me sleep on it," she said.

Ángel was about to protest, but thought better of it and, instead, offered her another drink.

"*La ultima bebida*," he said sadly — the last drink.

In the morning Ángel picked her up at noon in a bici-taxi. As they were pedalled along the Malecón she discreetly pressed a bundle of notes into his hand, ten fifties. "Try for the lowest price," she said, "And use the extra for his *comida*," — his food.

"Aieee, Rosamunda, I will wait for you," Ángel said with a big smile.

☙

Señora Amable Ponce

June 2007, Santiago de Cuba

SEÑORA AMABLE PONCE OPENED THE DOOR WIDE. I was
immediately riveted by her eyes, and only peripherally sensed
the grand entry hall. There was no doubting her identity.
Spanish to the core, her dark eyes smouldered with the history
of a people conquered, dominated for centuries, biding their
time until the tables turned and the Moors and Jews could be
driven out, no matter that their blood was by then irrevocably
mixed. The Spanish would be masters in their own house, as
was the Señora, *la dueña,* ushering us in with a languid gesture.

The ceiling rose forever, anchored from disappearance into
the heavens by a heavy cut-glass chandelier that swayed slightly
in the slipstream of a whirling fan. It was a minute or two before
I noticed her wounded leg, the crutches, her shrunken body,
and by then I had already a firm impression of grand stature
and fortitude. She had held me with her burning eyes, her red
lips, the elegant gestures of her hands, and now she was forever
indistinguishable from the grandeur of her family home. She
brushed aside my inquiry about her leg — nothing, a small

fracture — a blur of rapid-fire Cuban Spanish as she turned and led us, limping slowly across the expansive salon and down a wide corridor to our room. I glimpsed a child, a girl of perhaps eight or nine, through the half-open door of a large bedroom we passed.

Before opening our door with a key from a bunch dangling at her waist, the Señora gestured to a terrace spilling over with bougainvillea, the petals airborne like a cloud of butterflies. A table was set with green plastic mats and a condiment set. Would we like dinner? She could offer chicken, pork, prawns, as we wished. We settled on prawns, and Onaldo asked for beer. She called and a young woman appeared, wiping her hands on her skirt. Her head was wrapped in a turban and she had strange watery blue eyes, almost crossed, filled with a wounded light. Her mouth was soft and open like that of a baby. Señora Amable Ponce said something in a low voice and the girl left. A minute later I heard the big front door close.

As we entered our room they began talking, something about the dinner, no, the history of the house, the destination of the girl...consonants disappearing into a torrent of indistinguishable sound, drowning, lost to the ears of a foreigner. I turned away. A double-breasted wardrobe, inlaid with mahogany patterning, towered over the *cama de matrimonio*. Curlicued bedside tables sat sentinel on either side. In the mirror above a marble-topped bureau I saw the three of us, Onaldo's skin darkened by our whiteness. I only understood him fully when we lay together naked, the words that escaped my brain entering through my skin, spinning threads that wove us together after our long absence, creating pathways to intimacy across an impossible barrier to fluency. *Poco a poco.* This was our first reunion since meeting four months ago.

I hung my clothes in the wardrobe, savouring the dark aroma of the past that lingered there, an ancestral presence, and I thought of my brother and how he would stand in front of the long mirror inside the door of our Uncle Jim's wardrobe, arranging his tie, admiring himself. After Christopher died our mother's hair turned white and came out in chunks, lying on her pillow in the morning. She began to fall, head flung back, hitting the floor, like an angry child in the throes of a tantrum. My sisters had her kitchen carpeted to soften the blows. Like Christopher, she'd held to the concept of progress, moving forward determinedly like a crabbed turtle, clawed hands grasping at anything. Her house filled up with sticks, walkers, trolleys, all abandoned until finally her hip broke as she made one more determined lunge. After the operation we moved her into a nursing home and the floor of her room became a moving battlefield, a no-man's land to be negotiated with each trip to the toilet. Her every step was monitored by kind women trained to care for the infirm, and still she fell, with all that care, no one able to intervene in her battle with gravity. Finally she succumbed to a massive cerebral hemorrhage and we had let her go, speechless with the wonder of her helpless journey away from all that was familiar. A week later I was on the plane to Havana.

I heard the water from the shower, felt a warm dampness misting the air through the half-open door. By the time the girl brought our beer Onaldo was showered and changed, and he looked like a boy, fresh and light, cleansed of our long journey from Havana to Santiago de Cuba.

As we ate dinner — fleshy pink prawns with garlic and rice, a plate of bright tomato slices, *habichuela,* the long thin beans that Cubans carry like green bouquets dangling from their hands — I saw a balding man scuttle across the hallway. He wore shorts, nothing more, and his naked belly, round and full, glistened with sweat as he padded barefoot up a narrow staircase to one of those hidden second floors constructed to use a portion of the cavernous space — a *barbacoa,* the Cubans call it — a loft. Onaldo was sitting with his back to the hallway eating voraciously, so he hadn't seen the man. Had he come out of the child's bedroom? Was he Señora Amable Ponce's husband? He hardly looked worthy of her, but I lacked my usual certainty. Who could tell in this atmosphere of unsureness and multiple possibility? It wasn't only the language.

We left soon after, left the table with our cutlery splayed across the plates, and walked out onto the street together in the fragrant warmth of the night. The air felt like a huge and gentle animal lapping my skin.

At breakfast we were surprised by Cortés leaping onto the table.

"*¡Cortesito! ¡Abajo!*" Señora Amable Ponce demanded, but the cat ignored her. He twisted his neck away from the condiment set and began grooming himself, eyes slit, rough pink tongue working the fur of his left flank. I lifted him gingerly — he had that raunchy tomcat smell despite his obsessive grooming — and deposited him on the tiled floor. His tail rose stiffly in the air, quivering as he walked across the hallway and jumped into the Señora's lap. She had resumed her telephone conversation, a cigarette white against her red lip, smoke curling a shroud around her thick dark hair. She ignored Cortés.

Onaldo reached across the table and took my hand in his. We talked, making our plans for the day. No hurry. I felt languorous. Cuba does that to you. It's in the air, a kind of energetic laziness soaked in eroticism. Or maybe I was just relaxing finally. As we returned to our room the Señora said something to me, a question I didn't quite catch.

"*¿Perdoneme? No entiendo exactamente,*" I said.

"*No importa. El entiende,*" she replied and turned to Onaldo, dismissing me.

While they conversed I went into our room and prepared for the day. As I was applying lipstick in front of the mirror I saw Onaldo come up behind me. His hands on my hips, he turned me, his eyes dancing with merriment. He still seemed a miracle to me, already like a part of myself rooted in another place, in the rich soil of Baracoa. We had endured each other's absence, sustained by dreams and frequent e-mailings, and he had come all the way to Havana to meet me. The months of longing dissolved as he tumbled me again onto the big bed, his appetite insatiable.

While Onaldo slept I walked down the corridor towards the entrance salon. The little girl sat at a desk in her room, long hair snaking down her back. She wore a white dress, white socks, sandals. Her thin arms were bent, elbows resting on the edges of the desk as she bent over her paper, face concentrated with the effort of writing. I would have liked to speak to the child, but it seemed improper in that house imbued with a past I did not understand. In the morning light I had noticed the tired lines around the Señora's mouth, a furrow of pain in the centre of her brow. She seemed today a wounded woman struggling to maintain her dignity, a tired beauty playing the edges of her formidable presence.

In the centre of the salon a cushioned settee bore a large indentation. I pressed my hand into the warm depression. Another guest? Difficult to know who exactly lived behind the closed doors leading off the corridor — who had so recently vacated this settee. Each *casa particular* I'd stayed in during my visits held some mystery and many, like the house of Señora

Amable Ponce, housed ghosts from a past when Cuba was a playground for the rich. I heard the slight suction of a tongue against the roof of a mouth. I turned to meet the soft sucking sound and saw the child standing in the arched entrance to the corridor, her mouth open. She stared at me with liquid eyes slightly downturned, giving her an almost but not quite tragic look. Neither of us spoke, but slowly her lips curved into a smile and her head tilted back in a gesture of what . . . surrender? welcome? supplication? I spoke then, greeting her with my name as I rose from the settee.

"I am Marilenis," she replied. "I live here with my grandmother. I'm learning French. Do you speak French?"

"*Un petit peu,*" I said. In the broken silence we moved towards each other and I took her hand. "I am learning Spanish," I said. "Will you help me?"

Marilenis tossed her head and laughed. She spoke quickly now, her words tumbling as she tugged at my arm and pulled me along the corridor to her room. She showed me drawings of birds, trees, flowers, and told me stories, her face alive as scene after scene flashed through her, shaping and reshaping her features, with an eloquence that entered me and shimmered there. It was as though the child were a screen to be played upon and I had only to watch her with all my senses open. I noticed that in her drawings the sun always shone from the upper right hand corner.

She showed me frilly hair wraps adorned with butterflies and beads, a pair of shiny patent pumps waiting under a red velvet dress in her wardrobe, a green frog sitting on her bedside table. She bounced on the big double bed, laughing and beckoning.

I leapt onto the bed and bounced with her, the two of us laughing until the shrieking crescendo forced me to caution her. "Shhh! We must be quiet. Your grandma . . . "

Marilenis tossed her head and said something I didn't catch. She bounced off the bed, grabbed my hands and danced me around the room, leaping and twirling, pirouetting with her thin arms arched above her head.

When we collapsed onto the floor she began chattering again, accompanying her words with gestures, so that they entered me, the sense of them, like sign language, and I understood Marilenis as we understand each other in the world of childhood, easily, without the burden of personal involvement and without reference to past or future.

From the cupboard of her bedside table Marilenis brought two dolls. We conversed through them in a mixture of French and Spanish, and I told her that we had invented our very own language — *Frañol.* The little girl laughed, her soft brown eyes sparkling, and she was about to say something, leaning forward, an urgency about her, when I heard Onaldo calling me.

I stepped into the corridor and saw the balding man standing there, a loose tank top covering his belly. He nodded at me and smoothed a strand of hair over his head. I was about to speak, to bid him at least *buenas tardes,* when I saw Onaldo grinning at me from the open doorway of our room.

When we returned to the house in the late afternoon a large man was ensconced on the settee in the salon. I saw him first in the mirror and knew immediately that he was Canadian like me. Arelis, the young woman who worked for Señora Amable-Ponce, came running towards me as though she had been waiting.

"Please, ask him if he likes *camarones*," she said. "He doesn't understand what is *camarones.*"

"Prawns? Sure, I love prawns," the Canadian replied enthusiastically. He resembled a toad, his ample body perched on the edge of the settee as he leaned forward to reach for a full cup of something. Unperturbed by his lack of Spanish, he seemed untouchable, like the calm surface of a lake in a land without stones. I wondered if that was how I seemed to them — to Arelis, to the Señora, to Marilenis and the balding man. And where was he — still upstairs in the back of the house in what I now took to be their private apartment?

Onaldo took my hand, tugging, eager for the seclusion of our room. We had been wanting each other all afternoon, the intensity of our desire mounting. The door to Marilenis' room was open. As we walked past I saw her brushing her grandma's hair, the Señora seated before the dressing table, her crutches splayed on the floor. Her eyes were closed, her head tilting slightly as the brush tugged. Marilenis saw me in the mirror watching her, then Señora Amable Ponce opened her eyes and saw me too.

"*Buenas tardes,*" I said.

We passed the narrow staircase on the way to our room. I looked up, but there was nothing to see except the flickering light of a television, that alteration of the atmosphere so like the northern lights of the big Canadian sky. I heard the deep voice and rolling Rs of the news announcer. Then I heard another sound — a muffled protest alive with urgency. I stopped at the bottom of the staircase and listened. It was Arelis. Onaldo turned and beckoned me from the door of our room, his key already in the lock. I hesitated a moment, my foot on the first step, then I heard soft laughter, a sigh of surrender, and I followed Onaldo into our room.

We left early the next morning — the bus for Baracoa leaves Santiago at 7:45 AM — and the next time we called Señora Amable Ponce for a reservation her line had been disconnected.

❧

La Colonial

Baracoa, Cuba, just below the Tropic of Cancer, twenty degrees north of the equator, where the sun sets early and people eat late when the heat has ebbed from their bodies, making way for appetite to grow.

Don Antonio greeted me, rum on his breath as his fleshy hand grasped mine. He is *el dueño de La Colonial, un paladar* — literally palate or taste, the name given to Cuban restaurants run out of private homes. He seated me on the terrace and called to his son to bring me a beer. When it came, *cerveza Cristal*, I thanked Antonito, a younger version of his father, and gulped the first few mouthfuls, always thirsty. Then I waited for Onaldo, the sweating glass in my hand, the bottle half-full on the table.

We had eaten at La Colonial four months ago just after we met, Onaldo beaming at me, delighted by our surprising romance, and I unable to believe in the extraordinary magic which had come out of nowhere, like a plant that seems to have disappeared and is discovered years later in a new area of the garden. How can we ever know what occurs in the darkness of the earth? He had been wearing his new brown shoes that night, and was upset because he'd scuffed them on the broken steps of his building while hurrying to meet me. I'd shrugged it off — "It's only a pair of shoes, Onaldo" — but for him those shoes were of great importance — my first gift to him. After dinner we had danced again at the Casa de la Trova, his brown-shod feet nimble, moved by that effortless rhythm Cubans have. I'd thought him a wonderful dancer. *"Regulár,"* he'd said, and I'd taken it for modesty until I started watching the young men who stood in groups outside La Trova, jostling at the door to dance with the foreign *chicas.* Their skill was breathtaking. They all but made love on the dance floor, to the rhythm of the salsa, the merengue, the cha cha cha. And all their partners had to do was fuse and follow. I could hardly watch, the raw energy affected me so. When Onaldo and I had left La Trova we'd had to elbow our way through clusters of men on the street and I'd been glad of his arm around my shoulders — a gesture of ownership — protecting me.

I took another swig of beer and watched a man ride by on a bike too small for him — his knees jutting out, and a woman balanced side saddle behind him, her skinny arms around his waist — when I was surprised by Onaldo leaning down to kiss me, his lips firm and warm, his hand on my neck. *"Mi amor,"* he said, a tired smile creasing his face, and I noticed the greying of his hair, which gave him a distinguished look. "The meeting ended just now. My programme for September has been approved."

Onaldo works in promotions at the Casa de la Cultura, organizing cultural events in the neighbourhood of La Playa, which is bounded by two long streets — Mariana Grajales and Primero de Abril — and at the top by Calle Coronel Cardoza with its faded mural, drained of colour by the afternoon sun. That's where Onaldo had been living when I met him, in a small room in a broken down building. Now he lived two blocks away, in Migdalia's house.

We went inside and sat at the table by the window where we had dined the first time. We ordered our food and two *Cristal*, then the musicians appeared — a local band, Los Changeros, who always played at La Colonial. Onaldo knew the trumpeter, Modesto, a dark-skinned man with a shining bald head, thin and frail in his startling white shirt. I remembered how he'd played his trumpet last time, with passion, like a lover. Onaldo nodded to Modesto and as the music began — the first strains of *Strangers in the Night* — he bunched his fingers to his lips and let them go, like throwing a kiss. Modesto could make any old tune sound exquisite.

Our beers came and a plate of bread. I watched him as he began to eat. I could gaze at Onaldo for minutes at a time until he'd look up surprised, and then smile and shuffle with embarrassment as though he wasn't accustomed to being admired. Sometimes I watched him as he slept, feeling like a voyeur but unable to take my eyes off him. Once I'd photographed him, his body curved in sleep, one arm flung across his neck, the other resting on his thigh. I knew I was behaving like an idiot, but I didn't care. My genitals hummed with a damp desire, and I felt loved and cherished, marked by the fire of Onaldo's hands. I pressed my knee against his and he reached across the table and grasped my hand, looking into my eyes as he continued eating. He was completely focused, chewing the bread and butter, savouring it. He ate like he made love, with gusto and greed — a generosity of appetite — and with total concentration, eating steadily as though someone might steal it.

Behind him was a long table filled with German tourists. They were drinking *Bucanero*, a darker version of *Cristal*, and many of them were sunburnt, the men's necks red and puffy, the women with shiny faces and painful chests cooling under plain white blouses. Cubans have their own national beer named for Hatuey, a Taíno chief who led his people against the invading Spaniards. Hatuey was captured finally and burned alive, but in the chief's last minutes a priest asked him if he would accept Jesus and go to heaven. Hatuey asked, "Are there Spaniards in heaven?" When the priest assured him that there were, Hatuey replied, "If Christians go to heaven, I do not want to go there."

"*Extraños en la noche intercambiando miradas, preguntándose en la noche lo fueron las posibilidades . . .* " The song floated across the room, lyrics thick with sentiment, and then came the trumpet solo. Onaldo stopped eating and stared, something strangely removed about him — that concentration, and an intensity which belied his calm exterior. I touched his hand and he turned, his eyes upon me like birds landing.

"Did your father play this?"

He nodded, then took his handkerchief and dabbed at the corner of his mouth, greasy with the unaccustomed butter. Onaldo's father had died of arteriosclerosis after a lifetime of drinking. He'd played piano too, the same piano which now stood in the front room of Tia Dory's house and which I played when I went to visit her. Was Onaldo still carrying a childish guilt for his father's retreat into the rum bottle, or was he infected by his father's lifelong absence, carrying the torch of unavailability in some essential way? He didn't drink much himself, but the sins of the fathers take many forms. I remembered Chrisopher's long retreat from us, driven by the absence of the only other male in the family, our father — the only adult with whom he'd felt safe, he'd once confided to me.

Our salads arrived and Onaldo drenched his with oil and drizzled a little vinegar onto it. He sprinkled salt on top and filled his fork with lettuce.

"Any news of Fidel?"

Castro was ill, with cancer it was rumoured, although it was difficult to get accurate information other than the basic story that he'd temporarily stepped down from office due to illness. According to the internet, largely unavailable in Cuba, Castro was suffering from an intestinal disease — diverticulitis, a common condition of the aging colon — which required extensive surgery. His brother Raúl had been holding the fort for almost a year, but had made no public speeches. "Fidel will return," people said, "He has the best doctors, he will get better." Or they simply shook their heads, as Onaldo did now. In Miami the Communist-hating members of the exiled community exulted in what they took to be the approaching death of Fidel. Some even said he was already dead. Meanwhile Cuba was in a suspended state of silent anxiety, whether from lack of information or from fear of stating a true opinion, I could not fathom.

Our food arrived as Onaldo was mopping up dregs of oil and vinegar and a few tomato seeds with his last piece of bread. Crispy chicken and a mound of white rice for me, a dish of fat prawns steaming with an aroma of garlic and oil, and two large mounds of *congris* (rice mixed with beans, also known as *moros y cristianos)* for Onaldo, with a garnish of beetroot and wafer-thin carrot slices artfully arranged around the rims of our plates. It was a welcome change from the monotonous Cuban diet of rice and beans with perhaps a chicken leg once a month, or some illegal *camarones* if a friend managed to catch some. The best food was reserved for the tourists.

Onaldo looked at our full plates then glanced up at me, his face alight. He looked into my eyes as though he might consume me, then dropped his head and delved into the *congris.* I picked at my chicken leg, peeling off the burnt skin. When I reached for one of Onaldo's *camarones* he clasped my hand and teased me, his tongue quivering between his teeth, then he popped a prawn into my mouth. I wanted to share the pink flesh with him, probing past his teeth into the soft recess of his palate, my tongue tickling the roof of his mouth, exploring the soft mound under his tongue. I wanted all our food on one plate, to eat with him at the same trough, to merge and live inside him, privy to his language and the mysteries of his blood. I was in that state of constant desire that makes ecstatic fools of us. *"Como adolescentes,"* Onaldo joked about our mutual condition, but I had missed my adolescence. I had been absent from my body throughout my youth, like a sleepwalker going through the motions of life at a great distance from the experience. I suspect that none of us are what we appear to be. How appropriate to be living out my adolescence now in a country where governmental regulations render the entire population adolescent.

"*Mi amor*, what will happen when Fidel dies?"

"Fidel will recover."

"Perhaps, but eventually he's going to die. He's already eighty-one years old."

Onaldo shrugged. He'd been eleven when the Revolution triumphed. At sixteen he'd become a *brigadista* in the *alfabetización* programme, travelling the countryside with a group of *compañeros*, teaching *campesinos* to read and write.

"It will be the passing of an era," he said, "But our government will continue. Fidel has never governed alone. He has many advisers who have been in office for decades and are well qualified to continue his work."

"And Chavez?"

"Chavez is Fidel's political heir. He will carry the dream of a Latin America liberated from the American imperialists and the IMF. You're not going to eat any more? I'll take the bones for

Lolita," he said, reaching across, wrapping my half-eaten chicken in a napkin.

"What do you remember most from the early days when the Revolution was new and everything was changing?"

He paused in his wrapping, considering my question. "*Una cosa terrible* — A terrible thing... When I was a *brigadista*, we were in a village close to Camagüey and one of my *compañeros*..." He paused again, shaking his head. "We were swimming, a group of teenagers, it was a fast-moving river... the province of Camagüey is farming country — sugar cane and cattle — I don't remember his name... we called him Flaco, because was tall and skinny, always joking. I was a strong swimmer and I went after him, diving as fast as I could. Three times I went down, Karina, and finally I pulled him out. We tried to revive him, mouth to mouth, but it had been too long. He was dead."

"My love, how terrible for you. You were just a kid."

"The worst part was later. I had to tell his family."

"Why you?"

"I was in charge of our group that day. It was my responsibility." He looked down at his plate and I felt him leaving me, going back in time as though he had not thought of this in many years and found it fresh again. "They lived outside the city, on a small farm. His father came to the door... then his mother came and... I'll never forget her scream when he told her. 'Where is he? Where is he?' she shouted, 'I want to see my son.' They wanted to know everything, all the details, how it happened... It was the worst thing in my life."

I wanted to take him in my arms and smooth his grizzled head with my hands. So much of his life was a mystery to me, but when he opened up I was astounded by the depth of feeling there. He was an essentially private man. Thirty-five years a member of the Communist Party... It seemed that the words and opinions he was prohibited from sharing were stored in his body, packed tight inside his dark skin.

"Señorita?" The waiter at my elbow. "Would you like coffee, ice cream?"

"Just coffee, please."

"Don't worry, I'll eat yours," Onaldo said quickly, and grinned at me, his painful story folding back into his body. But I couldn't get the image out of my mind — Onaldo diving, over and over, searching for his friend, surfacing with a burst of breath, diving again, swimming the boy to shore full of hope, then laying him down, his mouth on the boy's mouth, breathing into him, waiting for the exhalation, the splutter of water, his compañeros standing over them in a circle, one of them saying finally, "Stop! Stop, Onaldo, he's dead."

"*Solo de pensar en ti amor . . .*" crooned the singer as Modesto moved through the room, pausing briefly at each table. He ended the number at our table and bowed to me as I pressed a three peso note into his hand. Modesto and Onaldo grasped hands and touched each other's shoulders, then he left, his gait slowed by a slight limp.

"Has Modesto played outside of Cuba?"

Onaldo shook his head. "His band plays in Guantánamo sometimes, and Santiago, *nada más.*" He shuffled in his seat. "I must go to Guantánamo to speak with Immigration about my *carta blanca.*"

"But you don't have your visa yet."

"They told me the *carta blanca* can take many months. I must apply now."

The seed we had planted in Santiago, daring to imagine Onaldo's first journey outside Cuba, had germinated, but it was a surprising plant that grew and began to flower during the process of sponsoring him. He seemed less interested now in going to Montréal to look for his daughter and her child. He had asked me about the possibility of doing a presentation on Afro-Caribbean culture at a Canadian university, presenting his research on the folkloric culture of Baracoa, perhaps selling some of his books, so I had made contact with Latin American Studies at the University of Toronto, and with York University where there was much interest, but I had not yet succeeded in firming up an official invitation. He seemed reluctant to speak further of his daughter. "Another time," he'd said when I'd suggested he fly direct to Montréal. "I want to stay with you in your house, and meet your friends. I want to discover the city of Toronto and understand how you live."

He was already trying to learn a few words of English, some basic phrases from the dictionary I had given him. His accent was totally charming and made me smile with something approaching what I suspected he might feel about my Spanish. It's amazing what assumptions are made about a person's maturity based upon their language skills, regardless of their obvious intelligence and accomplishment. We catch ourselves out all the time across our language barriers, condescending, patronizing, underestimating. There is something of the adult attitude to children who can both charm us and try our patience as they make their slow way into fluency.

Onaldo reached across the table for my hand and grasped it tight, looking at me with eyes full of hope. He was nervous, I could tell, about the outcome of his application. Many Cubans were refused visas by Canadian immigration. I had issued an official invitation in Spanish which he was to present at the Canadian embassy with his visa application. His *carta blanca* was the final step, permission from the Cuban government to travel.

"I must go to Havana. I have my appointment at the Canadian embassy for July first."

"Perfect! You can travel with me," I said, delighted. "I fly out of Baracoa on June 30th."

"What if I can't get on the plane?"

"We'll book you a ticket. It's cheap for Cubans with Air Cubana. I'll pay."

He sighed. "You don't understand, Karina. We can't buy tickets. We have to go on a waiting list and take whatever spaces are left after the tourists have boarded."

"I don't understand."

Impatient now, he continued, "We Cubans pay in *moneda nacional*, 240 pesos. As you say, it's cheap compared to what you pay — 120 *convertibles* — but still it's the equivalent of ten convertible pesos, sixty percent of a month's salary."

"So it's not about nationality, it's about money?"

He nodded.

"Every tourist who buys a ticket bumps a Cuban on the waiting list," Onaldo said. "A friend told me he was actually sitting in the plane waiting for takeoff, and he was bumped because a tourist arrived at the last minute. *Somos perros,*" he said. We are dogs. "But some Cubans pay in convertible pesos, the lucky ones who have help from relatives in Miami, or from friends . . . " he trailed off, his mouth turning down like a big fish. "There's a joke about people who have *fe* — they have faith — *familiares en el extranjero.*" He laughed bitterly.

"Onaldo, it's not a problem. We'll buy you a ticket in *convertibles*. Why didn't you ask me before?"

He shuffled in his chair, avoiding my eyes. "There's nothing left in my bank account . . . "

"*Mi amor,* I already said I'll pay."

"There are other expenses. The visa, the *carta blanca, muchos papeles* . . . "

"But I gave you money last week for your travel expenses."

"I had debts." He shrugged and smiled apologetically. "I have to borrow to survive, to have enough to eat each day. And there's the household expenses, Yarisel and her clothes for school. My granddaughter needs so many things. It's important for her to feel equal, to have what her friends have. Equality is the basis of our social and political system."

"Then why doesn't the government treat you as equal to foreigners and let you book plane tickets with *moneda nacional*?"

"Karina, you know that we're living off foreign currency. It's no secret. This is what funds our educational system, our health care, food subsidies, housing . . . "

I was feeling uneasy with the topic. It seemed vulgar to insist on clarification, especially when so many of the goings-on in Cuba made no sense to me despite elaborate explanation. I decided to let it drop.

"Just tell me how much you need . . . for Havana and Guantánamo. If the universities come through they'll give you an honorarium."

"How much?"

"I don't know. Maybe five-hundred dollars. Enough to buy some things for yourself. And they might even pay for your plane ticket."

"Our government takes eighty percent of foreign fees."

"You're kidding!"

Onaldo shook his head and raised his hands in a gesture of helplessness as though I were pointing a gun at him. Cubans don't get angry. There's a passivity about them that I didn't understand at that time and perhaps still don't fully comprehend. Cuba is a humbling place that defies analysis.

"Then don't declare it," I said. "How will they know?"

"It's an ethical matter, Karina . . . my conscience."

"Onaldo, you must be the only honest man in Cuba!" I said, and I was laughing, I don't know why. I felt I was in a maze, coming up against a wall at every turn.

As I waited for the bill, feeling more guiltily implicated every minute in Cuba's *doble cara*, I wondered if Onaldo really would give the chicken bones to Lolita, carrying them up to the rooftop for his little dog, or if he might gnaw at them on the way home, or give them to Yarisel and Migdalia because there was still some meat on them.

I had been to Onaldo's house and met Migdalia and her grandchild, Yarisel — a beautiful girl who adored Onaldo and called him Papi. Like all evening visits in Baracoa, it had taken place in front of the television with a background of urgent dialogue and hoarse weeping — *la novela* — the soap opera. When Onaldo had e-mailed me that he was moving back with Migdalia, I was glad for him to be out of that hovel on Calle Coronel Cardoza. Migdalia was having an operation and needed help with the heavy things, he'd said, carrying water and so on, in return for cooking and doing his laundry. It was impossible, he'd said, to find another room since he'd been evicted from the illegally rented *cuartito*, but I shouldn't worry because it was temporary, and he would sign in at my *casa particular* and stay with me there when I came to Baracoa.

I paid the bill and we left La Colonial, Onaldo's arm around my shoulders like a promise, but I began to feel uncertain as we stood on the street facing each other.

"You're going home?" I asked. His house was only a couple of blocks away, and my *casa particular* was on the other side of town. "Will you come later? I could meet you in the park. It's early."

"I have a meeting at seven in the morning." He massaged his belly, smoothing little circles around its tightness. Since eating, his energy had dissipated. I imagined him sitting in front of the television, falling into a half slumber.

"Another?"

He laughed. "Meetings, always meetings. It's my job, Karinita," he said, using the familiar form of my name. He leaned down to kiss me, his arm encircling my body, hand splayed at the base of my spine. "I'll see you in the afternoon," he whispered. Then he was gone, turning briefly with a smile, waving, and I watched him walk away, arms swinging loose at his sides, the chicken bones clutched in his left hand. When he turned down Calle 24 de febrero I turned and headed for La Trova.

⌁

Salón de Belleza

June — December 2007

WHEN THE GRAVEL ARRIVED AT MIGDALIA'S HOUSE it had to be hauled up to the second floor balcony bucket by bucket in the hot midday sun by two sweating men — one on the street shovelling, the other hauling the bucket up on a thick rope, tipping it onto the mounting pile. It took more than two hours. It was a big pile. The downstairs neighbour, Juanita, watched nervously, grout still drying between the new blue tiles on her front patio.

Everyone in Baracoa had received building materials. Some had been waiting more than a year, and now a boom was under way. El Caracol, the restaurant on the Malecón, was expanding, the Pentecostal church was being rebuilt, a huge and imposing bar was being constructed in the centre of El Patio, leaving little room for dancing or for Yerba Buena, the resident band. In front of almost every house was a pile of gravel mixed with sand, bags of cement leaning against half constructed walls, small towers of cinder blocks. New walls rose on the roofs of existing houses all over town causing visitors to the cemetery on the hill to look down in amazement at the changing skyline. Even hikers snapping photos of each other by the stone head of Antonio Maceo, kilometres away on the summit of El Yunque, turned in surprise to observe the changing landscape.

But nothing had changed yet at the corner of Flor Crombet and 24 de Febrero except for the settling of sand and gravel within its cinder block enclosure. Several times a day Migdalia opened her front door and gazed upon her mountain of promise.

"I'm going to build a *Salón de Belleza*," she told Juanita, "At the back of the house where the stairs are easier to climb." And Juanita passed the word until soon the whole neighbourhood was talking about it.

In effect there was no room for anything in front, especially with the gravel there. Out back there was a concrete patio, six feet by ten, with steps leading to the roof where Lolita lived. Loli was rat-like with bulging eyes and a quivering pink nose — part Chihuahua, part street dog. She had a high-pitched bark and like all the dogs of Baracoa she patrolled her territory vigilantly, barking at passers-by on the busy street. At night she slept under the stars and was sometimes transported by a mysterious winged creature to the street where she ran with abandon through the night, only to wake on the same barren rooftop amidst her own droppings.

Migdalia's husband looked askance at the pile of gravel. He was a man of few words who used the house as a convenience, eating and sleeping there, donning his freshly laundered clothing and striding proudly down the street to the Casa de la Cultura where he worked as Director of Promotions.

"Who's going to build it?" he asked.

"After the cement is delivered Raúl will come with his neighbour who works in construction." She tilted her head suggestively, staring at him as her tongue crept from the corner of her mouth, moistening her upper lip. "They can build a *salón* in less than a week."

Migdalia's husband didn't get along with her brother Raúl. He lived in Mosquitero, in *el campo*, and although Raúl was a good-hearted fellow Onaldo found nothing in common with him. There was something bullish about Onaldo, Migdalia thought, the way his thick neck was wedged between his shoulders as he frowned and hunched over his dinner plate. She noticed this particularly since she'd watched a Mexican movie on TV the previous night and there'd been a bullfighting scene, the crazed animal snorting and pawing as the picadors punctured its neck with their red flags. The bull had put up a brave fight, but the matador had dispatched it swiftly in the end and Migdalia had almost cried as the animal sank to its knees, blood bubbling from its foaming muzzle. But she'd caught herself. She wasn't given to strong emotion. She'd used it up in the early days. People had warned her. He'd had a reputation. But like every woman in love Migdalia had been unable to heed the warnings, until he began staying out all night, then taking weekend trips to Guantánamo, to Moa, to Santiago . . . She'd suffered silently, and had even retaliated with a half-hearted though noisy affair of her own, fuelled more by vengeance than lust. Finally she had closed her heart and opted for a career, something she could run from her own house.

Migdalia was a *peluquera* and a *manicurista*. She had accumulated a grand array of nail varnishes, two foam rubber devices for separating toes, and a metal trolley to trundle around the front room. But her specialty was hair colouring and she soon became busy because all the women of Baracoa wanted to be redheads or blondes like the women in the *novelas* they watched in the evenings, sprawled in their chairs by open doors, legs spread to receive the freshness of the night air.

It was Juanita who had given Migdalia the idea of a *Salón de Belleza*.

"*Mira*,"— Look, she'd said, "All that wasted space out back. You could build a room and receive your clients there, and have your *sala* free for visitors. No more smell of varnish and peroxide," she'd added with a mighty snort, tugging at the ends of the scarf which covered her fat hair rollers.

During their separation, when her husband had embarked on yet another affair, (with a foreigner this time, an annoyingly friendly Canadian), Migdalia had felt a dull ache somewhere in the region of her heart, but she had ignored it, and when Onaldo had brought the woman to her house, interrupting a particularly tense moment in the *novela*, she had seen her chance. That was in February. By the end of April she'd returned home from the hospital after her hysterectomy and Onaldo had moved back. She needed him to haul the heavy pails of water from the pump on the street, she'd told him, and to go to the market. In return she'd promised to cook for him and launder his clothes.

Juanita told Migdalia that Onaldo was a frequent visitor to the bank — she'd heard it from her daughter-in-law who had a cousin who was married to one of the tellers. So, when he arrived home one afternoon with a DVD player, and a few days later on a brand-new bicycle, and the following week with a laptop computer under his arm, Migdalia could only think that his Canadian had helped him to open a bank account and had deposited a sum for his security and well-being, thus she saw the possibility of further bargaining with Onaldo.

In the middle of May the gravel was delivered, and by the end of June Onaldo had become concerned about the weight of it piled on the balcony. After several unanswered questions about her brother's arrival and the commencement of the work he turned his attention to other things, specifically plans for a trip to Canada.

In June the Canadian had come back for another visit. Of course she hadn't stayed in Migdalia's house — it was illegal for tourists to stay in private homes unless the house was licenced as a *casa particular*, which required payment of a monthly tax of 100 convertible pesos for each room, thirty for the licence to serve food, and 6.50 for tourist passage through the house — so Onaldo went to Immigration to register himself as the Canadian's *acompañante* in Erminda León's *casa particular*, situated on the other side of town. But Baracoa is a small town and while Onaldo continued to work, saving his vacation time for October, Karina made efforts towards a friendship with Migdalia, who reassured her that there was nothing more between her and Onaldo than the press of circumstance.

"My heart has been numbed by the years," she said. "But we must live together, because there's nowhere else for him since he was evicted from his illegal *cuartito*. Aiee chica, there are many Cubans who suffer like this, estranged couples forced together in the same humble *casa*."

Migdalia sighed as she plunked Karina's hands into a dish of warm soapy water in preparation for her manicure. While she painted her nails bright red with white tips and a coat of sparkling *brillos*, she talked about her granddaughter's urgent need for new clothing, about her own struggle with the *Salón de Belleza* and all the things she lacked in order to run a successful business. "*La Lucha, tu sabes*," she sighed — The struggle, you know. Migdalia popped a Hershey's Kiss into her mouth and sucked thoughtfully before continuing, "We're going to build a room for Onaldo, independent from the rest of the house, with a private entrance off Calle 24 de Febrero."

She waited for a reaction, but there was none. Perhaps the Canadian had not understood, or maybe she was puzzling as to why Onaldo would need another room when he already had his own, separate from Migdalia as she had carefully pointed out. Perhaps she should have said they were going to build an office for his writing. Ah well, there were many possibilities.

The first crack appeared on June 30th, the day of Onaldo's departure for Havana to make application for a visa. No one noticed it but Lolita, who was standing directly above the mountain of gravel after a particularly ferocious barking session at the edge of the roof, and yelped when a sound like a pistol shot resounded in her shell-like ears. The crack itself was almost completely hidden under the pile of gravel. Only a spidery leg crept out at the very corner of the balcony where the cinder blocks separated their cargo from the rusted iron railings that gave onto the street below. Loli stood quivering, listening for the next shot, but nothing came and she pattered to the far corner of her rooftop where a withered plant provided sufficient shade for her small body.

It was said that in her younger days, with her husband gone from the house and her daughter in school, Migdalia had been easy prey. Juanita told of Migdalia's full skirt that billowed in the warm air blowing off the Malecón, and under which she'd worn no bloomers. When the bread man came to deliver, Juanita said, Migdalia would stand at the top of her spiral staircase smiling down at him, her skirt lifting in the breeze. But the stories in Baracoa are, as in all goldfish bowls, apocryphal and perhaps Juanita told this to save her friend's pride. Now, with her spreading girth, Migdalia had trouble negotiating the narrow staircase and rarely used the front entrance, so she didn't notice the crack, which could only be seen if one happened to glance up and over to the corner of the balcony while ascending the staircase. No one knew — except Loli, who felt only in the ringing of her ears that something fundamental was amiss.

In early September Onaldo returned with high hopes from his second encounter with the Canadian Embassy in Havana. His first visa application had been refused, so his Canadian had arranged for an official invitation from the University of Toronto, which he had duly presented with a fresh application. Even so, he told Migdalia, it was to be several weeks before matters were resolved, with many expenses for papers, stamps, his passport and *carta blanca*. He was away from the house more and more, sometimes not even returning for his meals. Juanita's cousin's sister-in-law, whose son managed Las Palmares, the government-run restaurant-bar on Parque Central, said that Onaldo had been a frequent visitor of late, treating himself to chicken dinners and sometimes a plate of spaghetti as well. He ate alone apparently, under the canopy of purple flowers which cascaded from the rooftop trellis, sinking his teeth into chicken thighs and legs, teasing the tendrils of white flesh off the bone with great enjoyment. But he didn't tip. And he even took the bones away in a napkin.

The second crack woke Lolita that very night, another pistol shot in her dreams, interrupting her foraging in the cemetery on the hill. With lightning speed she was lifted onto the wing of a graven angel and transported back to her rooftop, waking to a slight trembling under her paws, an uneasy sensation which seemed to presage something terrible. The little dog pulled back her ears and emitted a whimpery growl. Her gums were engorged with blood, her little teeth razor sharp after gnawing on the chicken bones that had miraculously appeared on her rooftop earlier that evening. She licked her chops, curled up like a snail in its shell, and slept with one ear cocked and one eye open while the second crack, which had started with a bang in the upper corner of the balcony by Migdalia's front door, crept northerly, widening through the night and, by morning, had arrived at the outer limits of the gravel pile, a short distance in front of the spidery end of the first crack.

Migdalia rarely left the house. She received her clients in the *sala* where the television and her plastic-covered furniture dominated. The conversation, after covering the latest gossip, inevitably turned to her building project. The *Salón de Belleza*, since her conversation with the Canadian, had begun to expand into a new bedroom, a bathroom, an extension of the kitchen. Juanita's bright eyes darted back and forth, marking the acquisitions to the house — the DVD player nestled under the television, Onaldo's laptop computer lying open on the table in his room, his new shoes placed carefully together at the foot of the bed, a set of plastic table mats from Niagara Falls, the box of Hershey's Kisses . . .

"You could open a store with all this new stuff," she quipped with a click of her tongue.

"*Aiee chica*," Migdalia sighed, "*La lucha, tu sabes.*"

"Don't I know it. I had to wait seven years to buy the tiles for my patio, washing people's dirty underwear and scrubbing their floors."

"It was worth it, Juanita. Your patio is the talk of the neighbourhood."

"Really? What do people say?"

"They're jealous."

"Of a poor widow?" she snorted.

Migdalia popped a Kiss between her pink lips and offered the box to Juanita.

"You're getting fat, Migdalia."

Migdalia wriggled in her chair, her denim miniskirt straining at the seams. "My operation," she offered, shrugging her plump shoulders.

"And how is Onaldo?" Juanita asked, leaning back in her chair, eyes closed as Migdalia began plucking her eyebrows, shaping them into two fine arches.

"He's preparing for his trip to Canada," Migdalia replied, bristling with an uncomfortable mixture of importance and humiliation. "His visa has been approved."

The ladies made out their shopping lists — bras with cups C and double D, bloomers XL and XXL, perfume, hair combs and brushes, nail polish in red, pink and purple . . .

Onaldo left for Havana on the 15th of October, and while he was gone construction projects continued all over Baracoa. Sand and gravel were shovelled into wheelbarrows, cement was mixed with water flowing from the mountains into the many rivers that held the town in their embrace, earthy materials were formed into man-made structures rising from the levelled ground, baked in the sun, rasped and smoothed, painted and furnished. Finally the empty spaces were inhabited. Newlyweds made love within still-damp walls, children dreamed, grandparents died, mothers cooked and cleaned, men watched baseball on the televisions which stood in every front parlour. Empty rum bottles accumulated in corners, bottles filled with the repetitive rambling of their drinkers, drunken dreams of another world. *Otro mundo es posible,* the Baracoa children wrote on the walls of their school, quoting Fidel, who quoted José Martí, whose writings had inspired his Revolution.

Migdalia took delivery of four bags of cement, and had the men pile them against the kitchen wall, between fridge and stove where they were secure from the rain which though rare was torrential when it came. She gave the men cool glasses of water and when they'd gone she turned on the television and lay back in her chair, her shapely legs parted to let the cool air from the fan play on her thighs. The *novela* came on with its romantic music, faces filling the screen with furrowed brows and lips caught between white teeth, the camera panning slowly from heaving breasts to manicured fingers twisting lace handkerchiefs. Somewhere far off a neighbour was singing to her child, Lolita's tiny feet pattered on the roof, and a low rumble came from the pile of sand and gravel as, Migdalia imagined, it prepared itself, rearranging its molecular structure, imagining itself into the perfect form — a *salón*, a *cuarto*, a *palacio* — and Migdalia in the centre with her blonde hair shining, her dark eyes heavily outlined, and each nail a miniature work of artistry.

The balcony held, despite the crossed lines of its double crack. It held through to the end of October and Onaldo's return from Toronto. It held through the hurricane season when the wind carries the rain in horizontal sheets, flooding the streets of Baracoa. It held through many nights of dreams and torment, nights when Loli whined and fretted, her little head cocked at the moon as Yerba Buena's clarinetist pierced the sky with his music. It held until Onaldo's Canadian returned in mid-December.

On December 21st Migdalia was preparing rice and beans with fried chicken for Onaldo's lunch when the third shot rang out. Loli started barking and Migdalia ran to her front door, but there was nothing to see except the usual pile of sand and gravel. Despite the innocent appearance of her silent mountain of dreams Migdalia felt a twinge of uneasiness, a premonition of something indefinable.

Onaldo came home, his step springy on the circular staircase, stopping for a moment, then continuing. He peeled off his shirt, sat at the table and began to eat. As he was finishing, wiping the grease of a chicken leg from his mouth, he mentioned to Migdalia that there were cracks on the balcony . . . "The weight of the sand and gravel," he said. "I told you, Migdalia."

She went out to look for herself, but still saw nothing until she'd squeezed her way down the spiral staircase, turned, and immediately saw a hairline crack creeping out from under her pile, centred exactly between the other two spidery lines. A sense of urgency entered her, a sensation of energy tugging at her as she felt its movement within the magic pile, like a creature taking on its own life, preparing to rise and walk.

"I'm going to Lidia's house to phone my brother tonight," she said, patting her hair. "I'll ask him to start work tomorrow." The materials must take their own form, she thought. They will become a room, and that room will create its own function. Onaldo nodded and when he went to his room to lie down Migdalia turned on the television and settled herself for the afternoon *novela*. She was soon engrossed and, as she watched and he dozed, a fourth crack began its slow course silently, from the lower corner of the balcony, across the centre of the pile where it met with three intersecting faultlines, and on upwards heading for the wall beside the front door. Only Lolita heard the crackling of the parting cement. The little dog paced and whined, then she began to bark, louder and louder. Onaldo stirred in his sleep, too sated to rouse himself, and Migdalia raised her hand in a half-hearted gesture, then the plot turned and she was drawn back to the screen.

There was no piercing crack as one might expect, only a soft rumbling which alarmed Loli even more than the gun shots. Dogs have a sense for earthquakes and if she'd had the power of thought she would have thought that this was it, as indeed it was in a manner of speaking, within her small rooftop world. The rumbling grew until it was swallowed by a grinding sound, and then came the cracks, like pellets fired from a gun, preceding the final crash as one side of Migdalia's front balcony fell onto Juanita's blue-tiled patio, smashing her tiles with chunks of concrete, followed by an avalanche of sand and gravel.

↭

Creative Non-Fiction

Early September, 2007

ONALDO SETTLED INTO HIS WINDOW SEAT ON the left side of
the bus, protected from the afternoon sun as they travelled
westward along the coast to Santiago de Cuba where he would
change buses for Havana. He had already laid the foundations
of his story and now he began to fill in the details, letting his
mind wander through the leafy streets of suburban Havana
towards the Canadian embassy. He remembered well from his
last visit the elegance and promise of the Miramar building. It
was far from the crowded streets of central Havana where he
would again lodge overnight with his cousin Rafaelito on San
Juan de Dios, a dark narrow street tumbling with overcrowded
buildings.

He strolled in his mind's eye down a fresh green street towards
the embassy, nodding to the occasional passer-by, a smile of
anticipation on his sun-dappled face. But in reality the people
in Havana were not like Baracoans. In Baracoa everyone knew
Onaldo and greeted him, but the *Habaneros* kept to themselves.
He felt like a nobody in Havana. No matter. He had a passport to

success this time. With an official invitation from the University of Toronto in hand surely they would not refuse him again.

The fat woman sitting next to him was peeling an orange. The tangy aroma filled his mouth with saliva and he swallowed as he took a notebook from his pocket and began to jot down a few phrases, capturing his thoughts before they fled, water down the drain. Onaldo was a compulsive note taker. He knew from bitter experience the elusive nature of his story ideas. By the time the bus reached Imías he was immersed, eyes glazing over as he anticipated the climax, so he did not see Anamaría board the bus, her fragile form sinking into an aisle seat two rows ahead. As the bus lurched forward she waved to her mamá standing anxiously on the sidewalk, then rested her hands on her belly, still tender from the operation.

Anamaría's husband, Carlos, was a marine engineer with the merchant navy, and was away on cargo boats for months at a time. She had waited until he was halfway around the world to make her arrangements. She lived with Carlos' parents, and she'd told them that her mother was ill — an emergency — she must go to Oriente to look after her. The *Habaneros* called the *Orientales* 'Palestinos.' Though they loved to visit in Santiago, Baracoa, and along the southern coast for vacations, (those who could afford it or had family to stay with), they knew that Havana was the international face of Cuba and that each one of them was a proud feature of it. Since she'd begun working at the gallery Anamaría had felt like a proud *Habanera* too, but three months at home had brought her back to her Caribbean roots.

She closed her eyes and began to drift, back to the hospital in Baracóa where she had waited each day for the handsome face of Léster, her surgeon, to loom over her, drawing her back from that dark place of massive infection that had followed her hysterectomy. She'd lost all sense of time, waking only at the insistence of the nurses who wanted to change her intravenous bottle and dressing, or for Léster to feel for a faint pulse and question her in his gentle manner, and for Mami who was always there at her bedside. She had long ago accepted that she could not have children, but now she felt bereft of everything, even of the faint hope that had shadowed her existence, an aura of possibility. She was vaguely aware of a pulsing around her as she drifted into a merciful half-sleep.

Onaldo's heart raced as the *prieto* approached him stealthily. The stranger's energy spreading around him like oil as he was jostled suddenly, the thief reaching in that moment of disequilibrium into Onaldo's *mochila*. He lived once again the heart-stopping panic which had inspired his carefully chosen prose. Karina would most surely be at his side on that street in Miramar when she read his story. He knew the power of her imagination, her appreciation of literature. Since their first meeting in the bar in Baracoa when he had twisted his story slightly to appear in a better light, Karina had entered whole-heartedly into his creative life, listening intently to his accounts, telling him about 'creative non-fiction,' a popular kind of writing in Canada, and he had begun to understand the creative importance of lies.

In shaping a story one could also shape one's life. It was not lying exactly, but more like rearranging the facts in order to elicit a higher truth. He was a master at it. Karina didn't need to know that Migdalia had driven him out of the house by bringing another man there and having noisy sex with him in the next room, tormenting him with her grunting and moaning. He'd told Karina that the situation had become intolerable, which was true. If she chose to believe that he was like her and needed solitude for his writing then he would allow her that belief. What woman wants another woman's castoff? Karina had given him back his manhood and he had given her the story she wanted to hear, political as well as personal. She'd been so excited about marching in a Havana demonstration against the US embargo, about seeing Chavez and Fidel in the Plaza de la Revolución, and so Onaldo had responded with enthusiasm, taking his lead from her and simply reflecting back. That's what he'd been trained to do. Revolution sells — Che T-shirts, Fidel paintings and postcards, cigars . . .

His communist stance was indeed empty, though he had believed in it when he was young. But now, after a lifetime of waiting and waiting, nothing had changed — in fact the situation only grew worse — until this opportunity which he had grasped like a lover. How could he have guessed that at fifty-seven he would meet the woman of his dreams? A man of many words but few divulgences he'd held the facts close and walked proudly on the streets of Baracoa with Karina on his arm, a permanent grin plastered on his face. Onaldo had felt so flooded with good fortune that he'd been loath to disabuse her of the exact truth, and now it was too late. One half-truth seemed to lead to another, until he himself was caught in a fantasy, unable to distinguish fact from fiction.

Karina had e-mailed him about his second trip to Havana — *Take the plane, mi amor, you deserve to travel in comfort. Why travel twenty-one hours on the bus when you can be in Havana in two hours? I've sent enough money to cover all your expenses and the plane ticket to Toronto. I know we will be successful this time.*

Ah, she didn't understand how many expenses he had, and how carefully he must use the money. *Extranjeros* were accustomed to luxury and convenience; they always took the easy way without a second thought. *Why travel twenty-one hours?* . . . because that's what we Cubans do. It's normal. We can sleep on the bus . . . think our thoughts . . . we're used to waiting . . . we have patience. Hmm, perhaps he could incorporate something of the travel arrangements into his story, some pertinent details that might further authenticate it.

Migdalia, as he'd anticipated, had been delighted when he'd taken Karina to the house to meet her. It was then that her plan for the *Salón de Belleza* had taken hold. Karina had inspired them both and had gained him re-entry to the house, Migdalia allowing him to move back with the promise of foreign money for house repairs — their bargain. Once again he had his own room and felt comfortable surrounded by a growing accumulation of clothing, computerware, shoes, books and mementos.

Always quick to draw similarities between them and jump to false conclusions, Karina in fact knew little of Cuban customs, but Onaldo had instructed her enthusiastically, sharing a wealth of passionate knowledge gleaned from years of investigation, digging at his own roots. When he had written to her about moving back to Migdalia's house — his own house she had presumed, telling him what a *caballero* he was for allowing his wife to continue living there while he moved to the tiny room on Coronel Cardoza — Karina had, surprisingly, responded with joy that he would live in the better conditions that he deserved. He had reassured her that there was no cause for jealousy, but she seemed not to understand the word, and to be so entirely trusting that he had not pressed it. Accustomed to the possessive nature of Cuban women Onaldo had realized that there was much to learn about foreigners. He would watch carefully the customs of Canada during his visit there and gather information as was his manner — *investigador de costumbres folkloricas*. His head filled with visions of abundance as he imagined Toronto's Chinatown which Karinita had described to him and where he planned to shop for souvenirs. Everyone in Baracoa would expect a share of his luck. He could hardly come back empty handed.

As they drew into the Guantánamo bus depot Anamaría woke with a jolt and pressed gently with manicured fingers on her freshly tinted hair. It seemed to spring with a life of its own, expanding as she slept. She collected herself and rose gingerly, almost colliding with Onaldo as he strode down the aisle. "*Disculpeme*," he said and held her arm, seeing that she was fragile. After they'd dismounted he headed straight for the *baño* to relieve himself while Anamaría took a few steps and stood near the bus, hand on her belly like a pregnant woman holding an invisible child. She wondered how old the child was now, Carlos' child — perhaps five or six years old. She tried not to think about it but, especially now, the episode sprang to mind frequently. She'd only seen the woman from a distance — an old school friend of Carlos — they'd met on the street one day, he said. She'd been in Matanzas serving with the military and had returned to Havana to study at the university.

Anamaría's first lie had been about her age. "I'm twenty-three," she'd said, lopping off four years when Carlos told her he was twenty. They often joked about her being an 'older woman' seducing him, an 'innocent boy'. If only he knew. Her family was sworn to secrecy, nevertheless she always insisted on celebrating her birthday alone with Carlos. When he'd wanted to surprise her for her thirtieth birthday she'd insisted that they go away together, "Just the two of us, my love."

In the first years of their marriage Carlos had never mentioned anything about children. It was not what he, a young man, was thinking of, although there was a tacit assumption that children would come in time. They used no birth control and Anamaría expected every month to find herself pregnant. After her true thirtieth birthday she'd been to a gynecologist for tests. There was scarring in her fallopian tubes, the doctor said — they could try a procedure perhaps, to clear the way? Anamaría had arranged a short 'vacation' with her sister in Pinar del Rio. It had been easy because Carlos was by then a qualified engineer and was at sea on a cargo boat, but she still had to keep up appearances for her parents-in-law.

She made love to him with renewed hope on his return, falling over and over in love with the man she called her *'media naranja'* — her other half. Anamaría had an identical twin sister, a voluptuous woman with two fat children. But her real twin was Carlos. She could not live without him. She would do anything to keep him. When six more months passed without a pregnancy she began to wonder about his sperm count. They never spoke of his infidelity though she knew that he must have sex with other women when he was away. "Be careful, my love," she always said when he left, looking deeply into his eyes so that he would have no doubt as to what she really meant. In moments of intimacy like this, when he understood her perfectly, beyond words, she felt as though they were one flesh, triumphant over the web of lies she was weaving and which she hoped to break with the birth of their child.

Two years passed and then someone at work told her, "There's a rumour. A woman who lives in Marianao. She's pregnant and she says that your Carlos is the father."

Anamaría had been unable to return to work that afternoon. She went home and crept into the house so that her mother-in-law would not hear her, and lay on the bed until Carlos came home. He didn't try to deny it. He wasn't even shamed or remorseful. He simply said, "Why can't *we* have a child, Anamaría?" So it was she who felt shamed because she knew then that the failure was hers.

"Don't ever speak to me about this woman," she'd said, but then she'd sought her out, found where she lived and waited there, a block from the house, to watch her waddle down the street with her big belly. Her name was Yoani. When the baby was born Anamaría watched Yoani's mother take care of the little boy while Yoani went to her classes at the university. When Carlito began to walk and she saw his father in him — in his features and his gestures — something dropped into her belly, like a stone landing there, and she did not return.

Onaldo squeezed past the fat woman, found a couple of bananas in his *mochila* and was just sinking his teeth into one when the driver started up for the final leg of the journey to Santiago and drove them off in a cloud of exhaust. There would be at least a two hour wait in Santiago. He would buy a sandwich there to sustain him through the long night-drive to Havana. The banana was sweet and meaty, substantial and yet ephemeral. He smacked his lips, savouring the aftertaste. He would save the second one for later. He remembered too well the pangs and cramps he had suffered, the loosening of his teeth during the 'Special Period.' He was deeply afraid of the feeling of hunger. *Gracias a Diós* for his diabetic condition which demanded that he eat frequently. "*Mi enfermedad*," he would explain, delving into whatever was at hand.

He was familiar with fear — that feeling that sat on top of all the old feelings, crowing like a rooster. "It wasn't my fault," he'd protested when the police questioned him, Flaco's body lying there, his lips pale and cold. "It wasn't my fault! It wasn't my fault!" over and over until he was hoarse, and the policeman had written down his words, filling out the report, and told him that he must go to the boy's house and inform the parents of his drowning. When *la policia* had come to the *casa particular* where he was staying with Karina and left a note demanding that he report to the station next day, it had all come rushing back, fear upon fear, burying him in fear until his lungs were bursting.

Onaldo balled up his jacket and put it between his head and the window. He closed his eyes and tried to re-enter his story in Miramar, but he could not recapture it. The story never quite ended no matter how many times he wrote it in his head. Endings were often elusive but this one was particularly so. After the robbery, what then? The robbery clearly was the climax, so there must be a resolution, a calming descent into normalcy, a regaining of equilibrium. Oh, how he loved the words, the repetitions, the synonyms and antonyms, like music, sweet and rhythmic, the music of his papá's trumpet, his papá who had wanted Onaldo to learn. He had sat on Papi's knee at the piano in Tia Dory's house, the sharp smell of rum on Papi's breath, the hard muscles of his thighs under Onaldo's buttocks, but all he had wanted was to jump down and run to the *biblioteca* and read, read, read, the words and the music all one, but he couldn't read music, that was Papi's world.

When his father fell ill Onaldo sat with him, held his gnarled old hands and sang to him, a childish song his father had sung to him when he was little.

Duermete mi niño
duermete mi amor
duermete pedazo
de mi corazón

Papi no longer remembered his life; all that remained were the songs, the music, his fingers thrumming their rhythm like the nervous twitches of a dying creature. Onaldo knew it was the rum that had destroyed his father's mind and he was determined not to follow. He rarely drank, and when he did he was moderate, but an appetite for excess filled his body, consuming him with sexual desires which, no matter how often he made love or to how many women, were unabated. Sex was like a kind of therapy, an escape from an overwhelming reality. When the tension was released and his body flooded with that peaceful feeling his mind relaxed from its habitual worrying, at least for a short while. Onaldo needed it all the time — at work with a *compañera* in the hidden corners of the building, in the park on the Malecón fumbling with a *chica's* clothing in the darkness, every night with his wife, like a drug to bring him sleep and keep the fear at bay. Sex had become for Onaldo like gambling — a compulsion to stake everything, win or lose. He felt like a man in perpetual motion, running away from himself.

Anamaría sat in the Santiago bus station, her face tilted upwards, staring at the television screen. In her bag was a package of food prepared by her mother — chicken and rice in a plastic container, a sliced mango from the tree behind their house, two bread rolls, some sliced tomatoes — but she had no appetite. She felt gutted, of her uterus, her heart, everything. On the television screen a shapely young woman swung her hips in the familiar gesture of the Cuban dancers, on her head a spray of pink feathers, her breasts bulging out of a sequined pink bra. Tears gathered in Anamaría's eyes. She felt the sharp sting of something that might be called grief but was perhaps more like self-pity for she was alone in it, trapped inside her secret world.

She noticed a man striding across the waiting room with a loping gait — a mulatto with greying hair cropped close to his skull, and a *mochila* slung from one shoulder. He caught her eye and smiled, and she saw then that it was the man who had taken her elbow and helped her down from the bus. She managed a half smile and turned again to the television.

"*Vámonos,*" he said. Let's go. For a moment she thought he was inviting her, then she realized that everyone was gathering up their things, forming a line by the door. Finally, the bus to

Havana. Carlos would not be home for two months — time for her scar to heal. She preferred anyway to make love in the darkness, all her senses concentrated in her skin, his touch lifting her, tiny wings all over her body carrying her. She would return to La Galeria where she worked as curator, and was also responsible for the maintenance and exhibits of the permanent collection. It would be a relief to talk with Florissa and her other *compañeras* there, to be able to talk openly about her operation. Her parents-in-law would ask about her mother's health and she would lie as usual — *"Un poquito mejor, poco a poco."*

Anamaría had a window seat this time, near the back of the bus. The mulatto, she noticed, was near the front and when he turned to look for her she turned her head and closed her eyes. She had lost so much weight in the hospital that her ribs stood out under her blouse. She traced them now with her fingers, the white tips of her nails bringing her skin to life. Around her belly and along the lines of the scar she felt the patches adhering, releasing painkiller into her body — flesh-coloured circles, no bigger than her little fingernail, barely visible. "These will help you," Léster had said, his kind handsome face, his green eyes. If only Carlos could have been there to share her misfortune, but that was unthinkable. He must never know about the hyster-ectomy. On her next birthday she would be forty.

As the bus travelled north through the darkness, its floodlit bulk barrelling down the *carretera,* Onaldo slept and dreamed of *El Caimán,* the grand alligator that was Cuba and which had slept for centuries, half submerged, its jaw in Oriente, its tail in *el norte,* and its eyes slits behind which the force of nature dreamed. In Onaldo's dream he saw the creature's eyes open and they were gold and red like molten metal swirling in a vortex which drew him in. He was not afraid. He felt safe in the embrace of his island, his people, safe enough to let himself be pulled into another world where he travelled rapidly, wind rushing past his ears, until he found himself at rest suddenly, lying in a field of cool green grass. Karinita leaned over him, her skin soft and fragrant. He tried to speak but there were no words, only a kind of contented cooing, and then he realized that he was a baby with fat little arms and legs which waved and kicked vigorously. But he could not walk. He could not even roll over or sit up. He began to cry, his baby voice piercing the blue sky so high above him, causing it to bleed as Karinita picked him up and held him to her breast, rocking him, speaking softly to him in her foreign tongue as they walked through the green field smothered with red flowers of forgetfulness which sprang up where the bloody raindrops fell. He surrendered and woke with an erection and a terrible hunger. He delved in his *mochila* for the second banana which he devoured in two swift mouthfuls, then he ate his sandwich and swilled out his mouth with a bottle of water. Three o'clock. It was dark and quiet except for the snoring of an old man across the aisle.

Onaldo was wide awake now, so he began his story once again, entering the embassy, presenting his papers, waiting patiently to receive his travel visa for Canada. Thwack! His visa stamped, signed, success at last! He pulled out his wallet to pay the fee — sixty *convertibles* — his billfold fat with money for all the other expenses — *carta blanca*, passport, plane ticket, new clothes and shoes, gifts for Karinita and her friends . . . He strolled down the street once more, an innocent, anticipating all the pleasures of his Canadian vacation, straight into the arms of the evil *prieto*. But one must have compassion. A man in greater need than he, no doubt. And Karinita would surely send more money when she read his e-mail, so well written, so subtly nuanced, with a creative structure which would carry her emotions to a natural climax and leave her full of sympathy for his plight. He would not even have to ask. She would feel a commitment to the university that had so generously provided an official invitation and with whom she would now be discussing the amount of his honorarium.

He would wait until his return to Baracoa before writing so that he could describe the journey home, his mixed feelings of elation and loss, his dreadful dilemma — a Canadian visa in his pocket and no money for a ticket or the necessary papers, the clothes he was going to buy, the gifts. He would compose the story carefully on his laptop at home, transfer it to his *memoria flash*, and go with it to Elexi's house and send the message by dial-up internet.

Finally his story had come to a natural conclusion. His plans were made. It all depended on the granting of his visa. He had prayed for this and had a strong feeling that his prayers would be answered. Before drifting again into a deep sleep, longing for Karina's warmth and reassurance beside him, Onaldo imagined how he would spend the money — a new washing machine with a spin dryer, repairs to the roof and a proper shelter for Loli, a new pair of shoes and a pair of jeans for himself, a dress for Yarisel . . .

They arrived at 6.30 AM in the Havana bus terminal. Neither Onaldo nor Anamaría had anyone there to meet them, nor did they think to greet each other after the long and difficult night. The solidarity of passengers on the same journey breaks upon arrival as they each go in their separate direction. Onaldo shouldered his *mochila* and crossed the street to wait for the bus to Centro Habana.

Anamaría was groggy from a night of troubled sleep, interrupted by visions of Carlos in the arms of many different women, one after another, younger and younger. She dithered a moment, reluctant to return directly to her house where she would have to face, once again, her own deceptions. Though she was exhausted she decided to go to the gallery and talk to Florissa. She needed more than anything the understanding of someone who knew the truth about her life. Florissa would kiss her and stroke her face. The *compañeras* would gather around her, weeping and laughing. There would be coffee and the latest gossip, hands all over her, the blessed touch of friendship. She took the same bus as Onaldo, but they did not notice each other in the early morning turmoil of the city, and when they dismounted he stepped from the front entrance while she exited from the back. The sky was clear and blue with the promise of a fine day.

⌁

Her New Red Dress

LINANCIA LOOKED DOWN AT HER NEW SHOES and smiled. They were golden yellow with thin leather straps across her instep and toes, and high, pointy heels that made her feel as if she were tipping over. She smoothed her hand over the red silk sheath of her new dress. It felt too tight, but, "Yes," he'd said, "That's the one," his eyes on the swell of her buttocks. "Now you look like my girl." She'd felt so embarrassed with the way the shop assistant had looked at her as she'd packaged the dress that she had avoided meeting the doorman's eye as they'd left the store, Luigi's hand splayed possessively across her hip.

She looked again at her shoes and laughed. Linancia didn't recognize herself. She was still the little girl who'd grown up in Baracoa, even though she lived now with her *tia* Marcelina, in Centro Habana.

She tapped her red fingernails on the table and glanced again at her new watch. She felt self-conscious, sitting there alone in the bar of the Hotel Inglaterra, waiting for Luigi. He was twenty minutes late. She moistened her lips.

"Waiting for your *novio*?" the barman asked.

Linancia's face flushed. She thought he was being sarcastic, but when she looked up at him he had a kind face.

"My boyfriend said to wait for him at the Inglaterra. It's my first time here, I mean in the bar." Last night they'd gone straight up to his room.

"Try the terrace out front. That's probably what he meant."

She tripped but managed to catch herself without falling as she made her way across the marble floor of the hotel lobby and out onto the terrace. Suddenly she felt naked and tugged at the red silk, trying to hide her thighs.

"Linancia!" His gruff voice, heads turning. "Where you been, baby? You're late." Her face reddened as she took her place beside Luigi at a table ringed with damp circles.

"I'm sorry. I didn't know. I was waiting in . . . "

"Ah, never mind that. You're here now. Cubans are always late, right?" he laughed. "You want a mojito?"

"I'll have . . . one of those," she said, pointing at his bottle of Bucanero.

Luigi raised his eyebrows, then shrugged his shoulders and snapped his fingers at the waiter.

"We'll have a couple drinks then go on up to my room before dinner, yes?" He grinned at her and plunked his hand on her thigh, kneading her flesh.

By the time they got upstairs the world had softened to a pleasant blur. He grabbed her immediately, breathing heavily into her neck as he fumbled with the zipper of her dress.

"Be careful."

He jerked the dress, causing a tiny rip in the fabric where the zipper met her tailbone. Her intake of breath intoxicated him and before she knew it she was tossed onto the big bed, legs splayed like an accident victim, while Luigi struggled out of his pants. She caught a glimpse of his curved penis and then he was on her, pushing and shoving as he entered her body. She began to drift away, until she was aware of nothing but the bouncing of her body. "*Puta, puta, puta sucida*," she heard faintly in her ear, damp with his breath, the words almost familiar but not quite Spanish.

When he slumped on top of her it was a surprise, the weight of him bringing her back into her body. Silence. Was he dead, lying there on top of her? A dark prickle of horror crept through her, rising to her throat just as he stirred and rolled off. Luigi's hands went immediately to his head, smoothing the strands of hair that had fallen across his forehead. He sucked in his breath and sat up. Linancia smelled the beer on his breath as he leaned over and kissed her, then he tweaked her nipple hard, jumped off the bed and padded to the bathroom.

The throbbing of her nipple made her think of Hilberto who'd sat behind her in school when they were fourteen. He'd braided her hair like the girls did, slipping his fingers up into the nape of her neck, massaging it. His touch had made her nipples hard and filled her with a longing for something unknown — adventure, escape from Baracoa.

She heard Luigi hawking and spitting, water running. He was washing his penis. She saw the rubbing motions through the bathroom door. He hadn't even taken off his shirt.

They took a taxi to a restaurant in Vedado, a fancy place with a long walkway covered by an arched canopy of begonias. Another couple was waiting for them — a thin, fine-boned Italian man called Pietro — elderly, with thinning hair — and a *jinetera* who towered over him in her platform shoes, breasts and ass thrust out defiantly. She barely acknowledged Linancia, but hung onto her man's arm possessively, leaning into him as they sat down. Luigi draped his arm around Linancia's shoulders, his fingers pinching at her cheek as though she were a baby. They ordered drinks and he lit up a fat cigar that dwarfed his fingers. Linancia sipped her Bucanero and felt sick suddenly.

"I'm hungry," she whispered.

"You're always hungry, poor baby. You were born hungry." He leaned over and cupped her breast in his hand. Linancia blushed furiously and pulled away. Pietro smiled and turned to his companion who was laughing out loud. "Come on, let's order," Luigi said, "You heard the girl. She's hungry."

After dinner they went to the nightclub at the Hotel Nacional. Linancia had only seen it from the bus, riding in from her friend's house in La Lisa. It had always looked to her like a castle. She had tried to imagine what it might be like inside, and now that she was there she felt as though she'd walked into a dream. She hardly felt Luigi's hands on her as he steered her to their table, but on the dancefloor he leaned into her, his breath sticky on her neck, and licked the shell of her ear, whispering, "*Puta, puta, mi puta . . .*"

When the music stopped she excused herself and escaped down a flight of stairs papered with photos of movie stars and celebrities staring from the walls as she made her way to the washroom. She wished she could work in such a place instead of at La Época. The department store had a stagnant smell and half-filled display cases, not much better than Novedades, the dollar store back home in Baracoa.

She was shocked to see the woman in the red dress staring at her in the washroom mirror, hair piled on top of her head, long neck curved at the throat like a bird. She looked away and hurried into a bathroom stall. Perhaps Luigi would give her enough money to quit La Época, but she didn't want to think about him now.

On her way back she lingered on the stairs amid the gallery of stars. There was Meyer Lansky with Frank Sinatra, Fulgencio

Batista with Desi Arnaz, a young Fidel with Richard Nixon. The only one she recognized was Fidel and she smiled to see him there, young and handsome, smiling at her from the walls of the Hotel Nacional.

Luigi had a wife and grown children in Padua, his youngest daughter the same age as Linancia.

"It's business, Maria," he'd said. "Quit complaining. Pietro is coming with me. I told you, it's about the new resort. I'm coming back with a nice fat contract in my pocket." He'd taken her hand off his arm and turned to pick up his suitcase.

Maria didn't complain because he provided well for her and the children. She had spread, with each child, into the comfort of her forty-five years. She managed her house, her children, and a lover. She was discreet. They had their afternoons.

Luigi had been the brunt of merciless teasing at school. "*Nano porco, nano porco.*" Virgilio, the big boy who'd sat behind him in class, had kicked his desk incessantly, and always pushed Luigi in the schoolyard so that he stumbled and fell. One day when it had been raining the force of his landing had splashed his white shirt, dirty brown splotches spreading down the front. And his knees had bled.

"*Sucido, sucido,*" Virgilio and the others had chanted amidst their delighted laughter. "*Nano porco sucido.*"

He hadn't understood why they taunted him and called him a dirty dwarf pig. They hadn't eaten pork in Luigi's house, and they'd observed Shabbat each Friday and celebrated all the Jewish holidays. He had failed to grow and, at ten, still short, his mother's insistence that he eat in order to grow only made him fat.

Maria had been the first girl to look at him and smile kindly. She had been short herself, only three inches taller than Luigi, and she'd felt sorry for him. She'd been on the outer circle of chanting children, watching silently, her brown eyes filled with helpless tears — not for Luigi — she'd sat on the other side of the classroom and never had occasion to speak to him — but for the painful ache in her throat as she'd watched her classmates' faces.

Maria and Luigi had met at a dance years later and recognized each other from schooldays. Maria's shy smile had encouraged Luigi and when, later that night, he'd reached up to kiss her she'd bent her knees discreetly. The desire unleashed by her generosity was a shock to Maria. When she discovered herself pregnant she had no choice but to accept Luigi's proposal. On their wedding day he was so proud that he seemed to have grown three inches. Maria's acquiescence nourished him and he began to feel alive for the first time. Her encouragement only increased his keen appetite — his penis rose crowing at dawn, again in the afternoon when he hurried home for siesta, and nightly in their sagging bed. She bore him five children, but when her body had to be shared with their children, Luigi began to turn elsewhere — to the secretaries in his office, to prostitutes, and once to the wife of a colleague. Then the business trips to Cuba began.

Linancia slid into her seat next to Luigi. He was leaning forward talking to Pietro, his hands in constant motion, his words a stream of unintelligible sound. He didn't even notice her return.

"Did he buy that dress for you?" Linancia asked the woman on Pietro's arm. The *jinetera* stared right through her. She was a *mulata* with glassy green eyes and long braided hair laced with golden beads. The lime-green dress fit her like skin. She splayed her hands on the table in front of her and admired her blood-red nails. They looked to Linancia like the false nails she'd seen at the *manicurista*, but she was afraid to ask and to be ignored again. She leaned into Luigi and touched his arm tentatively. Without looking at her he draped his arm over her shoulder, squeezed her tight against him, still gesticulating with his free hand. She watched his mouth, the flash of gold as he laughed at something Pietro had said. Then Luigi turned to Linancia and kissed her on the mouth, his breath sweet and smoky. She nestled into him, her head resting on his shoulder. When she closed her eyes she could pretend he was Papi, the rich cigar smell of his jacket, the earthy resilience of his body.

Papi hadn't talked much, except when he'd been angry and burst out with a storm of words. And then the storm would be over and Papi would be her safe haven again. Until the day of his attack. They'd rushed him to the hospital but it had been too late. That's when the emptiness had begun, and her ravenous hunger. Her mother and sister teased her that she had hollow limbs, but she could never get enough to eat. After Papi's funeral Linancia's sister got married and went to live in *el campo*, and Hilberto went to live with his uncle in Miami. Linancia was left behind, and she had begun to fight with her mother about letting her go to Havana.

"I can stay with *tia* Marcelina," she'd said, "I'll be safe with her."

But in reality she had a wild and secret idea that she might be able to take a boat from Havana to Miami. She knew it wasn't far. And whatever happened she would be closer to Hilberto in Havana than in Baracoa. Mami had agreed finally and bought her a bus ticket.

Linancia closed her eyes and remembered the last time she had danced with Hilberto, at El Ranchón, up on the hill above Baracoa, with all their friends around them. She felt Luigi's hand squeezing her breast. What would it be like to lean her head on Hilberto's shoulder and feel his gentle fingers reaching up into the nape of her neck? She imagined him driving a big American car, riding next to him, his free hand massaging her neck, reaching down towards her breast. He would stop at a fancy hotel and take a room. No one would care that they weren't married, because in the United States everyone was free, you could do what you wanted. When the desk clerk asked him to pay, Hilberto would produce a fat wallet bulging with American dollars. They would take the elevator, up and up to the top floor of the hotel, and Hilberto would undress her very slowly, kissing and caressing her until she was wet with longing, then he would enter her gently, slowly, rocking her body back and forth under him as though they were boats on the ocean . . .

"Linancia!" His elbow in her ribs. "Wake up. Let's go."

"She's drunk," Pietro said, leaning across the table, slapping her cheeks lightly with his long cold fingers.

"She's just tired," the *jinetera* said and yawned, raising a scarlet-nailed hand to her own mouth.

Linancia pulled herself up on her high-heeled shoes and let Luigi steer her out. She looked down at his hand clamped on her arm, at his head that barely grazed her shoulder. The *mulata* was so much taller, striding along on Pietro's skinny old arm. Linancia kept her eyes downcast on the dizzying patterns of the marbled floor. She wanted them all to be invisible.

They stood on the sidewalk in front of the Inglaterra. Pietro and his *mulata* had already gone in and the streets were almost deserted, except for a man sprawled on a bench in Parque Central opposite the hotel, and a pair of lovers sitting, arms entwined, lips joined in a long kiss.

Linancia began to protest as Luigi tugged at her arm. "I must go home. My aunt will be worried about me and tomorrow I have to . . ."

"Whoa there," he cut in, grabbing her by both arms, pulling the sleeve off her shoulder. "You aren't going anywhere. You're coming with me."

"No!" She pulled free and backed away from him. "*Tia* Marcelina will be mad with me. She'll telephone to Baracoa and tell Mami, and then she will . . ."

"Oh, grow up! You're a big girl now."

"I have to go to work tomorrow. This was my only day off."

"Don't worry, I'll set you up in your own place. You can quit your job. You've just started a new one." He threw back his head and laughed, his belly shaking.

"I don't want a new job. I have my own life." She felt the tears welling hot behind her eyes as she remembered Hilberto lying on their bed in the hotel room in Miami, but now he was with an American girl, her blonde hair spread on his shoulder. She turned and took a few steps towards the corner of San Rafael.

Luigi shouted after her. "Go then, you little *puta*! You think I can't get another one? There are *jineteras* all over Havana. You're just a kid. You don't know how lucky you had it. Wait till the next one. You'll have a nasty surprise."

Linancia turned and ran down San Rafael, the heels of her golden shoes clicking on the wet stones. Street cleaners had already been at work, hosing away the day's accumulation of dust and dog shit. She heard the rip of red fabric as she fell. The heel of one shoe was separated from its sole and her ankle was throbbing. She took the shoes off, struggled to her feet, and stood there a moment, until a slight movement caught her eye — someone standing in the darkness of the grocery store, behind the glass. A chill of recognition shuddered through her.

"I can't go home like this. Marcelina will kill me."

She started walking quickly towards Parque Central, hugging the darkness of the storefronts.

When Luigi heard the timid knock he smiled and opened the door. After a moment's hesitation, she came into his arms, her body convulsed with sobbing. She was cut down to size without her heels. His swollen penis pressed hard against her belly, but she was oblivious. He led her over to the bed, pulled back the sheet, and undressed her slowly. The last thing Linancia saw before she drifted into sleep was the plastic bag from the dress shop resting in the corner, her old clothes sticking out — the leg of her jeans, a scrap of green tank top. She was hungry, so hungry.

What's So Special?

December 17th , 2007

THE SMALL PLANE LEAVES BOYEROS AIRPORT, RATTLES down the runway and abruptly lifts, banking west, hugging the Caribbean coast. I heave a sigh of relief after a heart-stopping and protracted misadventure at the airport.

When I'd presented my electronic ticket at the check-in, the miniskirted attendant had frowned then spoken rapidly to her *compañero*, who had signalled me to follow him. I'd been conducted into an office where an official looked at my ticket and informed me that it was not valid and that I would have to buy a new ticket. I explained that I'd bought and paid for this ticket online, but my explanation was met with a stony stare and the repetition that I could buy a ticket now for the Baracoa flight — it would cost me 120 convertible pesos. Aside from the knowledge that I would very likely be bumping a Cuban off the flight, I was incensed at having to pay twice, but after five minutes of arguing there seemed no choice. The man was rigidly inflexible, and was backed up by his *compañero* who stood passively at attention, ready to remove me if I became a threat.

I was so afraid of missing the twice-weekly flight that I finally produced my credit card, but no, they did not deal in credit cards, I must pay cash. I had only seventy-five pesos on me, enough, I had thought, to see me through until I could change money in the Baracoa bank the next day.

What to do? I looked around wildly, panic rising in my throat. I felt like screaming but I could hardly breathe. Yes, I could exchange money at the bank in the main hall, the official informed me calmly. I hurried out, dragging my suitcases, and found the bank closed. No one knew when it would open. Perhaps they had gone for a *merienda* — a snack. I ran back to the office, desperate now, and started shouting, but it got me nowhere — Cubans are maddenly calm in the face of tourist frustration. They have a wall of bureaucracy to shelter them and are invulnerable to any amount of abuse.

I dashed out into the hall, heading again for the check-in, and collided with a couple of foreigners who were also travelling to Baracoa and happily lent me 100 pesos. I began to laugh as my panic subsided, and hugged the American couple who were young and in love, and quite carefree. I ran back to the office with the money and waited impatiently while the official studied my passport, shuffled a sheaf of papers in search of a blank ticket, picked up a leaky pen and very slowly entered the necessary data, double and triple checking his entries and stopping to conduct a complicated conversation with another official before handing the ticket to me with a final flourish. I checked my bags, then waited two hours in the holding lounge. I have learned that the Baracoa plane is always delayed.

I sleep through the flight, or perhaps I am only half asleep, because some part of me is remembering November in Toronto, just after Onaldo left, when Leila and I began our drawings. In my dream I recall how we tacked huge strips of paper, thick and creamy, onto the wall and stood on chairs to draw, Leila reaching higher than me because she is petite with birdlike hands and feet and quick movements, except when she is drawing and becomes herself dreamy.

Before we started, our dancer friend Vida had come to model for us and we sketched all day, then the three of us ate olives and soft cheeses with butter and crusty bread, and drank wine and laughed, throwing our heads back, delirious with the accumulation of our lives together.

The next day we climbed onto our chairs and started drawing, and continued for days through the first Toronto snow, themes emerging as we drew ourselves into the darkness. We travelled down a long tunnel, tracing the way with our fingers on walls leading to a series of illuminated caves. The woman's heart appeared first, a pale disembodied thing hanging limpid in the air, darkening with the softness of Leila's pencil into the bloodiness of its essential nature. Lungs appeared in the man I drew, suspended in his chest cavity, with bronchioles branching out like seaweed. Then the liver, stomach, and intestines pressed in, filling his body, grounding it as he froze in a leap above the map of Havana, suspended in a gesture of desire, reaching across the US divide to his Canadian counterpart, a woman with hair a banner flying behind her, striding through the Toronto sky. I thought of Onaldo all the time. My drawing became an evocation of him.

When we drew a satellite suspended above our creatures we began to see them as objects of global surveillance rather than as the passionate lovers who had dominated the landscape, and they seemed diminished. With the addition of the satellite their words and gestures were ready to be recorded, decoded, analyzed, and so we became the investigators, tearing smaller rectangles of paper on which we drew magnified images of the eye, the inner ear, the brain stem and genitals, kidney, foetus, heartlines of the hand.

In mid-December we took our drawings down and rolled them into a long tube. We were done, besides which I had a ticket for Havana December 16th with a connection to Baracoa the following day.

We're beginning our descent and I'm wide awake now, looking down, searching for a glimpse of that achingly familiar place, nestled between coast and mountains on the southeastern corner of the alligator-shaped island that is Cuba. Baracoa is, aptly, the eye of *El Caimán*.

"What's so special about Baracoa?" Vida had asked as she'd struck a new pose.

"It's the oldest Spanish settlement in Cuba. Columbus landed there and built the first Catholic church in the Americas," I said. "I go there most Sundays and sit with all the locals just to hear the children sing. Hernando Cortés was married in that church, to Catalina Juárez, before he set out to conquer the Aztecs." Leila and I sketched rapidly, trying to capture her gesture. "And Diego Velasquez set up the first seat of government in Baracoa with Cortés as mayor."

"I've heard that Baracoa is full of artists," Leila said, "and that they keep the indigenous Taíno mythology alive in their paintings."

"The Taíno are very much alive in the faces of the people, in their features and bone structure. Baracoa is an aboriginal word. It means the sea's presence."

I see the green-skinned mountains rising out of a thickly textured jungle. I see the devastation of the Canadian Sherritt nickel mine based around Moa — a tangle of red earth churned by heavy machinery into roads snaking up mountains.

"And there's a small archaeological museum in a neighbourhood called Paradise — *Reparto Paraíso*. Evidence of pre-Colombian life is everywhere, just under the earth, but there's no money to excavate."

"Cuba has an amazing history of resistance," Leila said, "It started with the African slaves who were brought over to work on the sugar plantations. The rebels were called *cimarrónes* and they escaped and set up their own communities called *palenques*. Many of them fought in the war of independence against the Spanish."

"Cuba has achieved what no other country could," I said, "Half a century of triumph over the bullying, blackmailing pressure of the US government's embargo."

"But when Fidel Castro dies it could all be for nothing if the Americans take over," Vida said, shaking out her arms as she dropped the pose.

"You don't understand," I said, feeling defensive and possessive of an extraordinary culture whose endurance seems a miracle to me. "Cubans would never let that happen. They have a powerful sense of identity and a lot of political smarts. They're way ahead of us in so many ways. The Revolution may be old and tired, but Cuba is still an inspiration to the world."

"What about the human rights abuses against the dissidents and against homosexuals?"

"There's no country in the world that has a clean record. Why should Cuba be any different?" I flipped the paper over, dissatisfied with what I'd done, and started a new sketch as Vida showed us her classic profile in a warrior stance.

"Baracoa is a second home for me. I try to make my own sense of it. I'm aware of the injustices and of my own complicity — my privilege, the unfairness of it, the ease with which I live compared to the Cubans' daily struggle. It's only tourism that allows the country to survive, but at the same time it creates an appalling gap between us, mediating all our relations."

Had I said that to Vida, that mouthful of pompousness? Or am I just thinking in quotations, after the fact, the way that writers often do, trying to justify the unjustifiable? At any rate I'm definitely too earnest.

We're over the water now, descending rapidly, wheels thunking down on what becomes, at the very last second, a runway. All my old thoughts disappear and I am exultant as I descend the rickety steps onto the tarmac, enter the holding room, and join the press of travellers waiting for luggage to be brought in.

There's a rush of people claiming their bags and I lunge to grab one of mine, then the other — the dusty rose-coloured one, which was my mother's and which is filled with gifts — and push my way across the room to the glass wall where I see Onaldo waving on the other side. It's like the movies, where lovers meet and everything goes into slow motion, closing down and focusing in on the lover. I'm oblivious to the din of the holding room, to the push and shove of my fellow travellers. I am held by Onaldo's eyes, his smiling face, and everything around me is blurred as though I am underwater, except for Onaldo who is crystal clear. Then I find myself at the gate, an official taking my baggage checks, and at last, finally, finally I am in Onaldo's arms, remembering everything I had forgotten, the smell and touch of him, the words that exist between us flooding in as though memory existed in relation to place — my place here within the circle of his arms in Baracoa.

There are no taxis, so we walk to Hotel Porto Santo next to the airport and wait there, clinging to each other while the receptionist phones for one. Then we are riding through the familiar streets, joy bubbling up inside me as I melt into Onaldo's embrace, memory rebounding as though I'd never left. We are almost at Erminda's house on Calle Moncada when he tells me that he won't be able to stay with me.

"Remember, Karina, when *la policia* came to the house last time and summoned me to the police station? It's too much of a risk for me. I could be expelled from the Party and lose my job."

I hear myself protesting, my voice rising as it had at the Boyeros airport — the same feeling, a brick wall, and no gringos to bail me out.

"Remember the neighbour across the street from Erminda? She's the President of the CDR (Committee for the Defense of the Revolution). She's always watching — when I enter the house, when I come out — she could report me. You must understand, *mi amor*, life in Cuba is not easy."

I am alone here, learning the language, clinging to Onaldo who seems to be abandoning me. I feel all the energy drain from my body, but we have arrived at Erminda León's *casa particular* and there she is waiting on the front porch with old Hernando. She throws her arms around me. "Aieee, Karinita, we've been waiting for you! Welcome to my house! I've cleaned your room, it's all ready for you, come, come!" And she bustles me past Nando who gives me a kiss and mumbles something in his indecipherable Cuban Spanish, down the corridor, through the kitchen, and into my room.

"What will you eat, Karinita? I have fish, I have chicken. Onaldo says you like fish. And I have salad for you, and *papas fritas.*"

Everything is so familiar from the last time. The door to the courtyard is open, sunlight flooding in. I open my suitcase and give Erminda the first of her gifts — a cotton housedress, coral with white lacy trim. She laughs and twirls, holding it against her body like a dance partner.

"Karinita, *mi amor,* it's so beautiful. I must show it to Nando," and she waltzes out of my room.

I am sitting on the bed, trying to regain my equilibrium when Onaldo walks in. He sits beside me and puts his arm around me. "Don't worry, *mi amor.* I will find a place for us to be together. There's a *compañera* at work — she has a *casita* outside of Baracoa . . ."

"But Onaldo, I'm here for three months . . . "

"We can go away, to Guantánamo, to Santiago de Cuba . . . " He kisses me, thrusting his tongue into my mouth, but I don't want it, not now. I want us to be at the airport again, before everything became complicated. I feel immobilized, as though I'm trying to wade through thick syrup. How can you complain when you don't understand the situation?

Onaldo is on his feet, striding across the room. "I will come tomorrow," he says, standing in the doorway a moment, then he's gone.

I sit on the bed in shocked silence. Everything has turned white. I hear his deep voice bidding farewell to Nando and Erminda.

Soon Erminda comes to my door. She looks at me, then comes and sits beside me, her arm around my shoulders.

"It will be all right," she says. "You're in my house, Karinita. I will look after you."

The Death of Pedro Iván

Saturday, December 30th, 2007

THE OCEAN WAS A BRILLIANT TURQUOISE WITH waves crashing over the rocks, sending spume flying. Flecks of it stung me and dried instantly, leaving my skin salty, sticky. This was not the grand curving Malecón of Havana. I was at the other end of *El Caimán*, swept down from his tail in Pinar del Rio to the hungry jaw of Oriente. I was in Baracoa, the eye of the alligator, surrounded by mountainous jungle and, to the north, the flat-topped rock of El Yunque, a brooding presence shrouded with clouds — a sinister child dressed for a fiesta.

Something was bobbing on the cresting waves, sucked under and thrown back repeatedly. I couldn't tell if it was a pig or a dog — a *piñata* with rigid legs and inflated body. I remembered a dead dog I'd seen years ago, swollen like a balloon, the memory of it in my nostrils. I watched the creature for a while, waited for it to come ashore on the ragged tearing rocks that separated the ocean from the sea wall, but the waves threw and pulled with a great sucking sound, keeping the dead thing at a teasing distance.

He was late. I sat in the bar of the Hotel Rusa — the little round tables were dark brown, the bar a long slab of darkness — and looked up at the television suspended from the ceiling in the corner. The hotel receptionist slouched on a bar stool watching the afternoon *tele-novela*. No soap ads interrupt Cuban soap operas — the only propaganda is revolutionary. Every morning I listened to Radio Rebelde which broadcast old speeches by Fidel while we all waited for him to die. When I asked about him people were silent as though struck dumb by the possibility of change. *The Comandante is recuperating. He will come back.* Cuba hung by a thread, every pipe springing a leak, every chunk of masonry cracked and crumbling, gashes at intervals on the streets where the inner workings of the town's water system were revealed. The whole island was suspended in the grip of imminent death, as though a large hand squeezed its throat. I remembered how we had planned, my sisters and I, for our brother's final days, not realizing that we were living them. Impossible to believe in death. It had been impossible.

On the wall next to the television hung a portrait of La Rusa, a pale-skinned beauty of the Flapper era, an opera singer married to a wealthy New Yorker. She'd been famous in Baracoa for her support of the Revolution and for her elegant hotel on the Malecón with its sun-bleached ochre exterior and a handful of rooms looking out to sea. They say that Che Guevara stayed at La Rusa, Camilo Cienfuegos, perhaps even Fidel.

"The woman in the *novela* looks like La Rusa in the painting," I said, "Her pale skin, her blonde hair . . . "

The receptionist gave a slow nod, a twitch at the corner of her mouth. I'd become accustomed to the restraint of Cuban service employees. It was like a kind of glazed absence, especially evident in the frigidly air conditioned dollar stores where stony-faced women went through the motions of service while queues of shoppers grew longer, jostling for position. I recognized that state from my own childhood — a paralysis that occurs when every energetic impulse is blocked, until the body becomes a closed system housing a fugitive spirit. In Cuba there seemed a lack of incentive for people stuck in the same make-work jobs for twenty or thirty years at a subsistence salary — that, and perhaps lack of protein, lack of possibility to imagine a world beyond the floating back of El Caimán.

When Onaldo arrived finally in a bici-taxi he seemed surprised to find me there. "I was at your house," he said accusingly.

"But Onaldo, we arranged to meet here, didn't we?"

He asked for money to pay the bici-boy and when he came back he was looking at his watch. Another rushed afternoon meeting.

We ordered two beers and while we waited for the barman to bring them, I gave him a bundle of Chinese temple papers I'd sewn into a book for him, with a poem for Año Nuevo. The papers were red and gold, the ink a startling blue. Onaldo read the poem slowly. He was a man of words himself, though strangely he did not speak much. He used his words on paper — sometimes poetic, sometimes archival, drawn from the mouths of a dying generation — and even his books were small and thin. But there was a richness to his body that hinted at a wealth within the secrecy of his dark skin. Onaldo's body had been my home since our first encounter, the solidity of him, the changing hue of his skin from dark to brown to ruddy gold.

He read my poem carefully and, ever the editor, corrected one of the words. Other than that, not much but a slow nod of appreciation. Then he picked up a book that lay on the table — Santería: African Magic in Latin America. The cover was red and bore an oval image of Christ crucified, a rooster, a ladder, a snake.

Circling the egg were likenesses of the major *orishas* — Changó, Oshún, Yemayá, Obatalá, Elegguá, Oggún — each doubled with a Catholic saint; originally a ruse to disguise the true religion of the Africans brought to the Americas as slaves.

Onaldo frowned as he leafed through the book, his glasses resting on the bridge of his nose. He couldn't read English but I'd often found him poring over one of my books, holding it in those pale-palmed hands, staring at the words as though he might absorb the sense of them by an effort of will and handling. I showed him the illustrations — black and white photographs of processions in Havana in honour of Yemayá and Oshún, of animal offerings, ritual objects and talismans used to cast spells and protect the home, grainy photographs of *santeros* possessed by their *orishas*. I'd been reading about possession when Onaldo arrived, about the initiation ceremony called *asiento* where the saints mount their initiates and ride them.

I thought of Fidel who'd been known in his younger days as *El Caballo* — the horse — presumably a reference to his sexual potency. But I'd also read that Fidel owed his success to the blessing of the *babalawos*, the high priests of Santería, and I wondered if it was indeed he who was mounted and ridden by the African deities who thus held him in a position of power, concealing their own powers, as Celia Sanchez had concealed herself in Fidel's huge shadow while she called the shots. It is a well-kept secret amongst the Cuban people that the Revolution was led by Celia, a gentle woman from Media Luna who determined to oust Batista when a child was raped to death in Havana by American *mafiosos*. Celia had been at the child's birth, assisting her father who was a doctor, and she had known the little girl all of her short life. It was Celia who gathered troops and ammunition in the Sierra Maestra, and when Fidel, Che, Camilo and their men arrived from Mexico in the famous yacht, the Granma, she chose Fidel as their leader. But he never made a decision without her. She always had the last word until her death in 1980.

Onaldo began to speak rapidly and my mind raced to keep up. We volleyed words back and forth and as I spoke he glanced again at his watch. Only an hour until he had to return to work. We'd wasted precious time with the misunderstanding about our rendezvous. I felt his impatience with my slow Spanish as he broke in again, all the while touching me, holding my arm and releasing it, punctuating his words. At first I'd thought him unique, but now I saw his gestures and heard his intonations everywhere — an entire island of people in lingual and gestural harmony, contained in a bell jar.

"Yarisel needs new clothes for *Año Nuevo*," he said, "She was crying last night. She has nothing to wear for the fiesta . . ."

I'd heard the same story too often in the past few days. Something in me kicked and I said, "If I could be included in your life, if I could get to know your granddaughter, feel free to visit in your house, then of course . . . "

I had not been invited to Migdalia's house as on my previous two visits, and whenever I mentioned it Onaldo was vague, preoccupied. We'd been to Guantánamo for Christmas at his sister's house where I had met their mother, a dear little woman who had embraced me with a warmth equal to Onaldo's. But even though Christmas was no big deal in Cuba, everyone saving themselves for New Year and the anniversary of the Revolution, it had seemed odd to me that there'd been absolutely no mention in Guantánamo of Migdalia or Yarisel.

"You know I want to help, Onaldo, but I feel used."

His response was rapid, his dark eyes flashing unforgettably, then he was on his feet, hovering in the doorway as I paid the bill. We went outside and stood on the sidewalk in awkward silence.

"I'll see you tomorrow," he said finally. "We will forget about this."

Then he leaned down to kiss my cheek and we parted. I walked back along the Malecón, and because I was on the other side of the street I forgot to look for the swollen creature tossing there.

I turned onto Calle Moncada and entered the bright house where I rented a room. The front wall was yellow ochre and on it were inscribed the names of my hosts — Erminda Léon and Hernándo Puentes — with a painted palm, *la palma real*, the symbol of Cuba. I had an office in back of the house where I worked in the cool early mornings sitting at a rickety table covered with Erminda's best cloth, light filtering through the wooden shutters and a double door like a stable-gate opening onto a garden lush with banana palms, papaya and baricoci trees, and Erminda's many plants which she used for healing teas. As I tapped out my stories I was accompanied by the grunting and squealing of the neighbours' pigs, the crowing of roosters and clucking of chickens as they laid their eggs, and the barking of the neighbourhood dogs that set each other going in chorus throughout the day. Occasionally someone made it past Erminda's vigilant guarding of my privacy to distract me with a gift of oranges or bananas and some delightful conversation. They thought me odd to spend my mornings so, but then I was a foreigner and they could no more understand me than I them. We would question and puzzle at each other, then bypass our confusion with laughter.

During the first week in my office I had struggled with a new novel I was writing, about my father who had been a Mosleyite and had spent the war years as a detainee in a British labour camp. After several days of shuffling papers around, reading and re-reading my research notes and the first chapters I had drafted, I had to admit to the incompatibility of imagining wartime Europe while living in Cuba. So that is how I began to write my Cuban stories, in a spirit of self-preservation, reeling from the shock of Onaldo's unexpected behaviour. Rosamund's story was one of the first. We'd met on my first visit to Baracoa and her situation had captured my imagination in a way that I now began to see as prescient. Onaldo and I had been wry observers of her doomed affair with Ángel, but I had felt some solidarity with her as a fellow *extranjera* and had been moved to imagine her predicament.

My stories grew and developed into a celebration as time went on and my circle of friends and acquaintances grew. The best of ventures often creep up on us in the guise of playfulness, as something temporary and incidental, not to be taken seriously. These stories, however, eventually became vital to my understanding of the situation I found myself in.

I stopped in the kitchen to talk with Erminda, hiding behind the brightness that came so easily to me in Spanish, a new language that made me feel like a child again with the possibility of a new beginning. Every morning we greeted each other in the courtyard in our white nightgowns. A wrought iron gate led off my bedroom and I would open the wooden shutters, unlock the gate from the inside and step out to embrace Erminda. We would look up at the sky where often clouds were gathered, threatening rain, but on this morning the sky had been a clear blue. I told her about the dog-pig and Erminda laughed.

"Just a dead animal," she said and teased me about my refusal to eat the neighbour's pig they'd killed for her grandson's birthday. There was to be a fiesta for him the next day — New

Year's Eve. The pig had screamed horribly, a piercing sound which had faded gradually as it bled to death.

As we stood talking by the kitchen table a woman entered, grim-faced, but unmistakably related.

"Ah, another sister," I said.

There were fifteen in Erminda's family, and as I got to know them, a warm and inclusive clan, we joked that I was #16, an honorary sister.

"Alina," Erminda said, and embraced her sister in that gentle way she had, laying her head on Alina's shoulder. Then everything changed. There were some rapid words, too fast for me to understand. I saw several women clustering in the doorway. I saw Erminda recoil, her arms flying in the air, then collapsing around her head.

"*Esta muy grave*, Erminda," — it's very serious — Alina said, her voice expressionless.

"*¡No, no, Dios mío, no!*" Erminda wailed, and the women moved to surround her.

I slipped into my room and closed the door. I sat on the bed and picked up my Spanish grammar book. *Yo normalmente me despierto a las seis.* Wailing sounds from the kitchen, from the *sala*, more people entering the house, many voices rising and falling. *Entonces, yo me levanto a las seis y me baño.* I should go to her. Something is terribly wrong. But there are too many people and I don't understand. *¿A qué hora se acuestan los niños?* I read the words over and over, nothing making sense. In my throat a bird beat its wings, trying to escape. I smelled the swollen dog and my gorge rose.

"Karinita?" Erminda's voice at the door.

"Erminda, what is it? What's happened?"

"My nephew is dead, an accident . . . "

I thought it was a niece, confusing my genders once again.

"No, no," she grasped my hands, "Pedro Iván, my nephew who works in Moa for the Canadian mining company. He fell from the balcony of his apartment."

Erminda had talked about this man almost every day. He was like a son, and she worried about his drinking. She'd raised him since he was four when his mother, Erminda's sister, had died in childbirth.

"I was expecting him. He always comes for *Año Nuevo*."

I held Erminda, but she was stiff and unyielding. "When someone dies in Canada we light a candle for their soul," I said, "And place their photo near to it."

Erminda rustled in the drawer of the kitchen dresser and turned to me. In her arthritic fingers she held a black and white photo of a twelve year old boy. His face was solemn and he wore a Russian school uniform with a loose tie around his neck. I lit one of the scented candles I'd brought from Canada. I'd bought them thinking they'd make a good gift for someone, never imagining this light flickering on a dead boy's face as the aroma of ginger and lemon filled the room. Erminda began talking with that animation that often signals a state of shock. She kept on talking as Alina entered from the *sala* and sat in the kitchen rocker. Then her brother Francisco came, a tall handsome man, his body stiff and awkward in the women's kitchen as he leaned down to kiss Erminda. I slipped past the women sitting in the front room, and out onto the street.

It was late as I approached the funeral parlour. I'd been walking for hours. Earlier the dim streets had been lit by flickering television screens, everyone watching *la novela*. I'd seen a large woman, her hair braided in a circle on her crown, knitting in front of the screen, a fat baby girl wobbling on pudgy legs, clinging to the woman's knees. From every open doorway a room was revealed — a gleaming motorcycle leaning against the wall, a long corridor leading to a tiled kitchen with a faded blue refrigerator, an old woman rocking, children playing, Christmas trees with lights still blinking — lives spilling onto the street. Some homes were dark holes boarded with broken planks, dogs patrolling the rooftops, snarling and setting up a chain of barking as I passed.

I'd glanced into the Casa de la Trova to see if Onaldo was there, wondering if he was still angry. I'd wanted to join the dancers and lose myself in the piercing trill of the clarinet, the rhythm of *la musica tradicional*. Swivel-hipped men danced as they breathed, effortlessly, dark hands on white skin, bodies snaking and pressing as they guided tattooed foreigners around the tight dance floor. But I'd walked on, the music filling my mind, until I'd found myself on a corner, recognition creeping in slowly as I'd looked up at the spiral staircase ascending into the emptiness of Onaldo's collapsed balcony. Rubble was piled on the sidewalk where the downstairs neighbour had been sweeping the ruins of her patio.

From the upstairs window an irregular blue pulsing had signalled the changing images on a television screen. I'd heard voices in dialogue — perhaps a movie on the DVD player which Onaldo insisted Migdalia had bought with the proceeds of her hairdressing business. I'd paced the block, always returning to the shadows, staring up into the impossibility of our own dialogue. Finally the patterning changed and I'd heard Fidel's voice. He was talking about refrigerators, giving detailed statistics — it was the same speech I'd heard him deliver in the Plaza de la Revolution when Chavez had visited Havana a year ago. I imagined the old man's long finger stabbing the air with each statistic, his youthful passion grown pedantic. I imagined

Onaldo's face locked on the screen, the curve of his upper lip, his glowing skin.

The funeral parlour was next door to Mirian Zelda's house. I'd seen her sitting in the open doorway every night as I walked home, a hibiscus flower in her hair, the lights of a tiny Christmas tree blinking behind her. Her parlour was a hive of light with golden walls. She was a handsome woman who had two daughters by Erminda's son, Hernandito. Everyone seemed connected in Baracoa, but the order was breaking down. The mouth of the alligator, after years of hunger, now fed on foreign visitors and their influence. Mirian Zelda's younger daughter had an Italian lover more than twice her age. He came three times a year loaded with gifts and all the family benefitted, turning the blind eye that enables and normalizes in the clasp of necessity. But he couldn't marry Linancia because he had a wife and children in Italy. He bought her instead hand-made shoes with stiletto heels, clothing that was tight and revealing, and a startling array of nail polishes. She'd quit her job in order to be available for Luigi, but had begun offering manicures to alleviate her boredom.

As I walked past the funeral parlour light spilled from the double doors, open to the street where people clustered like guests at a dance waiting for the music to begin. Women sat inside, heads tilted in conversation. A white-tiled cafeteria displaying the inevitable ham and cheese sandwiches separated Mirian Zelda's house from the funeral parlour. The prospect of food so close to death turned my stomach. I wondered if Erminda was there. I wanted to cross the street and look for her, to join in the wake and bathe in the flood of light, but I walked past slowly, careful not to stare, and turned the corner to my house.

The funeral was arranged for four in the afternoon of the next day. The birthday lunch had been cancelled. "We'll have it tomorrow for New Year's Day," Erminda said. "We must eat the pig." She was trembling, her shoulders hunched, her brow furrowed and anxious, as though she could prevent Iván's fall with her worrying. I held her hand and talked to her, trying to bring her back from that strange zone of magical possibility.

"You must eat something, Erminda. Have some bread with a slice of cheese, or a plate of rice and beans," but she shook her head and went to sit at the funeral parlour. She would stay there all day, until it was time for the procession to the cemetery. I sat on the front terrace waiting for Onaldo. He came at noon. "There's been a tragedy in our house," I said, and he listened while I told him, the death holding us, banishing our discord.

We walked over to the funeral parlour where the women sat inside on stiff, high-backed chairs, talking and wringing their hands, while the men stood out front, all zipped up. I looked for Erminda while Onaldo greeted the mourners, shaking the men's hands, kissing the women's damp cheeks. In back of the dense parlour was the casket. It seemed so small, so narrow and inconspicuous. All the women were gathered there, the sisters and aunts and cousins, clustered around Iván's head. Erminda called to me and Onaldo, reaching out her arms to us.

"*Mira, mira,*" she said urgently, "How beautiful his face, not even damaged. His hair, his skin . . . "

The casket was closed except for a sheet of glass covering his face. Onaldo stood on one side, looking directly down at Iván, while I leaned over from the other side, grasping Erminda's hand. I saw the startling whiteness of his skin, like marble against a shock of black hair and his moustache, and of course I remembered our brother lying on the hospital trestle, his beauty taking my breath away. I wanted to look and look at Iván, the communion with death never enough for me, but the blood family was gathered at his head, jewels in the crown of his death, and I felt myself an intruder.

I wondered if it was suicide. No one had said that word, but I'd heard the story of his father, a *combatiente* and loyal member of *El Partido,* who had been accused by the police of attempting to sell a television. He had been found at the kitchen table slumped by the television set, a note stuck to the screen. *No pretendia vender este televisor. Se lo estaba arreglando a mi vecino* — I did not intend to sell this television. I was minding it for my neighbour. He had stabbed himself many times in the chest, then slashed his throat. No one spoke of the blood, only of the television and the terrible accusation the police had made against a man whose life had been devoted to a Revolution that strove to resist the marketplace.

Suicides are different from accidental deaths, the mystery of a suicide haunting us as we try to imagine that extremity. My father's death still shadows me. I dream of him, and of my brother as I wander through a dark night carrying their bodies, searching for a place to bury them. We carry our dead with us wherever we go, and the grief continues until we are able to integrate those who have passed and allow them to live through us, enriching us. In Cuba one is encouraged to think about family, to clothe yourself with them, because to Cubans, family is everything. People will ask you, "And how is your family?" even though they know nothing of your relatives — it is simply an extension of "How are you?" because we are indeed inextricable from our families, and this is recognized in Cuba. I remembered the power of Christopher's dying, his breathing raw and laboured, the silence of his bones jutting as we stood around his bed in the hospital room, my hand on the wing of his pelvis, the city street below us, land stretching thousands of miles to the ocean, re-emerging on the other side of the world, minds and hearts stretching all the way across, and my brother labouring on his last lap to leave this world, how he breathed himself out and flew straight as an arrow, the peace and completion of that sureness. But we were bereft. It is we, the survivors, who suffer our inability to understand such willingness to let go of the world. I stared down at Pedro Iván's face beneath the glass and wondered what his final expression had been before his face had been set into repose.

The alarm rang, pulling me from a dream where Onaldo was calling to me down a long corridor. He'd gone back to work, saying he would return in the afternoon to walk with me in the funeral procession. I dressed quickly and arrived in time to see the coffin being carried to the hearse. The roof of the car was piled with red and orange-petalled flowers. I hung back, looking for Onaldo, and felt the ocean trembling in my throat, the dead dog jiggling. I saw Erminda finally, standing behind the hearse with her daughter, Irma, their backs rounded as they walked, oh so slowly, hands pressed against the crawling hearse, heads bent, pushing. It was the gesture of Erminda's sweeping, her endless washing and scrubbing, pushing and pulling, the gesture of a lifetime of domestic toil. The procession snaked behind them, curving round potholes filled with filthy water and stretches of sidewalk gaping like broken-toothed mouths.

The cemetery was high above the town. As we approached the tower at the cemetery gates I realized that Onaldo was not coming. The procession halted and everyone stood around as the *despedida de duelos* was spoken for the family, acknowledging the life of Pedro Iván, his achievements, the eternal love of his family. When the speech was over, many of the mourners slipped away, back to their homes, while the hearse crept forward with the family through the gates of the sprawling cemetery where generations of Baracoans lay in close communion under marble slabs topped with crosses and heavy-winged angels. There was one angel in particular that towered over all the others. Despite an androgynous form, she seemed quintessentially female. She had huge wings which, though they were obviously heavy, gave me the feeling that she could be lifted by the wind and carried by the power of those wings high above the town, swooping down to the shore.

I saw the ocean in the distance, a streak of aquamarine under a pure blue sky with banks of engorged cloud on the horizon. I picked up a small stone from the well-trodden path and held it in my palm, smooth. Sunday, the eve of a new year.

The men set to work opening the tomb where Erminda's parents were interred with their daughter. After thirty-eight years Pedro Iván was to be reunited finally with his mother. The coffin was lowered into the tomb on long ropes, the men struggling with the weight of it, their muscles bulging dangerously. A terrible wail split the air, and it was seconds before I realized it was Erminda, her hands flying once again above her bowed head, grieving as her dead sister would have done had she been alive. Hernandito and Francisco took her arms and walked her up the path and sat with her on the edge of another grave at a distance from Pedro Iván's grave. Irma joined them, her face like a stone.

Pedro Iván's friend, Pancho, mixed a pile of cement in the middle of the path. He spaded three shovelfuls into a bucket that was passed, hand by hand, down the line to a rake-thin man in a loose shirt standing inside the grave. He tipped the cement onto the coffin, beginning at the head, covering that face under the glass, and leveled it out with a spatula. Only his head and shoulders were visible as he worked, as if he were a baby struggling to come into the world. He continued until the cement was finished, the coffin covered, then he climbed out. But before it was done, Erminda and Irma began to walk down the sloping path to the cemetery gates, Irma's sons on either side, a line of blood linked. I followed them and after a while, without looking back, Irma reached for my hand. We walked together, arms linked, then she slipped back, the boys dropped away and I walked alone with Erminda, supporting her, through the cemetery gates where Oya, the Yoruba goddess of death and rebirth, holds sway as Keeper of the Cemetery and guide to the spirits of the dead. I turned then and looked at the angel. That's her, I thought, that's where she resides.

Erminda kicked off her shoes and curled into the kitchen rocker. I relit the candle and picked up the photo of Pedro Iván, holding it between my fingers.

"What was he like?"

I leaned forward to listen, replacing the photo by the flickering candle. Behind Erminda's flood of words was a bright-eyed grief too fresh yet to know itself. I remembered my last reading, before Onaldo had arrived at La Rusa, about the law of similarity pertaining to sympathetic magic — the contagion of an inexplicable attraction between objects that have been in contact and continue to affect each other long after physical contact has been broken. Erminda was on her feet now, searching in the drawer amongst the photos. She'd remembered something. She turned with a small stone in the palm of her hand, a face painted there, its mouth a flower of faded red petals.

"He painted it at school," she said, "when he was seven years old, and he gave it to me for my birthday."

"Put this with it," I said, unfolding my fingers. "A gift from Oya."

The family began to arrive from the cemetery — Irma, Hernandito, Alina, Francisco, old Nando, his voice gruff. Erminda went into the *sala* to greet them, still clasping her stone. I watched the candle fade and sputter, drowning in its pool of wax, then I picked it up and poured the wax into the palm of my hand where it burned, gathering all my senses. As the wax cooled and set, I exhaled and set the candle, burning brightly now, back in its saucer. I blinked my wet lashes and felt the ocean subside in my throat. Then I turned and entered my room, closed the door behind me, sat on my bed and molded the warm amber wax. It smelled of ginger and lemon. As I worked a familiar form began to emerge — high cheek-bones, broad nostrils, ears flat to the head, heavy-lidded eyes, strong teeth pushing the mouth forward. A disembodied head, carrying all the force of his powerful body, had emerged, unbidden, from my burning hands.

I went out later to walk on the Malecón, half expecting to see the dog-pig floating, but there was nothing visible in the darkening ocean. I looked up into the sky, bruised deep red with the promise of a better day. I walked the entire length of the Malecón and when I returned, at the very end of that day, the end of the year, I saw him standing at the corner of Calle Moncada. My hand went automatically to my mouth and I smelled the warmth of my own waxen palm.

⌁

The Barbacoa

DOÑA FLORA SAT IN THE CENTRE OF an old blue mattress, her stumps tangled in the greyish sheet that swathed her hips. Her ears were sharp with listening. She could see nothing beyond the faded blue walls of her room save a corner of the kitchen where the *gallina* foraged on the earthen floor tugging at the string tied tight around her leg. A little light filtered from the courtyard, but Flora could only imagine the cloudless sky, the plants that her granddaughter Sonia had told her grew in the corners of the yard soaking up the water that splashed from the stone *pila* as she washed the children's clothes.

They all lived together, four generations of women — Flora, with her daughter Tamara, granddaughter Sonia, and great granddaughters Marielena and Mumu. It was a small wooden house with a stable door onto the street, the top flap always open, and gaps in the high ceiling where water flooded in when it rained. Flora had been born there, Tamara too, but after the Revolution more hospitals were built and that's where the women went now when their labour started. Doña Flora had brought many souls into the world before her profession had died out. There were no more midwives. Now the babies were delivered by caesarean sections performed by male surgeons.

The front room was dominated by a television and a rusty old refrigerator which hadn't functioned in two years. It was barely ten steps, (the memory of those steps in Flora's phantom feet), to the room where Sonia and her mother shared a bed, and the girls their outgrown cot.

Sonia was thin and drawn from long nights of studying. She worked all day then picked the children up from *Circulo Infantíl*, brought them home and hurried to a friend's house to study on the computer. How many meals had she missed? Flora had watched her grow from a fat little girl into a voluptuous teenager. She'd been only sixteen when she'd met Arturo, recently moved from his parents' house in *el campo* to work in construction. On her eighteenth birthday she gave birth to Marielena, two years later came Mumu, a tiny curly haired girl with a high chirping voice and huge dark eyes — the image of her mother.

There was no room for Arturo in their house. He'd slept here and there, camping out with friends, and had eventually moved in with the mother of his third child — it was the only solution — she had a house. But Sonia still loved him and the children adored their Papi. Flora would hear them scream as he roared up the muddy street on his motorbike, and she would gather her nightdress around her and pat her hair into place.

With the money sent from the girls' godmother in Canada, Sonia was gradually accumulating materials to build a small room on the roof, a *barbacoa* where she and Arturo could be together finally. First they had to fix the water cistern and wait for a new refrigerator — these were priorities, for the children. Flora imagined her beautiful granddaughter making love with handsome Arturo on the roof above her bed, safe in each other's arms in their *barbacoa*, a thousand stars falling on them, blessing them.

In the silence of dawn's light Flora's head was inclined, her eyes fixed on the eyes of the Virgin, whose face was beatific, rays of light streaming from her exposed heart. Yesterday the Canadian had come and hung the Virgin on her wall. She'd heard the knocking, Tamara running, the little girls chirping — "¡Hada madrina, Hada madrina!" There'd been shouting and squealing, the children jumping up and down, Tamara exclaiming, "¡Aieee mi madre! ¡Karinita!"

Doña Flora wondered if Karina had smelled urine from her bedpan. Tamara never seemed to get around to emptying it in the dark hole of the courtyard toilet that Flora hadn't seen in three years. She no longer noticed the acrid smell, but she'd seen Karina recoil, then gather herself with a sudden shallowness of breath before she leaned to kiss her and stroke her freshly washed hair, drying in a cloud around her head. Tamara washed her hair every week and massaged her back and arms, and Marielena brushed her hair for hours while Flora told her the story of *Blanca Nieves y Los Siete Enanitos*. But with the Canadian, Flora had been aware of her soiled nightgown gaping at the arms. She didn't care that her withered breasts might show, dangling uselessly — it was her stumps she had wanted to hide. Surprising that a second loss could be so hard — the pride of that one leg swinging over the bed, able to support her weight during the Canadian's summer visit. She didn't want to use the wheelchair that Sonia had brought home. She was ashamed to go out on the street.

"I'll come back in the afternoon," Karina had said, "When Sonia is here."

Sonia had been gone since nine that morning, writing her final examination. She would be the first in the family to receive her *Licenciatura*, in psychology. Tamara worked at the hospital as a nursing assistant, changing dressings and emptying bedpans.

Sonia had returned at midday, too excited to eat with Tamara and the children. "Mami, I got a high score on the exam," she'd said, trembling, "I'm going to have my graduation!" Tamara had let out a high-pitched whoop, and Mumu had screamed as Sonia picked her up and whirled her around the kitchen. Marielena had hugged her mother's hips, her little face plump with smiling.

In the afternoon Doña Flora had been roused from a half-sleep by more shouting. The Canadian had returned and this time it was Sonia's voice she'd heard, quivering as she jumped up and down, hugging Karinita. She'd heard the Canadian giving out gifts with her faltering Spanish. Soon they'd come to her room, Mumu in a tiny red dress with a string of pearls floating in a tight net held by red ribbons, Marielena in a pink butterfly top, her little round bottom resilient inside tight black pants. They'd paraded back and forth practicing the drum majorette routine they'd learned in school band. "¡Aieee, Dios mío!" Tamara had exclaimed, spinning in a black sequinned skirt and a gold knit top that hugged her plunging breasts.

Sonia had stood at Flora's bedside, the skirt of a bright new dress spread between her outstretched arms. "Now we can all present ourselves proudly for my graduation," she'd said. And she'd turned and taken the picture of the Virgin down from the wall, kissed it, and gently replaced it.

Karina had sat smiling at the end of Flora's bed, Marielena and Mumu hanging onto her. She had tickled Mumu's arm. "Hormiga, hormiga, hormiga corre," she'd chanted, imitating an ant running up and down the child's arm. Mumu had giggled and Marielena had held out her arm to be tickled. After Karina left, the fun had continued for a while, until the house subsided into a long night.

Doña Flora hardly ever slept deeply now. Her life was a reverie of half-sleep, drifting in and out of consciousness, travelling through time as memories of her youth returned.

She'd had her own Arturo and she had entwined her shapely legs around his hips every night as he moved against her, cupping her buttocks in his hands. When Tamara was ten years old he'd gone to Havana to look for work. He never returned.

All her life was contained within those walls, a shroud of memories swirling around her, binding and containing her with all that had passed. She would never again step out of the house, until one day her legs would return and she would look down at her delicate turn of ankle, her broad feet with toes slanting in two perfect lines, and she would stand up and float out the door, along Calle Rubert Lopez, down to Parque Central where lovers would be lounging, leaning into each other, passing the time until night came to envelop them. Artisans would be selling their wares in front of the Catholic church, the oldest in all of the Americas, and she would float down to the ocean, to the Malecón where spumy waves crashed against the stone parapet, spraying her legs. She would run along the sea wall, her arms outspread, and rise like a bird to Las Terrazas de Yara where her ancestors had lived before Columbus came. She remembered how cool it was there amidst the Royal Palms, the ground thick with their débris. She would drink coconut milk, the thin cool liquid running down her chin and neck, trickling between her breasts and onto her belly. Flora would make her descent along ancient stone pathways, the air thickening as she came closer to the water, and there she would bathe in the Rio Miel, as she had bathed with Arturo, to ensure his eventual return, according to the legend. As she emerged, dripping, a wet cloth of hair clinging to her head, the red earth would pull her forward, westward along the sand. Her muscles would strain for purchase in the shifting sand, then she would be on solid ground climbing towards the cemetery where all the dead look out over the town of Baracoa.

La Terraza

SONIA HAD NEVER BEEN INSIDE LA TERRAZA Tropical, even though the nightclub was right in front of her house and she'd lain in bed listening to the cabaret music for many years. Of course she knew all the songs by heart, and she knew the dancers and singers too because she saw them on the street every day — Misha, Odalis, Lobo, Iliana — but in their show costumes they would be transformed.

She had never imagined that she might go there with Arturo. He was such a dancer! And Karinita was paying for everything — for her new dress, for the *entrada*, for a bottle of rum.

Last night she'd been up till three in the morning at Isaida's house studying for her exam until her eyes felt full of sand. But it had been worth it because she'd studied all the right things and had been able to answer everything. After Karinita's visit Mami looked after the girls and gave them their supper while Sonia lay down for a nap, but she only tossed and turned so finally she took a shower to refresh herself and tried on her new dress and the shoes Isaida had lent her.

"Look, Abuela!" Sonia twirled around her grandma's bed and plunked herself down beside Doña Flora, laughing and kissing her soft cheeks.

"*Aiee chica!*" her *abuela* had exclaimed, stroking Sonia's cheeks with her papery hands, "You will be the most beautiful girl at La Terraza."

By the time Arturo arrived she'd checked her makeup and combed out her tangled hair a dozen times so she was more than ready. They tucked Mumu and Marielena into their cot together and kissed them goodnight.

"Marielena must have her own bed," Sonia said, "*Mira,* Arturo, she's getting too big."

"First the *barbacoa,*" he said, "So that we can be together, *mi amor.*" And he had grasped her hair in his big hand and kissed her mouth so tenderly that she didn't care that her lipstick was smeared and her hair messed up after all that fussing.

Karinita met them at the entrance and they climbed the stairs together to the rooftop dance floor of La Terraza. Sonia's eyes grew big and round. She was beyond smiling. She was in a dream world, looking down on the top of her own *casita,* imagining the *barbacoa* Arturo would build with his *amigo* César. As Arturo turned her and held her hips, pulling her against him, Sonia saw herself lying under the stars with him, making love in their own private room, with a roof made of leaves and the moon shining through, patterning their bodies with light. They would be like two lizards dropped from above, surprised to find themselves in a bed of their own. Isaida even knew someone with a good mattress and she was saving it for Sonia.

She longed for Arturo to leave the other house and come to live with her. She couldn't bear to think of him in that woman's bed, sleeping with her every night — though she would rather share him than live without him. He was her *gordo*. Like Marielena, he loved to eat, and his solid body gave Sonia comfort and pleasure. She tried not to think of Arturo at night, lying in the sagging bed she shared with her mamá, but often he entered her dreams and made love to her there, and the dream would carry her through the day.

Sometimes they argued about money, and about why he didn't visit the girls more often, then she would feel so angry and helpless that she refused to let him touch her. But she always returned to him in the end, into his arms, strong from building *casas*, from riding to *el campo* gripping the handles of his motorbike. She loved his smooth, brown hands, cool like the water of Rio Miel. He knew exactly how to touch her — every time she was lost. They danced, swaying in circles, bending rhythmically, living for another day.

The moon had almost disappeared behind *El Castillo*, the big hotel up on the hill, when Sonia crept into bed beside Mami, who was on her back, mouth open, snoring. No sound from Abuela or the children. Sonia fell asleep immediately, but she woke early as dawn was breaking and crept out past Abuela's room to the courtyard to pee. As she tiptoed back she saw her grandma sitting up in bed looking at the wall. The sheet was tangled around her and there was something odd about her stillness, as though she were propped there by invisible hands.

"Abuela!" Sonia whispered, but Doña Flora didn't move. A dog began to bark somewhere down the street, then another and another, roosters crowing, but her *abuela* was silent. Sonia reached out to touch her, but even before her hand reached her grandma's shoulder she felt the coldness. She touched Abuela's cheek, quite, quite cold, her eyes wide open, staring at the Virgin, as though she waited for something, someone.

"*Mi abuela,*" Sonia whispered, and she began to cry because she couldn't bear the loss. All her life Abuela had been there with her loving arms, her patient smile, her laughter. Sonia stared into her eyes a long time before she touched her fingers to the lids and closed them. She gathered the small body, so light in her arms, and laid her down with her head on the pillow. She fluffed Abuela's hair around her like a halo and sat with her until Mami and the children woke.

Palace of the Princess

DURING HIS SECOND YEAR IN AFRICA LÉSTER had e-mailed his
fiancé, Inés, part of a story he was writing. It was a fairytale
about a Princess who was locked in a castle. Her father invited
suitors for her hand, but each suitor was required to answer a
series of questions. Only the suitor who gave a perfect set of
answers would be successful in his quest for the hand of the
Princess. Each hopeful was greeted and entertained personally
by the King. He would lull the young man into a sense of
confidence, giving him wine to drink and rich foods to eat. He
would converse with him about many things, then abruptly turn
to the questions.

How many brothers do you have?
Where has the road led you?
How will you defend yourself against the enemy?

Some answered literally *–I have three brothers, your Majesty,
brave and strong. If aught should assail me my brothers would
take care of my wife.*

Some answered philosophically — *Oh, your Highness, the
world is filled with my brothers.*

The practical suitors would reply — *The road, your Majesty,
has led to your magnificent palace.*

Or, for the broader and more imaginative, *the road has led me to the crossroads of my life where I have the choice to continue as a merry bachelor, or to enter into the holy bond of marriage which will hold me in honour for the rest of my life.*

Given the challenge, your Majesty, I will defend myself and my property with a crossbow and sword. Whosoever would threaten my livelihood or my home will lose his head to the sharpness of my broadsword.

The less literal-minded answered — *If I have enemies I will stand my ground until they are convinced and turn to friendship with me. Two wrongs never made a right, and the course of life is not to be hurried.*

Some of the suitors answered one question correctly and faltered on the others, some answered two correctly, and mistook only one, some answered all the questions falsely, but none answered all correctly. Until one day came a hunchbacked youth with bent spine and straggling dark hair. His eyes shone with an extraordinary green light as though all the foliage of the forest lived within him.

The King, who was a wise and exacting ruler, sat up and paid a different quality of attention to this suitor — he recognized something in him — (which surprised the Queen and all the courtiers who laughed and did not take him seriously). Furthermore the King had come from his daughter's quarters where she lay sick with longing.

Father, when will I marry? I grow old and tired waiting here for your approval of a perfect suitor.

There was something about the coincidence of the Princess's malaise with the arrival of the crookbacked youth which piqued the King's curiosity and he felt his own puzzle turn on him.

Inés had thought it a strange story. She'd asked Léster what happened to the Princess, but he had sent no more excerpts. He'd come home from his medical mission in Burkina Faso with more than fifty pages and offered them to her, but by then she'd lost interest.

Inés lay on the bed, her baby son nestled at her side, a cellular phone pressed to her ear. Léster was calling from the hospital — he had a long list of surgeries to perform — he wouldn't be home until late. *"Nos vemos, mi amor."* She clicked the phone off and let it drop onto the creamy bedspread. It was a languid afternoon and she was already sated with the long day. Her eyes rolled up into her head, but sleep would not come. She heard low voices murmuring from the foot of the bed — the *telenovela* — a tedious Brazilian romance.

Inés knew the exact placement of everything in her room — the computer next to the television, the picture of the Virgin on the wall above, and in the corner Lestercito's little empire — a crib draped with golden net, scallops of material ruched and bunched with yellow ribbons, toys hanging from the ribbons. She had discovered her pregnancy only a month after Léster's return. They had started to build their own house, next door to her parents, with the money Léster received from Fidel for his three year mission, but it was a slow process, waiting for the permit, the building materials, the workers. They'd lived with her parents and her brother Chucho while their house was being constructed on what had been her mother's rose garden. Now the earth beside their house, where roses once had bloomed, was barren, scarred with cement and gravel. Fresh from his voluntary service in Africa, Léster had become principal surgeon of the Baracoa Hospital.

Inés had been fascinated by his work from their first meeting. As he kissed her she would imagine his hands delving into dark places, holding life and death in the balance, cutting and sewing, joining threads like a seamstress, then walking home, casually shedding his clothes to lie with her, his hands on *her* body, entering *her* darkness. She'd questioned him about the heart surgeries, about the mastectomies and hysterectomies, the amputation of gangrenous limbs, trying to picture him operating on a human body, changing it forever, then washing his hands and eating lunch. She couldn't fathom the journey from one reality to another.

Diabetes was epidemic in Baracoa. Almost every other person she knew, including her own papá, had type 2 at least, often accelerating to type 1 with the unavoidable carbohydrate-based diet of rice and bread. Circulation worsened, amputations were common. What did they do with all those legs? Inés imagined them piling one on top of the other in the hospital basement like dolls' legs in a toy factory, patients limping home like war casualties, their names creeping slowly up *la lista de espera* as they waited for their prosthetic limbs while surviving on the prescribed three tablespoons of rice per meal so as to control their carbohydrate intake. For many people there was nothing else to eat, only rice and beans or starchy bread, insubstantial as the styrofoam that washed up on the beach.

One afternoon Léster came home stinking of something terrible underneath the familiar disinfectant smell that all the hospital workers carried. He'd smelled as Inés thought an unearthed corpse would smell, and he'd had to wash and scrub himself into the night, but still the smell had clung to him, the smell of a man who'd never complained, who'd lain in bed all day until his stomach swelled, and when the family had insisted on surgery Léster had found the man's innards putrefied and had sewn him up again. He'd doused his hands with lemon juice, and then with *Voltaje,* the cologne Inés had bought him for *Año Nuevo*, but nothing could mask the insistent smell that had permeated his skin.

Somewhere between her inability to solve the mystery of her husband's life and the numbness that had overtaken her since Lestercito's birth was a missed step, as though someone had cheated her of the reward for her patience. She had waited two more years for Léster after he had proposed to her and placed a ring on her engagement finger the day before he returned to Africa, only one year into his foreign mission. She was accustomed to waiting, like all Cubans. But he was home now, and she had her son, and she was still waiting, and for what?

Lestercito gurgled and hiccoughed. Inés sat up, swung her legs over the edge of the bed and picked him up. She walked to the window and stood there, swaying slightly, her hand patting the baby's tiny back as he nestled into her shoulder. She carried him across the hallway and into the nursery at the front of the house. It was a bright room with windows on two sides, a mobile with elephants, giraffes and lions hanging from the ceiling over the spot where Lestercito's crib would stand when he was old enough to be weaned from his nighttime feedings. The marbled floor swirled under Inés's bare feet, cooling them. She loved to stand there and muse about where the marble had come from, perhaps Italy, or India, perhaps a Greek island, to imagine herself walking there . . . she'd never been outside Cuba.

Lestercito's head wobbled as he squirmed and nuzzled her neck. Inés wanted her body back. She remembered when her breasts had begun to grow, hips swelling, buttocks flaring as she'd become an adolescent. There'd been an excitement then, with new feelings surging through her, accompanied by a sadness because she'd known that there would be no going back. How could this happen to her a second time? Her body was swollen and puffy despite her lack of appetite. She didn't want to look like her mother, like all the women she'd seen lose themselves in motherhood. She was sullen with Béatriz when she came to the door, all smiles and so tender with Lestercito. Béatriz always looked after him when Inés went out, her first grandchild, and a son — she couldn't help favouring the boys. Her own son, Chucho, was the apple of her eye.

"Inés?"

She walked through the *sala* to the kitchen where Yanelis had just finished mopping the floor. Inés had chosen Yanelis for her plainness, but she was also an excellent cook and cleaner, always eager to please. A pot of freshly cooked rice sat on the stove, and a casserole of chicken with root vegetables — *malanga* and *boniato* with a few carrots. Béatriz stood in the doorway, a big smile on her face.

"Inés, how are you, *mi amor*? And how's my little Lestercito? Aiee, *chicidito*, come to your *abuela*."

Inés surrendered her child into the arms of his grandma, where he grinned and wobbled with joy, waving his chubby arms. They're like lovers, she thought, a tiny boy and an old woman. Sometimes she carried him through to Béatriz's house and left him there, saying she had to go out, then she would go back to her empty house and simply lie on her bed and sleep, dropping into the heat of the afternoon.

Inés wandered into the *sala* and flopped down on the new red sofa, still covered in plastic. There were matching armchairs, big and red, on either side of the sofa. Everything was new — the walls freshly painted, a chandelier hanging over the dining table with its six matching chairs upholstered in gold brocade, Lestercito's playpen in the middle of the room, filled with toys and stuffed animals. On a shelf above the stereo was Léster's collection of replicas — Niagara Falls, the Eiffel Tower, the Colossus of Rhodes, the Sphynx, and the Great Pyramid of

Giza. Light filtered through the frosted panes of the front door, usually open onto the patio, but closed now against the stifling afternoon sun while the new ceiling fan whirred. Léster had promised her two rocking chairs for the front patio, which was handsomely tiled in black and white ceramic. Valentine's Day was coming and she expected the chairs to appear on that day, then she would rock there in the night and gaze at the stars as she fed Lestercito.

"*Mi amor,* do you want to go out for a walk along the Malecón? You're so pale since the delivery. You need fresh air. I can stay here with the baby. Chucho and Papi won't be home till later. You must come and eat with us if Léster is late at the hospital again."

Inés could barely summon the energy to reply. Her only sensation was a pang of jealousy at the mention of Chucho's name. He was still free and here she was a prisoner in her own house. He went out every day to the bar, talking with tourists from all over the world, dancing with *extranjeras.* It wasn't fair. He had money, fancy clothes and many pairs of shoes. Of course he'd been generous, but he'd always been the favourite, the golden boy standing in the spotlight. When she was a child she'd thought, I'll have my own son and he'll be all mine and people will pay attention to me. But she still felt invisible. When people walked up to her on the street it was Lestercito they wanted to see. When she came home and looked in the mirror she saw a beautiful woman, a stranger.

Somehow Inés managed to get up from the sofa and cross the room. She paused by the door and looked at herself in the mirror, lifting her hair, heavy on her neck, securing it to the top of her head with a large plastic clip, toothed like an open mouth. It was as though she were in slow motion, wading through deep water. She saw Lestercito in the mirror, lying in his playpen looking up at Béatriz. They were smiling and nodding at each other, quite absorbed. She slipped out the door unnoticed.

Inés remembered the story as she hugged the shaded side of Calle Rubert Lopez. *El Palacio de la Princesa.* She was puzzling over the correct answers when Fulgencia Sánchez called to her from across the street.

"*Buenas tardes, chica.* Where's Lestercito?"

"With Mami," she said and walked on.

She wanted to be invisible. She was tired of this small town where she'd lived all her life. She was tired of being observed, of being questioned about her mother, her brother, her baby, her husband. Nobody cared about *her.* At the corner, where the road jogged north and began again in full sun, Inés stopped abruptly, squinting into the brightness. Her breasts were heavy with milk and her pale skin began to burn. Something terrible is going to happen, she thought. I shouldn't have left home. But she walked on, like a sleepwalker now, as though something were drawing her to the edge of a cliff. I'll be punished for thinking badly of Chucho. He's a good brother. Madre María, forgive me for my bad thoughts . . .

Her heart was already pounding, sweat beading, bursting, trickling down her neck when she saw the hearse from the *funeraria* parked further up the street in front of one of the wooden houses. As she approached, two men opened the door as wide as it would go — it was a narrow door at best — and by tilting and turning managed to negotiate the opening with a body on a stretcher. Inés stood still. In a small town one is always afraid of death for it is likely to strike someone familiar. The body seemed slight and short, perhaps a child, wrapped in a greyish sheet. Standing in the doorway was a thin woman with a tangle of hair, tears streaming down her face, behind her an older woman with two little girls clinging to her hands. It was Sonia

Rojas, her grandma gone. Léster had done the amputation. Inés had been thinking of that at her delivery. She'd never expected to have a caesarean. She'd comforted herself with the thought that at least she would have something to show for it, not like Sonia's *abuela*, losing her second leg.

As she turned away from the hearse and began walking down towards the Malecón a weight lifted from her. A death, that was all, an old woman, it was normal. She'd thought that terrible feeling of dread had to do with Chucho, but it was only her guilty conscience. Everything was going to be all right. As she neared the ocean and felt the relief of a fresh breeze coming in off the Atlantic she began to puzzle again over the King's questions . . . the answers. She sat on a bench above the rocks and watched the waves lapping. A leaf brushed her face as she turned — a leaf from a golden chalice vine with yellow flowers big as wine goblets. Inés grasped the glossy green leaf and rubbed it between her fingers. Yes, that is me, she thought, feeling the fine-veined shining enter the whorled patterning of her fingertips. This is me. And she let the leaf go, springing back on its long vine.

⤚⊃

Mirian Zelda Dreams

MIRIAN ZELDA DREAMS OF THE DEAD EVERY night. Her house adjoins the *funeraria*, and her patio, bordering on the funeral parlour's drainage system, is filled with cascading flowers and foliage. When José Manuel sluices his embalming table a gob of bloody water gushes and splashes, divides into rivulets and runs, soaking into the dark earth, irrigating the roots of Mirian Zelda's plants.

Her bed tonight is drenched with golden light from a full moon which floods through her open window. It is too hot to close the shutters, and the fan is broken. She lays herself on her belly and drops like a stone into a dream in which she covers the corpse of Bismar Sanchez, carried away that morning in the midst of a hernia operation. His heart simply stopped beating and, despite the efforts of the medical team, refused to be revived, so they sewed him up, his soul already departed on its quest for freedom. In her dream Mirian Zelda feels the rhythm of Bismar's blood pulsing against her body, a wetness spreading under her belly.

When she first moved as a young bride into #19 Jose Martí, Mirian Zelda had woken with a silent shout, her blood racing each time the dead entered her house, but she had quickly accustomed herself to these nocturnal visits, and once she recognized herself a host for the dead she opened like a lover, offering her body as a last communion.

At her door in the front *sala* is an altar with offerings to Elegguá, guardian of the crossroads. His head — a hollow coconut with mouth and eyes made of cowrie shells — rests by a half bottle of rum, a thick cigar, a slice of coconut meat, and a vase of hibiscus which Mirian Zelda renews daily, picking the fleshy flowers with their quivering stamens from her own patio.

Hardly a day goes by without a funeral, and sometimes there are two or even three, the names and interment times of the dead written in chalk on a blackboard by the door to José Manuel's office. No matter who comes to honour the dead, to weep and do penance for past ills, to lay flowers on the coffin and pray for the soul of the departed, it is to Mirian Zelda that the disoriented souls turn in the night, seeking the refuge of a host who will guide them home.

The familiar smell of Bismar is mixed with an antiseptic hospital smell as Mirian Zelda gathers him in her arms, carrying him home to the *cementerio* high on the hill above Baracoa. Bismar hovers over his family grave in the shadow of a great stone angel and sees his bodily remains interred within a concrete skin, thin but firm, to be broken open in two years when the bones will be secreted into a small sack placed in a niche of the tomb. Interments are rapid in Baracoa, a race against decomposition, but his soul will not be rushed. It lags behind like a reluctant child. "Not yet, please, I'm not ready, I didn't think it would be so soon." Life, the blink of an eye. All his unfinished business, his new lover, her swelling hips and shapely bottom . . .

It is almost dawn when she returns, eyes heavy-lidded, skin permeated with the smell of death, and stumbles into her bathroom where the shelves are thick with creams and perfumes, powders and soaps. Some are gifts from foreign guests, but often the fragrant packages will appear on her doorstep or at her altar to Elegguá, mysterious acknowledgements of her nocturnal life. She adorns her body with Healing Rose cream, Magnolia Essence cologne, powder soft as the woodland violets clustered on the lid of the box.

Mirian Zelda washes the night from her body and emerges from her bathroom refreshed, but behind her glimmering green eyes dwell a clamour of souls. Despite her cleansing rituals each dream leaves her with a residue of fine dust upon her own soul. When Pedro Iván had fallen to his death from the fourth floor, climbing from one balcony to another to break into his own apartment because he'd forgotten the key, slipping insensibly between parapets in a haze of alcohol, Mirian Zelda had held his broken body for three nights, unable to guide him home. She'd feared his soul could not sustain the shock of separation from his body and might be lost forever. She wonders now, for the first time, who will guide *her* home when her time comes.

She is a woman in her prime, full and handsome with radiant eyes and red lips. Sometimes in the evening, as she sits in her front parlour, she places a hibiscus behind her ear, just where the tendrils of her hair escape onto a flawless neck. She has thickened with the years but anyone can see that she's been a stunning beauty in her day and is still, in her age of maturity — a creature of the night with a variety of lovers she could never have imagined.

The trouble with Pedro Iván was that he'd been right in the centre of his life when he'd fallen. Forty-two years old and everything unfinished — the bottle of rum sticking out of his back pocket, the half-eaten sandwich on the kitchen table, a bus ticket to Baracoa in his wallet, a date with his new girlfriend that very evening. He'd fallen on the eve of a new year which had held all the promise of a future he was just about ready to inhabit. Pedro Iván had vowed to give up drinking. As he'd fallen he'd been filled with disbelief, a disbelief which inflated his soul, making it impossible for him to accept the final destruction of his body. Even though he'd known Mirian Zelda most of his life his soul's flight to her house was impersonal. And when he was driven out of her dreams, homeless and helpless, by the more recently dead, clamouring for their own safe passage, he began to haunt her.

This very afternoon as Bismar's soul whirls to freedom and the lifeless body of old Flora Rojas is laid out for viewing, Mirian Zelda rocks in her chair in the front parlour. She never sleeps during the day. She runs a *casa particular*, a bed and breakfast for tourists. She has three rooms and the house is full now with a newly married couple from Switzerland, two Canadian girls, and a middle-aged Czech who has arrived this very day. He looks, Mirian Zelda thinks, rather predatory. She will keep an eye on him. She runs a strict house.

An aroma of fried chicken and garlic fills the kitchen and wafts down the corridor into the front room. As it creeps into Mirian Zelda's nostrils her mouth waters, saliva slipping down her throat. She begins to feel drowsy as though someone were tugging at her, trying to pull her down. Irresistibly her eyes roll up into her head, the iridescent green disappearing under heavy lids, and suddenly there's a jostling in her body, a multitude of lights and movements in front of her closed eyes. A small man jumps up and down, a red halo enveloping him with his dark moustache and familiar face, his lips moving soundlessly. Mirian Zelda stretches out her arms — *Ven, ven aquí, Pedro Iván* — but he won't come. She is enveloped by his anger, his refusal to be guided home. She cannot believe she's really asleep, she tries to move, but she's paralyzed, held under, suffocating. When she wakes finally the room is dark and she's sticky with sweat. She raises her hand to wipe her brow with trembling fingers. All her muscles ache.

On this night she's afraid to sleep and lies wakeful until two in the morning. When she does sleep finally it is old Flora who comes, her gentle soul seeking a final reassurance. One second she's in Mirian Zelda's arms — the touch of her skin dry and crêpey with a sickly smell of funeral flowers in dank water — then she's gone as Mirian turns in the darkness, trying to hide from Pedro Iván.

When the Czech doesn't show up for breakfast they leave him to sleep, his place still set at the table, his plate of fruit in the refrigerator. By afternoon Mirian Zelda ventures a sharp knock at the door. Everything is silent but who knows, he might have a *chica* in there. She opens the door and finds the room empty. She laughs at herself and thinks no more of it, until the next day when he is still absent. She puts the word out, but no one has seen him, neither at La Trova, nor at La Terraza, nor at El Patio. He can't have left without paying because all his things are there — clothing, shoes, a handsome suitcase, a gold watch, books and papers . . . He is obviously a man of substance, not just a backpack tourist.

On the third day *la policia* are alerted. They examine the Czech's room, pack the suitcase with his things and take it to the station for safekeeping. After all, Mirian Zelda has to rent out the room — it's high season and she's already lost sixty pesos and the price of three breakfasts and dinners on top of it.

La policia visit all the tourist haunts asking questions, making notes, but no one has seen a dark-haired Czech with a mole on his left cheek, forty-two years old, tall and slim, wearing jeans and a white cotton shirt, with running shoes and blue socks, answering to the name of Marek Svoboda. However, as word of the mysterious disappearance spreads through Baracoa people begin to involve themselves, searching the bushy shorelines of the beaches, keeping a sharp eye on the clusters of tourists in Parque Central. Women with faces pulled tight by their hair rollers speculate on their patios — "Perhaps a love tryst with a *chica* in *el campo* . . . or a sudden heart attack brought on by high blood pressure, the unaccustomed heat . . . poor fellow, he must have drowned, that's why there's no trace. It's a curse on the house of Mirian Zelda — a death in her house, but no body — what will she do now with that room?"

As the weeks pass and the mystery is still unresolved it slides slowly into legend. A young woman swears she saw the handsome Czech rise dripping from the shores of Rio Miel one moonlit night as she was walking home along the Playa del Caribe. "He must have been enchanted by a Taíno maiden," people say, "and stepped back 500 years." Others accuse the girl of lying to get attention. Someone says he saw the Czech dancing at La Trova, a beer in one hand, a cigarette in the other, dancing remarkably well for an *extranjero*. Another says he's seen Pedro Iván, a bottle of rum sticking out of his back pocket, walking by the Rio Duaba. Memory marries with imagination and flowers with great variety, but no one really knows, they just talk, their words entering the water like stones, creating ever-widening circles on the smooth surface, sinking into silence.

Mirian Zelda scours the Czech's room top to bottom, puts fresh sheets on the bed and sleeps there herself one night to cleanse the room. She sleeps deeply and peacefully, and just before waking she has a gentle dream in which she sees Marek Svoboda walking down Calle Jose Martí, past her house, past the funeraria, with an expression of willing surrender on his face. He looks like a lover. He looks the way she feels as she receives the disembodied souls into her care.

But, after this night, she receives no more visitations, neither from Marek, nor from Pedro Iván, nor from the steady stream of departing souls next door. Mirian Zelda does not know exactly what has occurred — she knows only that her work is over and that someone else is guiding the souls of the dead.

❦

Erminda's House

January 2008

THE DOOR TO ERMINDA'S HOUSE IS OPEN. Sunlight sheds a bright path along the yellow-tiled parlour floor, saturating the dustballs collected in corners and along the side of the wall. She's an incidental housekeeper. Even though she always has a mop or a broom in her hand she is most often leaning on it, or using it to gesticulate wildly as she talks.

Erminda begins each day with great intent, then the visitors come — Evangelia from across the street, Clara with a packet of coffee, one of her hungry grandsons looking for a sandwich. Efforts are made to keep up with the housekeeping, but Erminda's passion is elsewhere — it shows in her smile and in her brown eyes, birdlike as they dart, taking note of everything. She is a paradox, a big spirit in a small body clothed in comfortable shorts (mended and extended with strips of mismatched fabric added on with her old sewing machine), and the ragged blouse she wears until late afternoon when it's time to shower and change into a loose dress, to sit down with Nando and snooze in front of their postage-stamp television.

Each morning as soon as I'm out of bed she's at the metal grille of my window.

"Karinita, what will you eat for breakfast?"

As we both know, I fix my own breakfast, but this is how we start. I open the door onto the narrow courtyard and we embrace and begin our conversation.

"Did you sleep well?" I ask.

"Like a *bandolera!*"

"You didn't hear me come in?"

"No, no, I took my pills and I was out like a power cut."

"How is Nando?"

"He's gone to *la bodega* to buy coffee and bread."

Since the death of Pedro Iván Erminda has been living over top of her grief in a flurry of words and activity, trying to keep it at bay lest she drown, but I see it in her eyes every morning, the darkness of the night tugging at her somewhere beyond the oblivion afforded by sleeping pills. And I feel for her, living as I do with my own losses — my father, my brother, my mother — and now Onaldo's growing absence.

Erminda loves to talk about the shortcomings of Cuban men. "They're all *bandoleros,*" she says enthusiastically, "*Bandoleros sin vergüenza!*" — shameless bandits. She considers Nando to be a rare prize because he neither drinks nor smokes, and he's never been a womanizer.

Onaldo hadn't turned up for our date at La Trova after *Año Nuevo*, after the death of Pedro Iván, and then something happened which put me on a different course. I had been hesitant, but Erminda had said, "Go out and enjoy yourself, Karinita. Dance and enjoy your life!" And that's how I became involved with Felix, with his light-hearted and engaging ways, and with his all-embracing family. But that's another story. I'm jumping ahead.

Erminda used to wash the clothes every morning, scrubbing away, arms up to her elbows in the outdoor sink, then she would climb the spiral staircase onto the roof to hang them dripping in the sun — until the washing machine arrived a week ago. I had paid my rent a few days previously, insisting on paying the going rate instead of the ridiculously low rate she proposed, knowing that they needed so many things, she and Nando. I'd been in my office at the back of the house when I'd heard a rumpus in the courtyard where there are two deep sinks for washing and a water cistern. Curious, I had walked down the corridor to see what was up. Erminda's daughter Irma was there with her husband, Oriól, who was installing a brand new washing machine while Nando looked on and Erminda ran back and forth, waving the instructions in her hand.

"It has a one year guarantee," she'd declared proudly, "And look, Karinita, there's a spin dryer!"

Old Nando had taken off his shirt for the occasion and was standing by ready to tackle the machine.

"We must test it," Irma said as Oriól had patiently followed the installation instructions, checking the plugs and dials, securing the hose.

I congratulated them on their purchase and we all grinned and said "*Felicidades!*" many times, then I went back to my office. But when the power went off five minutes later, I returned to investigate, thinking that maybe the new machine had blown their fragile electrical system. Oriól had his shirt off now and the machine was elevated on its own wooden throne. A hose ran from the spin dryer out into the courtyard and there were large puddles of water everywhere. Irma showed me a bucket of freshly spun clothing and Erminda came down from the roof where she'd hung the bed linen and towels.

"*Mira*, Karinita, it works!" she exclaimed. And then the power came back on.

Later that night Erminda and I sat in the kitchen talking about the new machine. "What will you call it?" I asked. "Your machine must have a name."

Erminda thought for a moment, then she said decisively, "La Favorita! Nando will sit in front of his TV in the afternoon and I will sit with La Favorita on the patio."

"What time are we going to the hospital?" she asks me for the third time as she passes through the kitchen, her hair done up in rollers. I'm just finishing breakfast, preparing to go to my office.

"Oh, around noon, is that okay?"

"Yes, yes, we'll take a bici-taxi. I'm going to wear my new blouse."

Erminda rarely ventures out and when she does it's usually round the corner to Mirian Zelda's house, or across the street to Evangelia's to sit with her on her bad days. Mostly she sits on her front porch with Nando who never goes further than *la panadería* and *la bodega* — he's a good deal older than Erminda. He gazes at her as she holds court, her voice competing with the barking of the rooftop dogs and with the ladies who are perched on the steps of her porch like a Greek chorus — "*Aiee chica*, the shame of it, how does he dare? . . . *Dios mío*, the price of *frijoles* . . . " They converse about rice and beans, cooking oil, light bulbs, refrigerators, and last night's *telenovela*.

"*Aieee, mis piernas*," Evangelia cries, clutching her painful legs. She's a loyal Party member and, during her years as president of the CDR she once travelled to Havana for a rally in the Plaza of the Revolution, and received a medal. But now she can no longer make it to the meetings. Diabetes has affected her legs and some days she can barely cross the street. Her house is a homage to the Revolution, filled with posters of Che, Fidel, Raúl and Camilo. In the corner is an altar to San Lazaro with a tiny glass of rum and a cigar stub, and above hangs a glossy picture of Santa Barbara. One afternoon on one of her good days Evangelia crossed Calle Moncada in full uniform with the medal hanging from her withered breast and sang a revolutionary song in her sweet and tremulous voice. The neighbourhood ladies applauded then continued with their gossiping, punctuated by the pained grunting of the palsied man next door as he paced his trembling path back and forth across the balcony.

"Is it time to go?" Erminda shifts nervously from foot to foot, a shopping bag in her hand. Who knows what we'll encounter on our way? A truckload of oranges from *el campo* or someone on the side of the road selling plastic bags of yogurt? In Cuba one must always be ready, a shopping bag as necessary as underwear. Much of the shopping is done in the doorways of people's homes where an old woman might sit with a tray of eggs secreted behind the door, or a chunk of crumbly white cheese fresh from Holguín — black market produce. Carts rumble down the street loaded with tomatoes or earthy root vegetables — "*boniato, malanga, ñame,*" the vendors cry, and people run to their doors to buy.

Erminda is wearing a shoulder-padded blouse and silk culottes from a Toronto thrift store. I wonder if she's looked in the mirror, or perhaps in the bottom of her stainless steel pot. "*Mira, mira!* A special pot from Canada. It's shiny as a mirror, and it heats the milk so fast!" For several days she had danced around the kitchen gazing at herself in it and showing it off to visitors.

Her hair, released from the rollers, has a mind of its own. She looks like a little chicken with her feathers sticking up, but I can tell she's pleased with the effect. She's splashed herself with perfume, and she would have gotten me too if I hadn't ducked. Her policy on personal appearance is like her housekeeping — you go through the motions and hope for the best. There are no completions in Cuba, just a long process of struggle, so one must enjoy the moment. The government invades every corner, dust accumulating, walls patterned with mildew.

We walk to the corner and wait for a bici-taxi. A driver stops for us and Erminda takes charge, negotiating the price, then we climb in and we're off, bumping along under our canopy, reggaetón blaring from a small radio attached to the handlebar.

"Panchito!" Erminda cries, twisting around to wave at a cousin, chattering to me at the same time, patio gossip, reiterating what the neighbours have said in her confidential tone which makes everything sound urgent and exciting. Many of our conversations I already know by heart. We spend afternoons under the kitchen ceiling fan talking about La Lucha, the struggle, and about the 'Special Period' — the years following the collapse of the Soviet Union when Cuba was literally starving from the loss of its major benefactor. "La cama, la cocina, el baño, nada más" — the bed, the kitchen, the bathroom, nothing more, she'll say, with a mighty snort. "We wore our clothes until they were rags, and we washed them with stones because there was no soap. You couldn't get clean in those days; there was no shampoo, no soap, nothing. I remember how Nando fixed our shoes — he cut pieces of rubber tire and tied them around our feet. We walked like ducks," she laughed, "Waddling down the street. But it saved our feet."

When we arrive in the forecourt of the hospital the hearse from the funeral parlour is parked in front of the main entrance. We deek around it and encounter a guard.

"Maternity ward, bed number 24," Erminda says.

"Visiting hours are four till six," the guard says.

"But they told us we could come from noon till three," I protest.

A slight shake of his head. A stream of words in a low voice. I am about to push my way through when Erminda grabs my arm and walks me outside.

"What is it? Where are we going?"

"He says we must wait." She plunks herself down on a stone bench in the shade and pats the cool stone next to her. "*Ven aquí,* Karinita. Sit."

I want to protect her. She seems so small and vulnerable out here in the real world, but at the same time I know that in reality it is I who need protection. Erminda belongs here, in this country, on these streets, even though she rarely goes out.

I look up at the sprawling three-storey building. The hospital seems to cling to the earth, taking life from it. It is a dilapidated structure, saved by the palm trees and flaming isora bushes which surround it, and by the horizontal hold of its stance. It is squat and grounded, a tenacious form. We are here to visit a newborn baby, Ariadne and Omar's first child, a son. Ariadne is Onaldo's cousin, but she has been steady in her friendship and reliably discreet. She doesn't ask about our relationship and only mentions Onaldo in passing. Like most Cubans, she is expert at turning a blind eye, having fostered an emotional neutrality essential in a country where everyone walks on eggshells with no reason to trust anyone.

We hover by the door now, near the empty hearse. There are many people milling about, waiting. I wonder if they know what they're waiting for, perhaps because I'm unclear myself. Will we eventually be admitted? Or will we be told to come back tomorrow? After ten minutes or so the guard touches Erminda's arm, his facial expression barely changing. She clasps my hand

and marches me down the corridor which has a strong odor of disinfectant. The walls are grimy and broken, pitted as though they've been shot at — a décor of such despair that I want to leave. I remember Onaldo taking me to the Moncada Barracks where the young revolutionaries were slaughtered on July 26th, 1953 — the bullet scarred walls there, marked up some say for the tourists.

We are directed to the next floor and climb sagging marble steps, chipped like the ancient teeth of a monumental sculpture. The grime of many hands is ingrained in the walls. As we walk down a windowed corridor I see a relief of palm fronds through slatted blinds, then we're in the maternity ward, a hushed place where young women shuffle along a corridor taking their first steps after, in most cases, a Caesarean section. Surgical delivery is now more common in Cuba than vaginal birth.

Ariadne moves towards us like an old woman, supported by Omar. Her face is shocked, her eyes dulled like the eyes of a stranger staring out of a grainy black and white photograph. Erminda kisses her and congratulates her. I show her the bananas and cakes we've brought, but she's far away, deep inside her assaulted body. After a while Omar takes us up to another floor to see his son in the incubator room. A nurse wheels a crib over to the viewing window and we stare at the tiny boy through glass. Omar is puffed with pride, soft as a feather cushion inside his hard muscled body. He can't stop grinning. I wonder how long it will last, before he begins going out without Ariadne. I see her face awakening from the shock, growing accustomed to a life which is not what she had imagined.

When we return to the maternity ward Erminda of course meets someone she knows, then someone else and soon the ward is transformed into her front patio. It seems that Omar's mother Mercedes knows Erminda's sister Nelvis — they did nurses' training together at the hospital in Santiago. While Erminda talks with Mercedes, the new grandma, I walk up and down the corridor with Ariadne and Omar.

"He's a beautiful baby," I say to Ariadne, holding onto her arm. "What will you call him?"

"Hilario Daniél, for my papá," Omar says cheerfully, and Ariadne nods.

I glance through the open doors of the rooms. Everything is so quiet and slow, the air thick with heat. There are no fans, and only makeshift beds, some of them brought in by the patients' families. There's no television, no radio, only a drugged silence humming with flies and visitors' voices. The undercurrent of pain is palpable. Is it really the miracle of new life that these women share, or perhaps like war veterans are they bonded in a pact of shocked silence?

Erminda is as animated as a rooster at dawn. She at least is not awed by the post-natal hush, having delivered two children herself, and being one of a family of fifteen. She grew up in *el campo* with plenty of food, she says, and with the freedom to run and play, surrounded by her siblings. But she's suffered the inevitable losses of a large clan, an ongoing grief held close to her heart as first a sister died, leaving four-year-old Pedro Iván and his three sisters who Erminda took in and raised with her own two children. Then her mother died, and after that two nephews — one burnt in an army accident, his brother killed in a car accident a year later — a handsome mustachioed fellow whose photo stares down from her kitchen wall. And finally Pedro Iván, tumbling through the air to meet his destiny on the eve of a new year.

On the way home we talk about Erminda's neighbours, all of whom seem to suffer with high blood pressure and sometimes have to be rushed to the Policlínica late at night, or even to the hospital — and the shortage of doctors now that they're all clamouring for foreign missions, desperate to resolve the gaping need in their lives before it's too late. And Fidel, still reeling off statistics about Cuban doctors, ophthalmologists and other medical specialists serving in Venezuela and Africa. Erminda pats her heart. *"Aiee, mi corazón,"* she says breathlessly and pops a diazepan capsule into her mouth. *"Mi presión alta,* Karinita, I feel it."

"Relax," I say, "You worry too much," though I know that relaxation is impossible for Erminda. She is permanently wound up and if she ever let go she might reel out, a kite in the wind, disappearing into the clouds banked over Las Terrazas de Yara. We joke that the whole island will one day explode like the government-issue pressure cookers everyone uses to cook their *frijoles.*

"Get your parachute ready," I tell her. "Soon the lids will blow and everyone will be parachuted to Miami, Spain . . . "

"To Canadá!" she interjects with enthusiasm, and we laugh at our ridiculous joke which nevertheless holds a ripe seed of truth, for a change is coming, undoubtedly. I am aware of witnessing perhaps the last moments before a combination of tourist influence and desperation combine to galvanize the youth of Cuba into some sort of action other than *jineterismo.* I see a gathering of young males, the lightning rods of any culture, with attitudes which have progressed from admiration to envy to resentment — boys on the street clustering against foreigners, shouting abuse at foreign women their grandmothers' age. Living off tourism is brutalizing to a people who seek to preserve their dignity. It's a balancing act I watch, waiting for the scale to drop. Will Cuba's inevitable change come from its own people, fuelled by foreign influence, or from a more direct outside intervention?

I had thought we might linger on the journey home and stop somewhere for a *refresco*, but Erminda is anxious. "Nando will be waiting," she says, and as we turn the corner we see him sitting on the porch gazing up at the blue sky. We wave but he doesn't see us until we're upon him. I go into the house and leave them to catch up on the events of the day.

I must have fallen asleep because the next thing I know I'm woken by the sound of rain thundering on the roof. There's a moment before I realize what it is, and by then it begins to taper off. Baracoa rainstorms are macho — they come on strong and are soon finished, leaving a trail of consequence — streams of water sluicing through gutters, pooling on porches and patios, dripping from trees. The smell of rain fills my room and I close my eyes and listen as the sweeping starts, an incessant swishing of water across the tiles — Erminda's broom, *swish, swish, swish*, from one end of the courtyard to the other, the neighbours' brooms echoing hers in the background.

I pad barefoot into the kitchen and find her standing in the archway between courtyard and kitchen, hugging a large green towel. On the table is a pile of laundry. She sees me and grins.

"I collected the washing before the rain started. Nando's towel," she says, nestling her face into it, and I feel the warmth of the sun-soaked cloth on her withered cheek. I laugh and walk out into the courtyard where all the flowers and leaves are dripping, their colours vibrant now that the dust of the day has been washed away. Amidst a profusion of jasmine, hibiscus and begonias are three plastic roses, their colours unnaturally cheerful. Along one side of the courtyard runs a plastered wall of bricks. Behind it is an empty space five feet deep between Erminda's house and the neighbouring house where the palsied man lives with his mother. Erminda has a plan to knock down this wall and expand her courtyard.

"I'll have a back patio," she says, "where Nando and I can sit peacefully without the noise of the street. But the government inspector must approve it. He refused me last time, but I can apply once a year until they give permission. *Ojalá*, one day I will have it, *si Diós lo quiere.*" If God wishes — there it is, the surrender to the old bearded man, Papa Fidel, the dying god.

I lean my back against the wall and feel the warmth of the sun in it, the long day held in those plastered bricks, all the days accumulated.

❧

Rio Miel

MY FIRST NIGHT WITH FELIX HE TOWERED over me, his head a halo of blue fire, his long arms reaching for me, hands filled with pleasure. I was amazed by the beauty of his body, the power and strength of his grip, the length and muscle of him as he pulled away suddenly and threw back his head, tipping the rum bottle to his mouth. His throat moved as he swallowed, then he walked towards me, his astonishing erection bouncing with each silent footfall. As he entered me again his voice was husky, smoky, rising and falling, his face wreathed in tenderness. Felix with his fine Taíno features and his eyes dark with memory as his black skin was swallowed by the night, only his cheeks shining where the bones pushed, straining at the surface.

We left the *casa clandestina* separately and met at the corner. He took my hand as we crossed the street and I saw in my mind's eye, because I'd seen and absorbed the geography of his flesh, his palm plumped against my own, scored with dark lines. We went to the park on José Martí, a quiet place, deserted now except for a boy playing his guitar, singing a song about the girl he loved who wouldn't have him. There was a peacefulness about Felix then, his dangerous edge tempered by a sweetness struggling for ascendance. A fugitive flashed across his face and disappeared, but I had seen him — a hidden fighter harbouring an insistent promise — and I wondered at who he was and what his story revealed.

Felix walked me home finally when everyone had left the bars and the streets were empty. He waited while I found my key, dangling from a red ribbon, then he kissed me, a brush of his lips, a flick of his pink cat-tongue, and walked away laughing, cupping his hands to his genitals, throwing them to me like a kiss, hands huge against the narrow bones of his wrists.

After Onaldo failed to appear at La Trova ten days passed without a word, then I'd seen him on the street and there had been an angry encounter between us. He'd tried to humour me, but I wanted truth from him and he couldn't give it. He could not match me. In the end he'd stormed away, the veins in his neck bulging. Since then I'd felt him everywhere although I could not call up his face exactly. His image had melted into my brain and disappeared, taking refuge in my body, controlling me silently.

My days were filled with smiling faces and lively conversation, one long Spanish class in which I found myself intensely engaged despite the fact that I had come to Cuba to be with Onaldo. I became part of Erminda's family, the sixteenth sister, exchanging daily visits with Alina and Clara, and with the many neighbours who called to me as I cycled by. I always took something — a pound of cheese, two or three plump tomatoes, a braid of garlic. Alina brought eggs still warm from her chickens, and I would often come home to find a bunch of mandarins from Teófilo, Erminda's nephew, or a block of *guayaba dulce* from Clara. I was cradled in the embrace of family and felt my angry heart dissolving in the long hot days, relieved by sudden tropical rain which gushed to the ocean through the many rivers that held the town — Rio Toa, Rio Duaba, Rio Miel, Rio Maguana, Rio Macaguanigua — and was swallowed there.

Felix had appeared beside me at the Casa de la Trova in the exact moment that I'd realized Onaldo was not coming. I remembered seeing him before, on the dance floor of La Trova the night I'd met Onaldo.

Felix asked me to dance and, in the rhythm of the salsa, our hips moving together, something surfaced, something long forgotten. I can only call it adolescent fear. When you are young you have no precedent, no experience to help you understand what is happening to you, so I hadn't known during my own adolescence, which was characterized by a mixture of fear and rebellion, how stereotypical I was. My mother had often said wistfully, "Oh, if I could live my life over, knowing what I know now." Well, here it was, a chance to do exactly that, to relive my youth with the benefit of a lifetime of experience. But I'm racing ahead. What I felt then was merely a premonition of what was to come. In that moment it was simply a dance, and I was thinking of Onaldo, longing to be in *his* arms.

Later, when Felix insisted on walking me home, I felt a mixture of fear, guilt, and excitement — or perhaps in reality the excitement came later, replacing my initial impatience with him. Though Felix behaved like a *caballero* — gentlemanly and considerate — perhaps he was just another fast-talking Cuban. I felt angry with Onaldo for deserting me, for exposing me to a younger man's flattery. With Onaldo at my side I'd been safe.

After a few nights of persistence met by disinterest on my part, Felix had an unwitting flash of inspiration — he invited me to dinner at his sister Yolanda's house in La Playa, to eat *pescado Santa Barbara*, a typical Baracoan dish, he said — fish from the Caribbean sea, cooked with fresh lime, cumin and coconut milk. When I arrived a man was sitting on the front steps cradling his head — Yolanda's husband, Calixto, recovering from Saturday night's rum party. Their grandchild, Susana Rosa, brought me a tiny pink rose, and the neighbourhood children came to stare at me, grinning, their gangly arms and legs draped around one another. The littlest one, Alejandra, threw her arms around my neck and gave me a smacker of a kiss on my mouth and whispered to me unintelligible sounds of sweetness, her petal lips in the shell of my ear.

We ate in the kitchen, balanced precariously on the edge of a wobbly table — there were no chairs — and afterwards Felix took my hand and walked with me onto the street. "I will take you to Playita," he said, and as we crossed the bridge over a sluggish canal he told me that boats loaded with coconuts had passed there in the old days, drifting down to the harbour. I heard frantic barking, and as we rounded the corner I saw a tight cluster of men, the muscles of their arms and necks corded from holding back dogs.

Felix smiled at me and flipped his white palm up, an inscrutable gesture. A couple of his friends joined us, emerging from nowhere, sidling over, palm slapping palm in a gesture of intimacy embedded deep within the male culture, while a group of women laughed and fingered each other's clothing, the husky honeyed buzz of their rapid exchange blurring the air.

I watched two dogs held with harnesses, straining and barking with bared teeth. *Pelea de perros,* Felix said, the Sunday dog fights. Twenty or thirty dogs barked furiously, some held in the firm grip of their owners, others kicking up the dust, jumping and whining, trying to join the fray. There was a sudden scuffle followed by a terrible screaming and snarling as one of the dogs broke free and sunk its teeth into the neck of another. Immediately the men closed in around the fighting couple. I thought they were trying to separate the dogs, but they were simply straining for a better look — they had money on the animals.

I grabbed Felix's hand and pulled him away. He laughed at me but let me lead him to the water's edge where the waves rolled in, lapping the shore. There were a couple of roosters each tied by one leg to a stake in the ground, their spurs erect and sharp. The flourish of their tail feathers reminded me of the tendrils of fire curling from the dragon's mouth on Felix's red T-shirt.

"I'll take you to the *pelea de gallos* next week," he said, "by Rio Macaguanigua."

We sat a while and talked, our feet scuffing the sand which was littered with coconut shells, but I was drawn back to the dog fights, fascinated. A handsome man with a brutish mouth held his dog by the skin of its back and with his other hand he slapped at the creature's haunches. I felt the slap of a hand on my butt and turned angrily. Felix grinned, pulled me against him and held me, the tendons of his arms like ropes. The dogs, straining to escape from their own skins, finally ripped loose and one was immediately pinned in the dust, jaws clamped on its throat.

Felix worked on Saturdays and I usually took a long bike ride, shopping and visiting along the way. That particular Saturday I had woken early with a feeling of excitement and anticipation. By 8 AM I was cycling towards Cabacú, when my sandal slipped off midway across the bridge. I braked and hopped off my bike. Below me the Rio Miel gurgled slowly towards the ocean, darkened with earth stirred up by the recent rains. There'd been a week of torrential downpours, interspersed with a buildup of thunderous clouds as everyone waited for the next storm. I balanced my bike and ran back to get the sandal, dodging a bici-taxi as it raced past, followed by a donkey trotting briskly, pulling a cartful of cabbages.

I flipped the metal stand and set off again, the river sparkling beneath me, rippling across a shallow riverbed of tiny stones to the far bank where the earth shadowed it a deep green. I'd bathed there with Onaldo almost a year ago. Legend had it that a Taíno maiden had been bathing in the river when a young man, drawn by her beauty, had slipped in to join her. Miel, the maiden, had wept lest her lover leave, and her tears had refreshed the salt water and made it sweet. The more she wept the sweeter grew the river, and the young man was enchanted and stayed in Baracoa with her for the rest of his life.

This was my third trip to the hydroponic gardens at Cabacú to buy lettuce. The first time, a Sunday, I'd spoken with the guard and marvelled at the acres of nascent green in shades from the newborn lime of baby lettuce to the darkly curled leaves of mature spinach and *acelga*. At the end of each row was a burst of oregano or a budding rosebush — companion plants. "*Mañana*," the guard had said, "The lettuce will be ready *mañana*," and he had directed me to the long nursery greenhouses draped in black, provided by Canadians in a programme of *amistad* with Cuba. As I'd touched the earth of the seedlings in the greenhouse I had smiled to see my nails, (usually short and embedded with dirt from my own garden), long and pink, the tips sickled with white like new moons hanging beneath showers of stars where Erminda had applied a final coat of silver sparkles. "Now you look like a Cuban," she'd said with a nod of satisfaction.

On Monday I had returned to find an empty stand with a bored attendant slouching in the shade, and had bounced over the curb and down the muddy incline to the gardens where a group of workers stopped their conversation to stare at me. When I asked about the lettuce, a woman with a rusted wheelbarrow loaded with bunches of *acelga* came to life and said there was no lettuce and that she didn't know when there would be, maybe *mañana,* maybe in a week, that I should ask the *compañera* at the roadside stand, and with a toss of her head she'd set off down a path pooled with red mud.

The ice cream is hard, I thought, my code for the ever-shifting realities of Cuba. I'd heard a story about a tourist who'd lined up for ice cream at the famous Copelia ice cream parlour in Havana, and had moved to the head of the queue several times to inquire about the reason for the long delay. "The ice cream is hard," he'd been told. When the patient crowd eventually received their ice cream after an hour of softening time the tourist was delighted and, having relished his first serving, he asked for a second. The woman shook her finger in that quintessential Cuban gesture. "The ice cream is hard," she said.

There had been other things to buy in Cabacú. Erminda had told me about Bebita, across from the gas station, who sold *habichuela* in vinegar dressing — the long green beans I'd seen at the market, dangling like wilted bouquets. Bebita's *habichuela* had a smoky flavour from being cooked over a wood fire. She made coleslaw too and I'd bought some for Erminda and Hernándo, and for the sisters, Alina, Clara, Aleida, and for old Evangelia across the street because she had trouble with her legs and couldn't get out. There'd been a girl selling soy yogurt at the roadside from a box filled with swollen plastic bags. And bananas, the curved blackish ones with a slightly orange tint inside, sweet and meaty, like fat little penises. But there were no mandarins, no lettuce, no tomatoes or eggs. In Cuba a shopping list is useless. The agenda is — always travel with plastic bags, keep your eyes open and buy what you can.

I pedalled hard and was already across the bridge, passing the cartful of cabbages and the trotting donkey, when I saw a man cycling ahead with a lettuce dangling from his left hand. I cycled alongside and asked him where he'd bought it. Earth crumbled from the trailing roots as he flung his arm back to indicate a *casa* at the side of the road. I doubled back and dismounted, trundling my bike as I approached the house. The woman sitting out front shook her finger at me and with an inclination of her head indicated another house.

At the fourth house a pot-bellied man in a faded red T-shirt took my arm and said, "Come with me." His name was Carlos Enrique, he told me, and I followed him along the narrow sidewalk, protesting that the man on the bike had definitely said he'd bought lettuce back there in the other direction. "Look," said Carlos Enrique, pointing to a lettuce leaf on the sidewalk, "Lettuce, in this direction." Despite his lack of logic I followed, muttering that it would be easier for me to carry on to the hydroponic gardens. "Don't be afraid," he said, "There will be lettuce, I promise."

We turned off the main street into a network of dirt roads bordered by *campesino* shacks that were dwarfed by huge mango trees, breadfruit and chirimoya, and shaded by banana and platano palms. Carlos Enrique, his belly swollen like a football under his red shirt, called out to each person we met and was directed ahead to look for Fidel or Gloria, Ramiro or Yuri — on and on we went, my wheels making ruts in the soft earth. "Wait here," said Yuri, and I waited with Carlos Enrique, growing more and more impatient. "Relax," Carlos said, "Here is the rhythm of Cuban life, here in *el campo.*"

Yuri returned finally to ask how many lettuces. "Six," I replied, and his mouth gaped in surprise. After Carlos had instructed me on the different types of mango trees, indicating a variety of budding fruits and decaying seeds, I leaned my bike against a fence of thin wooden stakes, and followed him down the path after Yuri. The ice cream was softening. We rounded the corner of a very poor house. In the doorway stood a shrivelled man with bumps and nodules all over his body, his shoulders hunched against whatever it was that pushed at him from within. He and Carlos exchanged a volley of unintelligible words, the short bursts that Cubans use to communicate, without consonants, most often accompanied by gestures more eloquent than the sounds. An old woman listed in a wheelchair in the space between house and garden. I had learned to expect an amputation when I saw a wheelchair, but as I passed her I saw that she was just old and withered, her legs like brittle sticks.

Ahead of us was a field flooded with lettuce, their brightness contrasting with the darker green of cabbage. The sight of all that fresh greenness, curling and twisting from the earth, was like a miracle. Yuri and two women, one elderly, the other young, bent over the green ocean, dipping and picking, as though they were collecting bouquets. Finally they came to me, their hands and arms filled, and I held my plastic bags open to receive six luxuriantly leafy lettuce. "Six pesos," Yuri said. I took a twenty peso note from my wallet and insisted that he take it, though he protested. But when I tried to give an additional ten pesos to the old woman, she refused. "Please," I insisted, pressing the note into her hand, "So much work, so much time, it's nothing for me."

When I got home there was a lettuce leaf on the doorstep, a curly green fragment, dropped like a clue in a treasure hunt. "Onaldo was here," Erminda said, all agog. "He brought you a lettuce, and some mandarins. He's waiting for you on the Malecón."

A gust of wind hit me in the face, taking my breath away as I turned the corner. The waves were deep turquoise, sparkling in the sun as they crashed over the seawall, the salt spray stinging my eyes. I saw Onaldo in the distance, standing there staring at the waves, and I walked slowly, savouring that moment, watching his shoulders hunched around his thick neck, the power of him softening inside an aging body. There was something poignant about seeing him that way — waiting alone, unaware that he was observed. With his face in repose I could see his mother inhabiting him, that androgynous quality men achieve with the accumulation of years, something both mysterious and vulnerable. He never turned until my hand was on his shoulder and in that moment, as our eyes met, I lost my power of observation.

"I've been waiting for you. How are you?"

The usual pleasantries. We spoke about his cousin who had died suddenly of a heart attack in La Playa, in the house before the bridge over coco canal. He spoke rapidly. He seemed upset. Then he turned to me, our burning topic breaking through his reserve.

"You move so fast, Karina. One week and . . . "

"Five weeks since *Año Nuevo*," I protested, anger flaring. "Five weeks since you stood me up at La Trova. How do you think I feel, a stranger in your country, waiting for you, with no control over my situation?"

His face was solemn. He'd been talking to a woman who lived in La Playa, he said, close to Yolanda's house. People gossiped, and of course, I'd been there every afternoon, and in the evenings, my bicycle out front, exposed by my foreignness. I had only to cycle down Calle Mariana Grajales and a dozen eyes were on me, marking my clothing, the time, my destination. Where do you go in Cuba for privacy? Everyone lives cramped in small spaces, three generations or more perched like chickens at different levels. Outside every house there's a pile of sand or gravel, half built structures, tiny *casitas* of palm leaves lashed together erected on rooftops.

After Onaldo's trip to Canada I had expected some kind of reciprocity. I had not fully understood but had accepted the clandestine nature of our relationship after his warnings against the vigilance of the Baracoa police, his neighbours, the CDR, and his fear of expulsion from *El Partido*. I moved in darkness, feeling my way through an impossible tangle of lies and contradictions. Cubans have a gesture, finger to eye, counselling vigilance, but wide-eyed foreigners cannot see because vision comes from within a culture and I stood outside.

Onaldo had arrived in Toronto with an insatiable appetite. I'd thought he would be shocked by the abundance of North American culture — "I want to see for myself the corruption of the capitalist system," he'd said — but he took it all in his stride, consuming enormous amounts of food — oatmeal, eggs, toast, ham, yogurt, cheese, coffee and orange juice for breakfast, and three hours later another meal — chicken, coleslaw, potatoes, bread, rice, juice, and bottle after bottle of water, an ocean churning inside him. In the late afternoon he would be ravenous again and we'd stop on the street for falafel and salad, or subway sandwiches, cakes, fruit, juice or mint tea. I'd often find him at the open refrigerator sinking his teeth into chunks of white cheese, spooning ice cream from the carton, one hand on the door handle, holding it open.

At night we would eat in restaurants with friends who questioned him about Fidel, about communism, about the Cuban socialist system of education and medical care. But Onaldo was a reluctant respondent, his face hovering close to his plate as he consumed vast amounts of spaghetti, meat, rice and bread, salads and wines, while I amplified my translations to fill out his sparse responses. At night he would turn to me and consume my body and I was glad then of his appetite and urgency.

Perhaps it had started there, the greed that had swept in like a tidal wave, crashing on the Malecón, swamping our love, making it impossible ever again to distinguish the purity of his heart from avarice. A slow sense dawned in me of my own culpability. Had I offered too much and corrupted him with my desire to give? And was that desire motivated more by the discomfort of guilt than by philanthropy?

I had laughed at Onaldo in Toronto when he missed his *frijoles.* I had not taken seriously the fact that rice and beans were his daily fare, that the government places restrictions to protect Cubans from the corruption of foreigners, at the same time protecting tourists from *jineteros,* and above all protecting tourism because Cuba needs foreign currency to keep its economy afloat. And yet I had taken him too seriously when he'd hinted at his larger needs, being programmed to jump in and 'fix' things. When Cubans ask for something they hold no grudge about an honest, 'No, I can't.' They are for the most part accepting and will shrug and say, 'No importa' — It doesn't matter. It was I who feared rejection if I did not jump.

Everyone greeted Onaldo as they passed, looking curiously at us.

"Let's walk to the beach," he said, taking my hand. "Too many people here."

We walked in silence, and I leaned into the soft cushion of his presence. In that silence we were reconciled by the pressure of normal everyday activity — the movement of our bodies in rhythm with all the thoughts and desires of our brief times together and long months apart, shot through with a seductive familiarity — and the desire, the constant desire for him that I sustained.

We sat together on a driftwood log high up on the Playa Caribe, sheltered by the tough green leaves of the *uva caleta* which grew all along the shore.

"I miss you all the time, Onaldo," I said, "In spite of everything. You can't imagine."

Part of me knew that I couldn't let Felix go, inextricable as he was from his sisters, his mother, the brothers-in-law, and the children. But neither could I resist all that I had with Onaldo. I wanted them both — there it was, that adolescent feeling, the insistence on having it all, from which arose a steamy guilt, stinking like skunk cabbage in spring.

Then Onaldo spoke with an honesty which surprised me, about his lifelong reticence, his fears, his desire to change, and before I knew it we were cementing with words what already existed between us, almost a year of shared passion and experience, satisfying our minds, saying it's all right, everything's normal again. But when he kissed me I was thinking of what I would say to Felix, how I must break with him, and how angry and hurt he would be.

I was sleeping when he came to the house. The heat was like a drug, and Spanish immersion wore me down by late afternoon. By evening my brain was slow and mushy, fit only for the swaying rhythm of the salsa, for the smoothness of rum down my throat, for *la cama*. Erminda called me and as I woke there was a blank white space without words. Then I remembered. "*Me voy*," I called and I walked through the kitchen and the *sala* to the front door, but when I looked out there was no one there. Then I saw him at the corner, the red of his dragon shirt swallowed by the night. Everything was black — his skin, his clothing, the night sky. Yet the shape of him was so familiar, standing like a boy, his arms swinging loose, an inscrutable gesture in the inclination of his head. I walked slowly towards him, trying to collect my thoughts.

His face was solemn and tight. I knew immediately and felt a knife edge of fear. I struggled to surface, heard my own garbled words, apologies.

"Let's walk," he said, and I was both afraid and comforted as he took my hand in his, cool and dry. We walked in silence to the Malecón and sat on the seawall.

Of course he knew. They'd spoken. The conspiracy of men, Cubans together in a struggle to win the foreigners they bond against in the daylight hours of ordinary activity, searching for lettuce, cheese, eggs, oranges, the things people converse about and build their lives around. I was able to avoid his eyes in the darkness. He talked, on and on as my senses flickered and closed, unable to listen to his harsh words. A wave of tiredness swept over me and all I could hear was the suck and swish of the ocean, the gravelly breath of a thousand stones being pulled and pushed by the tide.

"I need to go home," I said finally, and he stood, silenced, and walked with me. When we parted at the door of Erminda's house he walked away without looking back, something in him beaten, despite his warning against Onaldo.

"He will leave you and I'll be waiting," he'd said, something I only half understood because I didn't want to believe it. My understanding of Spanish was like the ocean and I adrift in the vast deep waters blackened by a moonless night, guessing at everything. Then the light would come, and the water would sparkle and turn turquoise and I would see the stones moving under me and try to touch them with my toes.

Onaldo seemed unable to recover himself. We went out together a few times, and promises were made about his friend's house — "She's away in Guantánamo, when she returns I'll ask her." Then I would see him on the street the next day, hurrying somewhere, preoccupied.

Time passed, punctuated by missed encounters. And of course, Felix appeared everywhere — at the door of La Trova as I danced with Onaldo, emerging from the darkness as I walked home at night, alone. He came out of nowhere, silently, insistently, like water. In Canada it would have been called stalking, but in Cuba everything seems different because the context is different. My feminist politics were confounded. I wasn't angered by him, I wasn't threatened, I was seduced, worn down, as stone is reshaped by water. But in the end it was his family that drew me back — Yolanda calling to me as I cycled past, "Where have you been? Why don't you come to my house anymore?"

"*Amistad*," I told Felix as he stood silently on the front porch of Yolanda's house, his dark hands spilling over with pleasure for the taking. "Only friendship."

We entered the house together and I walked behind him down the corridor to Yolanda's kitchen. Through the open window I watched a handsome rooster with shining feathers, iridescent in the sun, climb the ladder onto the roof. I heard him crowing from the rooftop. Then Susana Rosa ran into the kitchen and hugged me, pressing her head against my belly. Calixto slouched past me, grinning, and plunked a plastic bag of meat on the counter. When I turned round Felix had disappeared, as silently and fluidly as he'd appeared. But I was in his sister's house, on his street, drawn into his life by the daily press of events. And this is how I learned to know him.

Later that night, walking home, I heard my name and turned to see Onaldo standing at a distance, his face ghostly in the moonlight. But when he spoke he was strangely animated. And it was not to me he spoke, although he had called my name.

"*Felicidades*," he said, staring past me at Felix, his eyes shining. And I felt like that invisible thing he could not directly address, the foreigner who stands for everything that seeps like poison into the lives of Cubans and sets them in competition with each other, trying to climb the slippery walls of the old Fidelista Revolution.

～

The Same Mouth

THERE IS ALWAYS MEAT IN YOLANDA'S HOUSE. Her husband, Calixto, works in the slaughterhouse, *el matadero*. He comes home with chunks of liver, meaty bones, pigs' feet or tripe. He's bent over the sink with the tap drizzling, washing membranes and grit from slippery kidneys while Yolanda makes salad — bright lettuce curling around the edges of the plate, slices of tomato, oil and salt. Their daughter, Anaïs, sits on the back step picking meat from a crab shell. Her *novio*, Leóbis, is a fisherman — he catches crabs in a net cast into the Rio Duaba, where the creatures lurk in the muddy depths, scuttling sideways inside their soft-blue shells. Anaïs hands morsels of crabmeat to Susana Rosa, who dances around the kitchen as Calixto works stolidly, heating oil, plunking the wet kidneys into the sizzling pan.

"*¡Papi, Papi, mira, soy una bailarina!*"

On Saturday nights, after a couple of bottles of rum shared with his neighbours, Calixto is transformed into a grinning gargoyle, as though some spirit enters him and lights there the lamp of his soul.

It is Sunday and the streets of Baracoa are quiet, except for the glow of the television from each house, voices of the latest romance *novela* drifting on the soft warm air. Calixto spent the day on the front verandah, head in hands, recovering slowly until Elbis from across the street brought a mickey to *matar el rata* — kill the rat.

Felix slinks down the corridor and into the kitchen. I call him *el gato negro* — the black cat — not that he's lucky, on the contrary he seems to bring trouble. At forty-three he's lean as a youth and moves with a characteristic sway of his shoulders, his arms swinging loose. He touches my shoulder lightly and kisses me. "What's to eat?" he asks his sister.

"Ask Calixto. I'm going to church."

Yolanda's head is wrapped in a faded blue scarf to cover the rollers she's been wearing all day in preparation for the Pentecostal service in the pastor's house down the street. The Pentecostal church is under reconstruction so the congregation must gather locally in *casas cultos*, in small groups, until the new two-storey building is complete.

"My church is El Ranchon, Anaïs says, challenging. She's voluptuous, with a face as pure and beautiful as her mother's, but her appetite is for rum and dancing at the disco up on the hill where the youth of Baracoa gather.

The family tease Yolanda about her devotion to the Pentecostal church. I accompanied her once and heard her confess to a roomful of people how she had joined as a refuge from her suffering. "My husband had many wives," she said, blushing at her euphemism, "And now, *gracias a Diós*, he's stopped, but he still drinks too much."

She'll have plenty to tell them tonight. Yesterday was Anaïs's thirtieth birthday and Calixto had been up since dawn roasting a pig for the fiesta, so he was already drunk when Florencio arrived with his horse and wagon to take us to Rio Duaba where the river enters the sea, carrying the little blue crabs. Susana Rosa was whiny and clingy on the journey, and Yolanda sat cradling the child, her legs astride the blackened cauldron she uses to cook rice and root vegetables, while Anaïs huddled with Leóbis in the back of the wagon. We had to stop frequently along the way — to buy tomatoes and lettuce, oil for the salad, cigarettes for the men, a half dozen bottles of rum sneaked under the seat up front — then Susana wanted *caramelos*. The problem was that Alejandra couldn't come so there was no one for her to play with.

When we arrived at the beach Yolanda found a condom in Anaïs's bag and blew it up into a big white balloon for Susana, but when it landed on a sharp stick and exploded she began to wail, so Yolanda scooped her up and carried her to the circle where we were sprawled amidst the driftwood. No one had an instrument, but we improvised, Anaïs tapping with a spoon against an empty rum bottle, Calixto clapping his big hands rhythmically, a silly grin on his face as he lurched from side to side.

Elbis sang *Negro Bembón*. He's a handsome man, a musician with the municipal band at the cultural centre, and to see him performing in Parque Central you would have an impression of studiousness as he plays saxophone, his spectacles balanced astride wide nostrils. But now, almost as drunk as Calixto, Elbis contorted his face into a caricature of the negro stereotype, pushing out his lower lip, pulling on it as everyone laughed, even Yolanda, then Calixto thrust a plastic cup of rum at her and she threw her hands up, making the sign of the cross, and swatted at his head. Calixto rolled onto the sand, convulsed with laughter as Elbis' gravelly Louis Armstrong voice boomed forth, his bloodshot eyes popping and flashing.

"Chango!" someone shouted, "He's Chango!" Fiery orisha and companion to the Catholic Santa Barbara, Chango is the crazy man who dances menacingly with a stick under his arm, flourishing it, challenging everyone in his path as his reddened eyes flash and his dark skin glistens.

When Calixto passed out no one was able to rouse him. He had to be carried to Florencio's wagon and driven home, then carried to his bed still sleeping like the dead as we ate the cake that the neighbours brought over.

"Thirty-three years with that man," Yolanda sighs. The beauty of her face catches my breath as she smiles at me and disappears into her bedroom. There is a placid softness to her, centred in the curve of her mouth, the same mouth that all the family share — Mama Alicia, Felix, his older brothers who live in *el campo*, Amelia, the eldest sister, Adelis . . . I love to walk with Yolanda on the street. She's a moving poem of rounded forms swaying and jostling against each other, her elegant neck stretching as she greets people. "Who was that, Yolanda?"

"A brother from the church," she'll say, a smile lurking behind her lips.

Felix leans over Calixto's shoulder, pretends to steal a plump kidney and yelps as though he'd burnt his fingers. Then he doubles over with laughter and Calixto stares at him, his steady gaze inscrutable.

"More food, Mami, I'm hungry." Susana Rosa hops from foot to foot as Anaïs cracks the claws between her teeth. The smell of crab is stronger than the amount of meat warrants, as though the tiny creature carried all the richness and devastation of the ocean within its shell.

"Going to watch the baseball game?" Felix asks.

Calixto grunts as he dishes up the kidneys, spooning onions on top. He cuts a portion into small pieces and hands the plate to Susana Rosa, gesturing with his head for her to sit on the back step and eat. Felix eats quickly, standing with one hip jutting, then wipes his mouth with the back of his hand, licks his lips and rinses his plate and fork under the tap. Calixto reaches into his pocket and pushes a tattered packet of cigarettes across the counter. Felix takes one, searches his pockets for a match, then lights it from the stove and inhales. He heads down the corridor to the front room where the door is always open onto a verandah that has just enough room for a couple of rocking chairs, so close to the sidewalk that passers-by can whisper their greetings.

When Susana Rosa and I enter the *sala* Felix is dragging a chair inside, and he looks up at us briefly, then slumps in front of the television. The Cuban national anthem is playing, then the game begins — La Habana Industriales against Santiago de Cuba Avispas — and the first player is up to bat. Osmani Romero is pitching for Santiago. Felix supports Santiago like a true Oriental. His arm is smeared with pink icing still clinging to the arm of the chair from Anaïs's birthday cake. He licks it and wrinkles his nose in disgust, making Susana giggle as she sits on my knee and leans her head against my breast, sucking her thumb.

"*Tio, quiero mirar los muñequitos.*" She slides off my knee and throws herself into her uncle's lap, demanding to watch the cartoons.

"No, *chica,* I'm watching the baseball game. Go play with Alejandra across the street."

Susana pouts and squirms in his lap. Her springy hair is held in three tight braids tied on top of her head. She jumps up and flounces out the door. A group of boys are playing *pelota* with sticks and a ping-pong ball from a roll-on deodorant container. They dodge bicycles and horse-drawn carts in the gathering darkness, chasing the precious ball. Mariana Grajales is a busy street that runs the length of La Playa, crossing two bridges — the first over a narrow stream that runs to the ocean at Playita where faded blue cabins front the beach, the second extending across Rio Duaba which carries fresh water from the mountains into the warm salty ocean.

Yolanda emerges from her bedroom, hair brushed into rolling waves. She wears a white skirt which balloons around her legs as she passes by the fan. Her blouse is freshly ironed and over her arm she carries a blue cardigan from the recycled clothing store — in her hand a well-thumbed copy of the Bible.

"Where's Susana Rosa?" she asks, frowning.

"Playing in the street," I say.

"Take care in church," Felix warns her. "They're a bunch of *bandoleras*." He ducks as she swipes at his head.

"You going out?" she asks me, turning back, her hand on the door jamb.

"Maybe later," I shrug.

"Depends on the game," Felix says, looking by force of habit at the clock above the television. It's always six o'clock in Yolanda's house. Somehow no one gets around to replacing the battery. But we know it's seven, more or less, because Yolanda is on her way to church.

We'd all been relieved when Yolanda recovered and returned to work at the clinic across town, walking proudly in her white uniform and white shoes. She had to take time off for an operation to remove nodules from her vocal chords. Her already husky voice sounded hoarse and for days after the operation she was reduced to a whisper. Felix brought her home from the hospital and for two weeks a stream of Pentecostal sisters filled the house. There were Bible readings and blessings, prayers and entreaties in which everyone would join, echoing each other. From time to time someone would rise and give a lengthy oration, punctuated by cries of "*¡Hallelujah!*", "*¡Gracias a Diós!*", "*¡Glorifica el Señor!*" When Calixto walked in on this after a day's work, he narrowed his eyes and slouched down the corridor to the kitchen with his bag of raw meat. The pastor is a broad-beamed woman with an expansive bosom. She lives down the street on the opposite side and Calixto will go out of his way to cross the street and give her the evil eye as he passes. But she is impervious.

He comes down the corridor now, his arms reaching out. "Yolanda! Give me a kiss." His big hands are on her body and she swats at him and wriggles out of his grasp, her generous breasts and buttocks jiggling.

Calixto grins. "Tell the pastor I'm waiting for her in my bed."

Yolanda laughs in spite of herself. "Watch out for Susana," she calls as she steps out onto the street.

"I'll walk with you!" I jump up, Felix grabs my arm and tries to stop me, but I pull away and run after her.

"What will I do, Karinita?" Yolanda asks, her voice low as we walk down Mariana Grajales, past open doorways where neighbours sit chatting on the front steps. "This is my last chance to get away, to buy some nice things for my house, for my kitchen."

"What's stopping you, Yolanda?"

"It's a three year mission. Who will look after Susana Rosa?"

This is what we talk about now, since Yolanda has been offered work in Venezuela. She's a nurse and Cubans in the medical field are in demand there. She would be paid in convertible currency, flown home once a year and best of all she would have access to quality goods. When a Cuban returns from a Venezuelan mission he will come with a television, a DVD player, a washing machine, new suitcases full of clothing, shoes, cosmetics — and his family will kill a pig and invite everyone to the welcome-home fiesta.

"What did you tell them?" I ask her.

"I put my name down," she shrugs. "How can I refuse? It's my last chance before retirement, Karinita, my last chance to travel. When Calixto was on his mission in Angola I had Anaïs to look after, a baby just starting to walk. I worried about Calixto all the time, and at night I wept for him, I missed him so much. We were in love. He didn't drink then. And he was such a dancer." Her eyes are sparkling. "Now the church is my life, and Susana Rosa."

The transformation must have been imperceptible to her. That's how change occurs, by appearing temporary, tricking us with its novelty as it roots in us.

"He still is, Yolanda, but you never dance with him."

"My church forbids it. When he returned from Angola he started drinking — not normal drinking, but a whole bottle, and then another, all the men in the neighbourhood gathering at our house until he was gone so far away from me that I felt he was still in Angola."

"Felix won't talk about his time in Angola."

"Trauma," she states bluntly. "He was a child when he left, just seventeen, a *muchacho*. All the men were hurt by Angola." She shakes her head, her lips pursed. "But Venezuela is different. It's my chance. I've never left Cuba before. I want to travel before I die!" she cries passionately as we cross the bridge.

"Yolanda, I've heard it's dangerous for Cubans in Venezuela now. The Contras have started to attack Cuban doctors and medical staff."

"But Chavez is like a son to Fidel."

"Exactly. And there are many Venezuelans who are against him."

"God will protect me. The Brothers and Sisters have said they will pray for me, to keep me from harm."

When we reach the pastor's house I kiss Yolanda and turn back into the darkness, guided by the light from the doorways. There are no streetlights in Baracoa.

Top of the fourth, Industriales leading, César León up to bat. Felix jumps, surprised to see me, and swats at the mosquitoes circling his head.

"Where's Calixto?" he demands. "I want a cigarette. *Calixto?*" No answer. "*Aiee coño*, he's probably asleep with that mickey of rum empty beside him."

I squeeze into his chair and we cuddle until the game is over.

"I have a surprise for you." He takes my hand and leads me outside, up the street to Orestes' house. "Shhh. We have to be very quiet."

He leads me up the alley to the back of the house. Only when we're safely inside does he tell me that Orestes is at an all-night poker game and has given us his bed for the night. His wife is in Guantánamo visiting her sick father and she's taken the kids with her.

Later, as we lie in bed, Felix chain smoking, I begin to extract more of his story. He has thrown out fragments casually as we've walked on the street, teasers which have left me hanging as our conversations were interrupted by friends, or as he darted away, to appear mysteriously, minutes later. But now I have him and I probe gently, nibbling at his earlobe, curious as Cubans are incurious. Not naturally so. It is part of an enforced diplomacy in a minefield of 'illegal' activity.

I ask him about the slim scar shining the length of his forearm.

"I was lucky," he says. "But my friend, Alexis . . . I was talking to him, we were in the trench together, so close we were almost touching . . . and after I was hit I turned to Alexis for help, but he was dead, a cigarette still burning between his fingers."

He drags on his own cigarette, inhales deeply, and crushes the butt, sitting up abruptly, but I pull him down and kiss his smoky mouth.

"Yolanda was the one who always looked after me. When she married Calixto I felt lost. But I liked the army, the discipline, the company of men. I grew up surrounded by my sisters and my mama. Papi died when I was seven." He squirms and pulls a pained face.

"You look like Susana Rosa," I say, and he laughs and leans forward as I turn him and massage his shoulders. Little grunts and noises escape his throat as I knead his tight muscles, then after a while he begins to speak again.

"I felt guilty lying in a hospital bed. I wanted to return to the battlefield. I was lucky. So many of my friends had died or lost an arm, an eye, their legs. Some of them stayed in Angola or sought refuge in Mozambique, in Ethiopia, but I wanted to come home to my family. It was like a sickness, that feeling of longing. Everyone asked questions when I returned, but it was impossible to explain what it was like in Angola."

We have never spent a whole night together before. All our encounters have been snatched moments in clandestine houses, or at the beach, an aura of the forbidden surrounding us. His body twitches and convulses in the night, the sheet drawn up over his head while I lie awake listening to his laboured breathing. I must have fallen asleep finally, curved into him with my knees drawn up, because I wake like that, embracing the emptiness of his imprint. It is still early, the air pleasantly cool, but Felix is gone.

Rrradio Rrrebelde, the voice of Cuba, presents the Reflections of Fidel Castro Ruz on the 18th day of February, 2008 . . .

A booming voice shakes the small radio by Yolanda's bed. She slides out and starts dressing in her white uniform. She's bending to tie her shoes as Fidel's voice comes on.

Ésta es una época del cambio para Cuba . . . a time of change for the world, reeling from the economic collapse of the United States, which is mired in a hopeless war with the people of Iraq . . .

She sits up, her brow furrowed. It is not Fidel's voice, although it is a voice very much like his. Fidel used to speak for hours on end, a river of words flowing from his bearded mouth, but now he is old and sick. After a series of operations in the past eighteen months he has become silent. Only his pen moves, recording his daily reflections, which are read at night on the television, and in the morning on Radio Rebelde.

With my resignation as Comandante en Jefe after fifty years of service comes a transition into another government elected by the people. On Sunday February 24th the National Assembly will meet in La Habana. They will elect your new President . . .

Yolanda's eyes fill with tears once more. She wept at the first announcement of Fidel's retirement more than a week ago although, as Calixto pointed out to her, Fidel had in effect been retired already, his brother Raúl governing in his place for the past eighteen months. It was widely anticipated that Raúl would now be officially elected as President of the Cuban Government in a smooth and well-orchestrated transition designed to reassure the international community. The Minister of External Affairs, Felipe Roque Pérez, had been working with Fidel more than three decades — he had an expert finger on the international pulse.

The Cuban people will have the opportunity to participate directly in a democratic process of election. The representatives they have elected will travel to La Habana and sit in the National Assembly, where they will vote in the name of the people who have elected them to do so ...

Yolanda is not interested in politics per se. She thinks with her heart and, like most Cubans, she loves Fidel. Born two years before the Revolution, she's known only Castro's Cuba and now she's afraid. Everything is falling apart. Fidel is retiring and might pass away before she returns from Venezuela. With Calixto's drinking and Anaïs's neglect of Susana Rosa, what will happen to the child? And now Felix with his Canadian *novia* — surely Anilbis will find out sooner or later and cause trouble for him. She sighs and shuffles down the corridor to the kitchen just as Calixto groans and turns over, covering his ears.

The senior Bush started the war in Iraq, and the junior Bush continued it as president when the presidency should have gone to Al Gore. The junior Bush bought his way into the Casa Blanca with the blood money of the Cuban Mafia of Miami ...

Calixto rolls out of bed — another day at *el matadero*. He is the *jefe* of the slaughterhouse and spends much of the day walking the bloody corridors, supervising the men who butcher and cut the meat. Yolanda comes home with the smell of disinfectant on her, Calixto with the smell of blood and offal.

Our compañero Chavez is moving forward with the liberation of all Latin America and the Caribbean in his heart ... we have 685 doctors working in Venezuela, 472 medical technicians, and 720 eye specialists. Our compañero Evo Morales, President of Bolivia, has asked for our help and we have told him yes, we will send doctors and technicians. We will work together to solve all our problems ...

I'm waiting in the kitchen with fresh bread and coffee on the stove when Yolanda slouches in. Her face lights up and she embraces me, her body warm and damp from the night. I tell her that we slept in Orestes' house and she raises her eyebrows and laughs, teasing me. "Where's Felix?" she asks.

I shrug. "You know what he's like, there one minute, gone the next."

"He's gone to tend his animals," she says with sureness. "He keeps pigs and chickens at a friend's house." She kisses my cheek. "Sister," she whispers in her croaky voice. "Let's have some coffee."

The work distracts Felix — hauling buckets of water to sluice down his pigs. He's had bad dreams again, all that talking, he wants to forget, not stir it up. Ever since he danced with her that first night at La Trova, ever since he invited her to Yolanda's house for *pescado Santa Barbara,* Karina has become part of his family. He's danced with lots of women at the Casa de la Trova — with Germans, Italians, Swiss, Czech . . . But this one is different.

What if Anilbis finds out? She's never interfered with his affairs before, but he's seen her watching him, too closely. She senses something. She has a temper and if she wants to she can cause trouble. They've been discreet, but now, *coño,* Karinita is always at Yolanda's house and the neighbours are talking. The police could come down hard on him for involvement with a tourist.

The government protects their tourists because Cuba lives off tourism. Everyone who's old enough remembers the 'Special Period', the stories of people eating livers and kidneys stolen from funeral homes. Felix knows from his relatives in Havana that there was truth to those stories. It hadn't been as bad in Baracoa, with food coming in from the countryside. Every month or so there'd been a market, trucks trundling down the Malecón laden with cabbages, root vegetables, crates of tomatoes, sacks of beans, and children running behind, catching the onions and cabbages that bounced off, throwing them in the air, running home delighted with their prizes. But sometimes the vegetables had rotted in the fields because there'd been no fuel to transport them — until Fidel opened the door to tourism, then Hugo Chavez was elected President of Venezuela with its abundance of oil. Chavez had come at exactly the right moment, Fidel's political ally, stepping boldly into his big shoes.

Felix scrubs the sow's back. She throws her snout up in the air and snorts with pleasure. He pinches her belly and feels by its firmness that she's almost ready for slaughter. She's produced five litters for him and the best of them are breeding.

He knows he's walking a minefield. He has two friends in prison because of their affairs with foreigners — one a *maricón* whose Italian lover squealed on him, and now he's serving seven years. The other man was unfaithful to his American girlfriend and she caused trouble for him with *la policia*, told them he was a *jinetero*. Now he's serving a three year sentence.

He refills the bucket and starts scrubbing out the pig pen. I should have stayed in Leipzig, he thinks. After Angola he'd been restless so he signed on with a group of thirty-five men for a government sponsored programme in East Germany, apprenticing in metalwork. Suited up in a protective suit, with steel-capped boots, leather gloves, hardhat and goggles, he'd learned to pour molten metal into moulds for automotive and aviation parts and long sections of rail. He'd loved the heat and glow of the molten liquid and felt himself at once in hell and paradise, earning for the first time in his life a good salary in that cold drab city of Leipzig. Most of the men bought motorbikes. They bought expensive clothing too and finely made Italian shoes, and they made love to German girls who wound their long pale legs around the Cubans' dark hips.

For three years the men from Baracoa lived and worked together acquiring skills which most of them never used again after their mission was cut short by the reunification of Germany. Once again Felix was sent home, but this time he had a choice of sorts, although he felt he'd been cheated of it. He'd had sex with many German women attracted by his black skin and intrigued by the extraordinary control he had developed, but there was one woman, older than him, who wanted to marry him and keep him there. It had all happened so suddenly. He woke one morning in Ingrid's bed, her smooth white body pressed against him, Lorenzo shaking his shoulder.

"Come on!" he said. "We have to go. The wall's coming down. We've been called home. The plane's leaving in a few hours." Felix's mind was still fuzzy with sleep, but his body made the decision for him. He leapt out of bed, dragged his clothes on and stumbled out the door with Lorenzo.

He sweeps the filthy water into the gutter and throws a bucket of clean water to swill it away. The sow is rubbing up against the cement wall, scratching her thick hide. He tugs on her ears and scratches them, causing her to snort and grin in her piggish way. Soon enough her head will be hanging in the *matadero*.

The nightlife of Baracoa is a continuation of Felix's life in Leipzig — the bond with his friends in their search for women. They all want foreigners, women who can give them a taste of another world where personal freedom is taken for granted. But it isn't easy in Baracoa. How many times has he explained to the *turistas* the need for discretion? They mustn't be seen on the street with him at night. They can't sit in Parque Central with him except during the day. And when they sit together at La Trova or Las Palmares they must leave separately and meet on a dark corner a couple of blocks away. He served on the police force in Havana briefly, after his return from Leipzig — he understands the mentality. And everyone knows that Baracoa has the strictest *policia* in all of Cuba.

He takes a wafer of soap from his trouser pocket and lathers it between his hands, washing them, splashing his face with cold water. He can't stop now, the thoughts won't let him go. There was Anilbis, standing in the kitchen of a neighbour's house on one of his weekend trips to Baracoa. That was when he was working at the nickel mine in Moa after his return from Havana.

She must have gotten pregnant the first time. It was so fast, almost as sudden and shocking as leaving Ingrid. He'd had to sell the motorbike he'd brought from Germany to buy a small house, not far from Yolanda's. When their son was born the baby lay between them at night as Felix's legs twitched in his sleep. Soon he was out more and more often with his friends, reliving the old days in Leipzig, sharing the silence of Angola with his smiling *amigos*.

When his cousin Roberto began an affair with an Italian woman fifteen years older than him and started travelling to Europe, Felix began to imagine another life. All over Cuba are written the words of Jose Martí, quoted frequently by Fidel — *Otro mundo es posible*. Martí was thinking of political transformation, but his words took on a new significance for Felix. On his fortieth birthday he made a vow to himself and two weeks later he left Anilbis and their seven-year-old son, and moved into Yolanda's house.

After coffee with Yolanda and a slice of crumbly bread, I walk to the end of Mariana Grajales where it joins Primero de Abril. There's the ground floor apartment in the ugly concrete building where Yolanda's ninety-three-year-old mother Alicia lives with her daughter Adelis. They've lived here since '97 when a hurricane destroyed their wooden house with its many rooms

shaded by the giant mango tree out front. When Alicia broke
her hip they kept her in the hospital for observation until she
suffered a stroke, then they sent her home to die. But Alicia did
not die. She sits now, a year later, like a girl in a fresh cotton
nightgown gaping at the arms. Her bones are revealed under
rows of ribbed skin caging the beating of an unrelenting heart.
Her steel-grey hair is short and curly, soft as down. She speaks
in a barely audible whisper, like Yolanda after her nodules were
scraped.

I have brought a big red apple. A boy was selling them on
the street, a rare treat, apples from Washington state — the US
embargo is not all it's cracked up to be. Once the economy is
destroyed it's safe to trade silently.

Alicia gives me the ghost of a smile and looks up question-
ingly at her daughters. Amelia grins and takes the apple out
to the kitchen. I hear her washing it as Adelis rattles on with
her rapid-fire Spanish, massaging her mother's arms, pinching
her flesh to keep her alive. In Adelis's house Alicia is constantly
stimulated by the children who run in and out, planting sticky
kisses on her cheeks, by her handsome nephews who handle her
with their large brown hands, by her daughters who sit beside
her keeping up a constant stream of chatter, surrounding her
with the life she has engendered from her tiny body — twelve
children — Felix the youngest, and of course her favourite.

He appears suddenly in the doorway and her face lights up.
I feel her intake of breath, and a rising up within her like a plant
opening to receive the rain.

"Mami, why aren't you out playing in the sunshine? You're a
bandolera, lazing around in bed all day."

He picks her up in his arms and carries her to the window,
holding her there a while, talking softly to her. Their faces are
identical — the narrow bones of their Taíno ancestry, the smooth

African skin and softly curved lips. She murmurs something into his ear and Felix carries her back to bed, propping her up and kissing her forehead. Amelia is there holding half an apple, the flesh creamy against the shiny red skin. She gives it to Alicia, and a tin cup with a little water in the bottom.

"Come on, Mami. You must eat. You're too thin," she says.

"Remember, Mami, how you used to be a *gordita* with a great big bum?" Adelis asks, cackling.

The old lady nibbles at the apple and I see the pleasure on her face. It is like a child's first taste of fruit — the savouring of flavour, texture, conversion. She eats slowly, and they surround her, chattering, as she is consumed by her apple, occasionally glancing up at Amelia, Adelis, Felix, then staring at me with a bemused look, as though I were from another world, as indeed I am.

Alicia was born in 1915, forty-four years before the Revolution. She bore her children in the countryside, in a wooden house in Sabanilla, with a thatched roof of banana leaves. She cooked outdoors over an open woodfire, and in the yard there were mango and guayaba trees, bushes of black beans, red and yellow beans. Thick bunches of platanos and bananas grew as the red flower pods dropped from the trees that shaded her house. They had all slept together, the children rooting for space like puppies, always at least one nuzzling her breast, searching for the nipple. When her husband died she moved with the younger children to Baracoa, to the mango house.

It takes Alicia a very long time to finish the fruit. There's a tiny splash as she drops the half-core into her watery cup and looks up at us. Felix pulls me to him, his arm around my shoulders, his hand falling almost onto my breast, acknowledging me finally, as though the intimacy of last night had been too much for him. I kiss Alicia, and Felix runs his hands over her legs, pinching and smoothing her wrinkled flesh, then he kisses her too. As we leave the room I turn for a last glimpse, as I had done in childhood with my great grandma and great-great auntie Maude, never knowing if there would be another chance.

Between the Sheets

SUNLIGHT FELL IN SPLOTCHES AT THE SIDE of the road, patterned by the foliage of fat coco leaves and long palm fronds. I would have meandered slowly along the dusty road, soaking up the fragrance of the landscape bordering Finca Duaba, but the woman grabbed my hand to hurry me along and I felt the slippery sweat of her palm. I didn't know exactly who this woman was or where she was taking me. Felix's friend, Manolo, had brought me only so far then turned back towards the Finca as the woman appeared, beckoning. I thought of the cold war spy movies I'd grown up with, turning to my mother in the darkness. Where are they going? What's going to happen?

She said her name was Graciela. She walked fast with her head down, muttering to herself, "*Madre Maria, Dios mío.*" She was short and plump, perhaps in her fifties, hard to tell.

"Do you have children?" I asked.

"I had two sons. They're both dead. I live alone now." Her face was impassive and I wondered if I'd heard right. I noticed beads of sweat breaking out on her brow.

"Have you lived here all your life?"

She nodded curtly, and called out to a woman hanging wet clothes on a line — words too rapid for me to catch the sense — then she turned off the road and I followed her through the grass towards a wooden *casita* thatched with palm fronds, fenced with a thick wall of cactus. Inside the fence rose bushes bloomed yellow, white, and red. Wet clothes were stretched over the bushes, drying in the sun. Two black pigs rooted in the dry grass, and in the doorway a dog slept as though dead in the hot sun. Graciela climbed nimbly over the stile which had a stone step on either side, and I followed, my long legs clearing it easily. The dog came to life suddenly, its dusty golden body wriggling with pleasure as it wagged its tail. Then a puppy came round the side of the *casita*, jumping and squirming. They didn't bark, this was a silent place.

Graciela led me into a cool room with a cement floor worn smooth and shiny. It was spotlessly clean and sparsely furnished. She was more relaxed now that we were inside and a faint smile softened her face when I exclaimed at the beauty and tranquility of the house. I could hardly believe it. This was the house I had imagined Onaldo and I would live in, where we would write together when he retired from his job, where I would cook for him, and where we would sit together during the long evenings, embraced by the darkness that falls suddenly at the equator. But all my questions had met with complicated answers about government regulations, Party rules, special visas, and other bureaucratic threads contributing to the tangle that had suffocated my dreams. I'd given up and entered into the compromising relationship of foreigner to Cuban, signing Onaldo in as my *acompañante* at Erminda's *casa particular* — her protection against the inspectors who paid regular visits, ready to slap her with a fine.

"I pay Fidel 100 pesos a month for the privilege of renting out this room," Erminda said, "Plus thirty pesos for food service and

6.50 for passage through my house. Now he sends his inspectors around looking for more. *"¡Dios mío!"*

A tiny chick, no more than a ball of pale yellow fluff, ran around the room cheeping furiously. I stooped to pick it up, but it ran in circles, and disappeared under a chair. "It wants to get out," I said to Graciela. But she must have misunderstood me because she picked it up and put it into my hands. I held it a moment, my hand damp with the newness of it. I carried the chick out back and placed it in the dust with the hens and the other chicks, but the little chick immediately ran inside again and continued its cheeping. Graciela gestured for me to sit down, then she disappeared.

At fourteen I'd had my first, tentative romance with a Welsh farmer's son, and the front room of his family's house had felt like this — a low-ceilinged room darkened by oak beams and a thatched roof, the smell of animals and vegetation, a cleanness in the air which circulated with the memory of constant activity, and yet a kind of stillness as though the place were held in concentration. On the wall of Graciela's *sala* was the ubiquitous poster of a pastel Jesus. The walls were of faded blue wood, mottled in places with age and stress, like splotches on an old hand. This was it, this was the place I had imagined for us.

Felix appeared in the doorway with Graciela and there was a quick exchange then she disappeared again, round the back of the house. I was still watching the chick running in circles as Felix took my hand and led me into the bedroom. The bed had a thin blue cover, a threadbare pillow, and next to it a table crowded with *muñequitas* — little dolls dressed as Cuban peasants. She must sell them, I thought. She must buy them from the factory in town and sell them to tourists visiting the Finca. This is *her* bedroom.

Felix sat at the foot of the bed, one leg crossed, his ankle balanced on his knee, his foot jiggling. He held out his hand. There were slats in the walls, a glimpse of red — the flower of a banana palm — a rustling of fronds as a slight breeze stirred the walls.

I moved across the room and sat next to him.

"She's very nervous," he said. "She told us to be quick."

I felt as though there were eyes all around the room watching us.

"I can't do this, Felix. It's her bedroom, her house, she lives alone, her sons are dead, look at the *muñequitos.*"

I remembered my mother's suspicions, her unjust accusations, shame and guilt descending like a tightly woven mantle on my shoulders, contaminating the friendship with my farmboy. I thought I'd shrugged it off, but here it was again, in another country, a lifetime later. We had sought a private place, just as Cuban couples do, paying by the hour for a dingy room because they live in a tight press of family with no space for lovers. Even though Cubans speak all the time of 'amor', toasting it, dreaming of it, dancing it, the sex-sodden undercurrent of the culture is, paradoxically, evidence of the prohibitions and regulations that govern people's lives. Sexual liaisons have to be planned, time snatched opportunistically. There is little of the privacy or spontaneity that allows intimacy to grow naturally. The urgency in the air, poured into music and dance with an easy elegance, makes gnawing preoccupations of food and sex.

He didn't try to persuade me. He simply looked at me, his eyes questioning. A quickie? No, not what I had in mind, and I realized that it was all in my mind, the excitement, the anticipation, the mystery and forbidden nature of it. In reality my body had deserted me, floating like the sleepwalker I had been, waiting to be used. But I was the user now. I was the one who would pay Manolo and Graciela, pay for Felix's drinks that night.

"Let's go." Felix took my hand and pulled me up. "Don't worry. I'll find somewhere," he said, and he held me close, nothing between our invisible hearts but skin and bones.

"What about Graciela?"

"She's gone. We'll walk back to the Finca and I'll tell Manolo we couldn't stay."

"It's too much of a risk for her. If the neighbours talk she could get a fine."

He nodded and took my hand. "Come on, we'll cut through the trees."

I slipped twenty *convertibles* under the lumpy pillow, and as we left the house I looked back, trying to remember, but now that I'd seen it my fantasy was gone, crumbled in the face of Graciela's reality. I thought of Onaldo growing old in his room, surrounded by his Canadian mementos, sleeping in his lonely bed, retreating further into his research, sifting through the tendrils of his African roots until he was buried there, merged with his origins, and I felt glad to imagine him thus, more truly himself than his own fantasy of a Canadian life that would destroy him.

As I climbed over the stile my foot slid on the stone step, grazing my ankle, and bright beads of blood rose in a diamond pattern. I felt the pain, a sharpness with an ache underneath it. The little beads would harden and pucker my skin until they fell somewhere by the roadside, in the ocean, between the sheets. As we walked back to the Finca I looked up at the sky where a bank of clouds had gathered, swollen with a sullenness that presaged a storm.

⮾

Witnesses

MINUTES AFTER THE POLICE CAR DREW UP behind Chucho's gleaming white automobile the news was all over Baracoa. Few houses had telephones — people simply went next door to relay the news — but Vilma was one of the fortunate. When she heard the news from her son-in-law who was home with *la gripe*, she immediately 'phoned her husband Ernesto at work, her voice low and conspiratorial, her face solemn.

In her heart she felt a mixture of fear, outrage, and a secret gloating at the inevitability of it. She and Ernesto had often wondered where Chucho got the money for all his fancy toys, how long he'd get away with it. After all, this was not Havana where *hombres de negocios* could operate more or less freely, protected by the eye of the international media. Strange, thought Vilma, that this should happen just as Raúl Castro was promising an easing of prohibitions with more opportunity for private enterprise. *Dios mío,* there'd even been an announcement that Cubans were now permitted to stay in tourist hotels and eat in tourist restaurants, at tourist prices of course. Ernesto said it was a bad joke. They'd never stayed in a hotel and didn't expect to now. How could they ever get hold of convertible currency? Vilma was on disability pension since her fall, and Ernesto was only a year away from retirement. His pension, like hers, would be sixty percent of his salary which already was barely enough to survive on. She couldn't imagine what they would do to get by when the time came.

Chucho lived across the street. They'd watched his sister's house being built, the brand new furniture arriving, the black and white tiles being laid on the patio. They'd watched him come and go in his fancy shoes with a flashy gold chain around his neck, and although they never spoke of it, Vilma knew that she and Ernesto shared a secret desire to one day see Chucho caught. And she knew they were not alone. So, when the police knocked on her door and asked her to step across the street and be a witness to the removal of certain articles from the house, she flushed with guilt and complied immediately. She was dying of curiosity and shame. When she entered the house she saw Chucho sitting on a hard chair, his head bowed, hands folded in his lap. It was a relief. She'd half expected to see him handcuffed. His mother, Béatriz, was weeping noisily and her husband, Adolfo, was attempting to comfort her, his arm around her shoulders, his hand patting her breast ineffectually.

Fulgencia and Geraldo had been called as witnesses too. Fulgencia stood with her back to the wall, arms folded across her breast, puffed up with importance like a songbird. She had an 'I told you so' look on her face. She'd often tried to engage Vilma in gossip about Chucho's lifestyle. Geraldo, on the other hand, stood forlorn, his head bowed like Chucho's. He liked the boy. They played dominoes together down the street in front of Hector's place where it was shady in the afternoons. He'd often won a bundle through Chucho's negligence and the boy had simply laughed, his strong teeth gleaming. It gave Geraldo a feeling of good health to be around Chucho. It made him feel better, especially since he'd retired and begun to feel all the aches and pains of old age, not to mention trying to survive on his measly pension, going to bed hungry most nights, unless his daughter surprised him with a *potaje de frijoles*, or a little piece of chicken.

Two uniformed police were in the process of searching the house. They carried things into the front room and piled them in the corner — a computer monitor, a keyboard, a hard drive tower, a collection of CDs and what Vilma supposed to be computerware — various boxes and cases with wired objects trailing from them. On the table was a pile of magazines, a tattered address book, a photo album and, balanced on top, a cell phone and Chucho's car keys. They wheeled in a red bicycle with thick tires and a fancy arrangement of gears and brake cords. From Chucho's bedroom they brought a television set, a DVD player, a clock radio with a long cord, and a white telephone from his bedside table. How many telephones does a person need? Vilma wondered, then she heard Béatriz's renewed sobbing and she almost felt like crying herself. It wasn't fair to involve her. She knew she would be there for hours, and she was already hungry. She'd had only a piece of bread for breakfast with a cup of coffee.

When the police had completed their search, the younger of the two detectives from Guantánamo laboriously listed the articles to be removed from the house, which included all of Chucho's clothing — every sweater, every pair of shoes, a collection of baseball caps — the bicycle, Beatriz's new washing machine, and so on — all handwritten with a leaky pen sweating in the midday heat. Vilma fanned her face with one of the magazines from the living room table. She saw Béatriz watching her and she smiled apologetically. She was beginning to feel very uncomfortable. Her stomach growled and she asked the senior detective for a glass of water, but he seemed not to hear her.

Chucho had come to life and was arguing with him, insisting that the car was borrowed from a friend.

"How could I afford a car?" he protested, "I work in a tourist bar. They give good tips, but not that good, and anyway we all share. Everything is legal."

"And your friend's name?"

"Sandra Gonzalez," he said. "She went away and asked me to look after the car for her."

A discussion ensued from which it appeared that the said Señorita Gonzalez had no fixed address right now. She was out of the country, in Barcelona visiting friends. Chucho produced the registration and the detective bundled the papers, together with the address book and magazines, and secured them with an elastic band. There would be an investigation, he said. They would track down the Señorita. Meanwhile Chucho would be taken to Guantánamo and held there until the investigation was complete. There was a collective gasp in the sweltering room and Béatriz burst into a long wail.

"No, no, you can't take my son!" she wept. Adolfo embraced her, muffling her protest. It was no use. They all knew that when a suspect was taken to Guantánamo it was almost certain that the police had proof against him for drug trafficking. The Guantánamo prisons, like the water, were the worst in Cuba, distinct from the US prison in Guantánamo Bay where Arabs sweltered in cages, but bad enough by Cuban standards.

Fulgencia sidled forward to sign her name as witness to the list of confiscated goods, her mouth a thin line of concentration as she wielded the slippery pen. Then it was Geraldo's turn. He frowned, reading the list slowly, following the lines with his fingers, his lips working. He turned the pages slowly, reluctantly, a muscle in his jaw pulsing. Finally he signed his name, a slow scrawl, and when he looked up at Vilma his eyes were moist. She took the pen from him and patted his arm, then she signed, wanting only to get out of there and cross the street to her own home, to eat something, to rinse her mouth with cool water from the refrigerator, to get the bad taste of fear out of her mouth, to swallow it all because that was the only way.

In the ensuing days the first words on everyone's lips were, "Any news of Chucho?" Adolfo travelled to Guantánamo to inquire about his son and came back the same day. There was no news, only the assurance that Chucho would be held until the investigation was complete and a judgement made. If he was cleared they would allow him to go home. They were still looking for Sandra Gonzalez.

Three separate raids had been made on the same day. Benito, who ran a *casa particular* for tourists, had been taken away in handcuffs, accused of renting rooms illegally to couples by the hour. Don Antonio's *paladar*, La Colonial, was searched and his accounting books taken, but the general opinion was that Antonio would be exempt from whatever crimes he was suspected of because he paid more than a thousand pesos in taxes each month.

All over the town of Baracoa people scurried to cover their tracks. Teófilo hid his motorbike in a friend's house, boxed all the movie DVDs he rented out and hid them in the house of another friend, then he locked up and took the bus to Santiago to lie low for a couple of weeks. Toñiquito sold his new clothes, hid his gold rings in the urn with Abuelo's ashes, and concealed his illegally bought building materials with a thick covering of palm leaves. Baracoa became a warren of creatures running scared, disappearing into their burrows where they tunnelled and lay low with their ears back and their teeth bared.

Vilma rocked in front of the TV, fanning her thighs. She and Ernesto were watching an old Hollywood movie in black and white, but her mind was elsewhere. It wasn't the fact that she'd signed as witness to the removal of goods from Beatriz's house. After all, what choice had she had? It was something else — a niggling, a gnawing, like a small animal that would not let her rest — and sometimes, when she woke in the middle of the night to Ernesto's snoring, it was indistinguishable from her own hunger, and the rumbling of her fleshy stomach.

"Aiee, Ernesto," she sighed, "When are you going to take me to Hotel Porto Santo for a big dinner and a night of passion in a *cama de matrimonio?*" And she laughed so hard that her stomach hurt.

Lorenzo's Museum

A FILMY WHITE CURTAIN HANGS ACROSS THE doorway to Lorenzo's bedroom. We stand at the open door of the two-room *casita* and feel the wind gusting in from the ocean, lifting the curtain. The tiny front room is furnished with a table, two chairs, and a third chair in the corner, the back broken off.

"It's a humble house," Lorenzo says. "I wish I had something to offer . . . " He grins, revealing a lucky gap between his front teeth.

"Lorenzo, you have the ocean, the palm trees, the sound of the waves . . . What more could you offer?"

"The storm woke me. I stood on the beach and watched the waves splashing into the sky. I thought they would touch the stars," he says, his face tilting upwards.

Lorenzo lives in Reparto Turey, in the mouth of the bay, close to where Rio Macaguanigua meets the ocean like a twisted lizard, its tail snaking up under the bridge that crosses Calle Primero de Abril. For Lorenzo to have seen the spume across the spit of land that is called La Punta and that forms the narrow opening to Bahía de Baracoa, the waves must have been huge. With each storm they are higher. I have a sense of foreboding as I remember an article in *Granma* — *An iceberg in Antarctica,*

*four times the size of Paris, is breaking up and will eventually
disintegrate into the ocean, raising the global level irrevocably* ....

"You want to swim?" Felix asks.

"You can change in here," Lorenzo tells me, lifting the
curtain to his bedroom. "I'm going to my daughter's house to
get tomatoes."

His daughter, Cileña, lives next door, her mother down the
beach, with brothers, grandchildren, cousins and aunts nearby.

I slip behind the white curtain and Lorenzo lets it drop. I
hear his rubber sandals flopping, sending out little sprays of
sand as I stand motionless, staring at the wall where his clothes
are displayed. Pants hang side by side over a long pole, the ends
resting in grooves he's chipped out of the wood. Shirts and
sweaters hang above the pants in a bright array of colours. I
want to touch his clothing, feel the material brushing my face
and shoulders, but something stops me as I reach forward.

Leipzig before the wall came down. *Humpty Dumpty had a
great fall* . . . Thirty-five Cubans tumbling home after living in
exile, training in the foundry fifteen years ago.

Lorenzo's shoes are lined up side by side on a low shelf, above
them on a smaller shelf his shaving mirror, brush and comb, nail
clippers. I touch the tongues of a pair of large white shoes, and
I remember my brother's shoes, handed to me after his death
with his meagre belongings — the pain of a denied love inside
me still, unfolding like a late and stunted blossom. I shiver at
the stillness of the room and wonder at the grinning man who
sleeps here in this shrine to the past. Layers of chalky whitener
cover Lorenzo's shoes. When does he have the opportunity to
wear this finery? He's always in shorts and a T-shirt with rubber
chancletas, padding through the sand. I shed my clothes and
change quickly into a bikini, wrapping myself in a sarong. When

I turn towards the curtain and reach to lift it, a hand grasps me and pulls me onto the bed.

"Felix! You *bandolero!*"

I fall on top of him and we almost roll off the lumpy mattress, laughing as we save ourselves at the last minute. Then I spread my sarong, edging gingerly onto Lorenzo's bed, which is balanced on teetering piles of bricks. We lie there listening to the swish of the incoming waves, the suck and pull of the ebb against the stones until, with our caressing, I feel the rhythm of the ocean inside me. Felix slides across my body, his skin brushing mine like dark silk. He stands by the bed and pulls me up, close to him, licking the salt off my neck as he turns me slowly. We make love like this, and I am held by his strong hands, my own hands resting so lightly on the fragile bed. When I return to him, twisting into his embrace, I see behind him Lorenzo's German clothing museum, his shoe collection, the toiletries with the scrap of mirror balanced on the shelf, and I want to lie in his bed and savour his solitary dreams. We break apart and I wrap myself in the sarong and lift the white patterned net of the curtain which for a moment seems bridal, then Felix slaps my butt and I turn sharply to see him grinning.

To swim so soon after the storm thrills me, knowing as I do that these same waves, so gentle now, could have taken my breath away, dragged me under and thrashed me into darkness. The ocean is a miracle of duplicity, a lover dwelling in the body of a monster, inextricable, unfathomable. I emerge dripping with salt water, cleansed by the stink of the sea which transforms everything, and lie on the same thin cloth we spread on Lorenzo's bed, thrown now across the hot sand. Light sparkles on my eyelids and picks out a million points on my skin as it dries with a granular residue of salt.

When I return to the beach house I find Lorenzo and Felix out back in something that might pass for a kitchen, although it is not. Because they are chopping tomatoes and onions, shredding lettuce there, it has become for now a kitchen. Lorenzo squeezes lime onto the salad, pours sunflower oil from a bright bottle, crushes rough salt in his big hands and sprinkles it on the tomatoes. We sit at the table with one fork and three plastic cups between us while Felix uncaps the rum bottle and pours the first offering on the earthen floor in the corner for Elegguá. The rum burns my throat and belly, and as the heat spreads inside my body a world expands, pulling everyone in — Lorenzo and Felix, Cileña and her children, Yolanda and the people of La Playa, La Punta, Maisí, Imías, Santiago, reaching all the way to Havana, to Canada, no limits now.

Felix leans forward and touches me, smoothing my skin with his hand, caressing me, as he and his sisters touch their old mother, keeping her alive. I cannot tell if it is a gesture of ownership or reassurance and, if the latter, to reassure himself or me. Lorenzo fetches an album from his room, not the usual handful of photographs in a plastic skin, but an actual album with photos carefully pasted in. I lean forward, eager for a vision of his life in Leipzig. There are groups of smiling, well-dressed men with mugs of beer in their hands. Lorenzo is grinning as ever, a neatly trimmed moustache above his gap-toothed smile. He's younger, and I see that he has improved with age, a subtle quality, as though he had been beaten and had survived it with all his youthful exuberance, tempered and enriched rather than embittered, scrubbed clean by the salt air of the ocean that pounds inside his head day and night. He breaks my heart with his brave happiness.

Felix lights a cigarette and rocks back on the legs of his chair, eyes slit, staring at me through the smoke of his exhalation. I pour another round.

"I recognize those pants," I say, my finger on a photograph, then I lift the curtain and point to the striped pants hanging in the centre of the pole, green, white and orange like a deckchair. Lorenzo tilts his head and laughs. And I think of Onaldo with his Canadian thrift-store shirts, the pistachio-strawberry chequered one with short sleeves, his face captured in closeup, turning, smiling at me in Parque Céspedes in Santiago. I remember his brand new running shoes, large and white with blue trim and long floppy laces, the silver ring on the third finger of his right hand embossed with the symbol of eternity, matched on my own hand in gold. I imagine a bookshelf in his room, light flooding in, illuminating the titles — *Inés de mi Alma, El Alquimista, El Sendero Encarnado* . . . a plaster model of Niagara Falls, arced in a horseshoe, spray captured in a solid glob of whiteness, like toothpaste.

"We'll lose everything if you don't come back to me," he'd said as we'd sat on the Playa Caribe, "All that we've planned for our future."

The poignancy of that lament, his fear of losing what had already been lost, even in the imagining of it, laced as it was with expectation.

Perhaps I'll never be in Lorenzo's house again, I think, at the same time aware that everything about my presence in Lorenzo's house is based on the importance of being there again, seeing his pants lined up below his shirts, building on these observations.

"Live every moment as though it's your last . . ." My brother's smoky voice echoing. How do we develop the habit of annexing part of ourselves into the future? And how can we pull ourselves back into this moment, short of receiving a death sentence?

Felix pinches the tanned flesh of my arm — I look down and watch my slow skin regain its smoothness. His touch is an annoyance now, reminding me of the movement of my body ahead of his, aging, and he unaware inside his dark river of skin. But I have the sparkle of the ocean on me now, invisible, and salt on my tongue.

"Take a photo of us, Karinita," Lorenzo says. And he jumps up and beckons to Felix. They stand together, arms around each other's shoulders, grinning like two little boys, *click,* captured forever in this miraculous moment.

"And now one of me alone to show your friends," Lorenzo says. He drags one of the good chairs over to the Elegguá corner and sits there stiff and upright.

"A smile please," I say, and he grins, *click.*

"Let me see," he asks, and nods approvingly when I show him his digital portrait. "Please, bring me a copy when you come back."

It is a small thing, but I know it will become magnified as it is gazed upon, and this day remembered.

~

The Prisoner

THEY CAME TO HIS CELL IN THE late afternoon, just as he was remembering the golden light that enveloped the bay at dusk as he'd sat on the patio of his mother's house. His sentence was for seven years.

The two detectives seated themselves facing him. They offered him a cigarette, made their proposal. Of course he knew Chucho, who didn't? A handsome mulatto with luminous green eyes, always buying drinks for everyone, dancing with the pretty girls. But Mario didn't know him personally. He didn't know where he'd got his money, how he'd managed to buy a car, a computer, gold jewellery. He only knew that Chucho was generous and that everybody liked him and sought him out for games of dominoes, for loans and favours, to share a bottle of rum.

It was said that people who hung with Chucho always had good luck. Sure, his sister had a nice house, furnished like a palace. Everyone knew that Chucho had helped her, that's what families are for. Of course there were rumours. People said that Chucho and his father had found a package washed up on shore near Barigua on the road to Yumurí — drugs dropped off from Colombia wrapped in heavy plastic — cocaine, marijuana … meant for the traffickers who took it to La Habana, people said, to be smuggled in small packages to Miami. Cuban army officials were involved in a narcotics trafficking ring, they said, but maybe it was only a rumour, you never knew. He'd seen a movie on TV –*Miami Vice* – same kind of story. Sometimes people confused what they saw on TV with real life, didn't they? But where do they get those TV stories anyway if not from real life?

He figured Chucho had it coming to him. And after all what had *he* done other than dance with his lover and show him a good time. So, the Italian didn't like it when he danced with the Cuban *chica*, but she'd sat next to him in school and they'd always been buddies. And to report him to *la policia* in a fit of jealousy! No Cuban would have done that! *Coño* — here he was, the only *maricón* amongst drug dealers, *jineteros*, thieves.

The deal was a huge reduction in his sentence. He'd be free in six months. They wanted an answer immediately. There was no time to think. After they left, Mario took a swig of water. His mouth was dry and tasted bad after the cigarette. But the bad taste persisted. The Guantánamo water was filthy, not like the sweet water of Baracoa which flowed from the mountains in shining rivers.

Mario closed his eyes and imagined the sky over Playita as night fell turning the beach to gold. The radiance of that reflection entered his skin and made his throat ache. There was El Yunque in the distance, her smoky blue aura soft and mysterious as a *mulata gordita*, like his mamá.

↩

Faux Pas

June 2007 — April 2008

THERE'S A PHOTO OF ME TAKEN ON the night that I first asked Teófilo if he was a *maricón*. I'm standing in Parque Central with Mario (or María as he likes to be called), who was on weekend leave from prison, serving seven years for homosexuality.

We'd been dancing and drinking rum of course. María's arm is around me. I look tired and a bit drunk, but we're smiling into the camera, at Teófilo, who had nursed an orange soda all night, refusing to dance, rocking back on his chair legs, head tilted to one side, smiling. After he'd handed the camera back to me we stood together on the edge of the crowd and watched María camping around with some German tourists, fingering a tall blonde's necklace and dangly earrings. He's a makeup artist and had pencilled in his eyebrows dramatically at odds with his soft features and prison-short hair.

Everyone hangs out in Parque Central after La Trova closes, crowding in front of the Catholic church that sits at one end of the park, unwilling to end the evening, waiting for something wonderful to happen, or even for one more drink. I decided to ask him finally. It had been on my mind ever since I'd met him in Erminda's kitchen and immediately recognized our affinity. He's Erminda's nephew. As soon as she introduced him we began to talk like old friends, about movies, books, travel. He brought me DVDs of Cuban movies — *Fresa y Chocolate, Un Rey en La Habana, La Muerte de un Burócrata.* He has a small business, renting out movies from his house for five Cuban pesos a night — about twenty cents.

His response was subtle, a door closing gently so that no one would hear, as though I'd said something gauche and must be protected from my faux pas. At the same time it was a matter-of-fact denial, and though I didn't believe him I let it slide by. I was leaving Cuba soon. Onaldo was coming to Canada, and who knew then what might happen?

When I walked into Teófilo's house six months later he opened his arms and embraced me.

"My sister!" he exclaimed. "Where have you been? I've missed you."

We'd been e-mailing, but I'd forgotten the impact of his physical presence, the beauty of him, the sense of familiarity. Somehow, even though he spoke rapidly like all Cubans, I understood Teófilo in ways beyond language, as I understood Onaldo, through an orchestration of gesture and harmony that sidesteps the brain. He was tenor to my alto, different voice, same key.

He showed me all the changes in his house, the newly painted dining room, the plants climbing up the patio wall onto the rooftop, his sparkling kitchen filled with cheap 'made in China' gadgets. He's one of the few Cubans I know who gets things done, and gets them done fast. There is an aura of prosperity and ease around Teófilo, not that he has money, but he does have an energetic belief in possibility that carries him forward. In Cuba, personal ambition is so often blocked that people have internalized a kind of disability, an unquestioning acceptance that robs them of initiative. The ubiquitous phrase — *No es facil* — (like our 'You know' — a lifeline thrown into the void by the individualist seeking commonality) — carries beneath the words an actual belief that nothing is easy, nothing is possible because there is no money. Everyone understands this in Cuba. But it's not only about money. Teófilo's easy personality has drawn to him a network of foreign friends who provide him with clothing, shoes, and computer equipment. And he has friends who work in hotels with access to special foods such as cheese, apples, prawns or beef — illegal for Cubans because these 'luxuries' are conserved for the tourist industry.

"When are you coming to dinner?" Teófilo asked. He loves to cook. "We'll eat *pescado dorado* with *salsa de coco, platanos fritos*, and a big salad. Oh, I have a surprise!" He clasped my hand and led me into his bedroom to show me the kittens that had just been born in his closet where the tabby had made herself a nest. Another cat, Toto, lay on Teófilo's bed snoozing, and Bruno, a sleek daschund who persisted in eating the coconut offerings placed at Elegguá's shrine by the front door, padded into the bedroom to join us. Two large tortoises nestled in the foliage on the patio.

When we sat down finally to talk about everything that had happened, our conversation was strangely lopsided. My life in Canada had been eventful — a new book launched in the fall with a reading tour and a Spanish translation, the fall semester of teaching at the university, and work with Leila on a new project for a Havana gallery. As Teófilo spoke I began to realize I'd heard it all before . . . the girlfriends, the tourists, his desire to travel, his plans to open a *paladar* at his mother's house. I didn't mind repetition — how many conversations had

I had about the price of beans, the unusual weather, the lack of quality goods in the stores? I was willing to talk about anything so long as it was in Spanish, but Teófilo was more to me than someone to practice my Spanish with. He was a brother, the one I'd never had until the final weeks of Christopher's life when he had revealed himself at last and I had fallen in love with him.

Teófilo asked me, half joking, if I could find him a Canadian woman, someone mature, perhaps in her fifties.

"But Teófilo, aren't you gay?" His playfulness had somehow encouraged me to respond spontaneously, but Teófilo shut down immediately, a wounded expression on his face.

"I'm sorry, I've offended you," I said, feeling stupid, because of course he was simply asking for a passport out of Cuba.

"No, no." He looked down, avoiding my eyes as he crossed the room and began searching for something in the dresser drawer. I knew he'd had an early reputation as a womanizer — after all it was part of a Cuban male's identity — and he had a grown son, a grandson, and a teenage daughter who lived with him part time. I'd met her mother. All the people in Teófilo's world were connected as friends. He surrounded himself. What would he do in Canada, an immigrant without the language?

He came back with a sheaf of photographs. "This is my second wife," he said showing me a photograph of a trophy woman in high heels and a minidress with a plunging neckline, elaborate makeup and gorgeous hair. "We were together for six years. She lives in Paris now with her new husband."

In the photo she was standing next to Teófilo, holding onto his arm as they stared at the camera.

"She's beautiful, Teófilo," I reassured him, glossing over my faux pas.

Then he showed me a photograph of himself under a waterfall with two Italian men, tourists in Baracoa. "Claudio is here again, to see his girlfriend," Teófilo said, pointing to the one on the left, then he began to talk about his own girlfriends, listing them, one, two, three, "And there's another, she's only seventeen. But it's nothing really," he laughed, "She's a friend of my daughter. She has a crush on me so I have to be nice to her."

Teófilo lived round the corner from Yolanda and by then I was spending a lot of time at her house, so I dropped in at his house quite often too and that's how I met Claudio with his cowlick of dyed blond hair, gold chains at throat, wrist and ankle, stylish shorts that showed off his shaven legs, two large pinkie rings and a gold hooped earring. His arms were tattooed, he wore a Che muscle shirt, and he kissed me on both cheeks when Teófilo presented him, almost choking me with his pungent aftershave as I felt his silken-smooth cheeks brush my own. He exuded well-being. Teófilo stood on the sidelines, bathed in his friend's aura.

We didn't speak of it again, any of it. Teófilo didn't even tell me that Claudio had gone back to Italy until I asked. He was like the calm surface of a pond which I hesitated to disturb for fear of what might be rooted in the depths.

Teófilo's place was always bustling with comings and goings — clients at the door to rent movies, his neighbour, Reynaldo, who looked after the business when Teo was away from the house, Vladimir, a young man who arrived one day from Holguín and had been around ever since, looking after the animals and gardening on the patio. He too talked about his girlfriend but I never saw her, neither had I seen Claudio's girlfriend or any of the girls Teófilo spoke of. But Cuban women are often more talked about than seen. On *Día de San Valentín* — perhaps the most celebrated day in Cuba after *Año Nuevo* — I'd seen a group of men drinking rum and declaiming love poems late into the night — to each other it seemed, since there were no women in sight. It didn't necessarily mean that they were gay, but simply that they saved their deepest affection for each other. In their honouring of heterosexual romance they were perhaps elevating what in practice appeared to be a bodily need and the desire for the closeness of family. Cubans are floored by childless foreigners.

The day Vladimir arrived we were sitting on the patio drinking coffee with Reynaldo and his wife, Mirella. Vladimir appeared silently in the doorway and stood there smiling. He walked over and put out his hand, but Teófilo pulled back abruptly, his own hands turning into fists. There was a play of ducking and feinting, a flurry of mock aggression which I almost took seriously, then Teófilo's face broke into a grin, and the men embraced, Vladimir's throat angling against Teófilo's bull neck. Teo was not exactly chubby, but he had that softness which sets in between perfect ripeness and the beginning of decay. I watched as they talked and smiled, their teeth so white, lips moving in the full and fleshy dance of speech. It seemed they were old friends who hadn't seen each other in several years. When I told Teo later that they had seemed to me almost like lovers his aggression was real, the word 'normál' jumping out at me repeatedly while Reynaldo and Mirella squirmed and sniggered. The fact was that many people in Baracoa either suspected or assumed that Teófilo was gay.

I wondered what our friendship was based on. Did Teófilo like me because I was a foreigner who recognized and challenged him? Or was it because I brought him things from Canada — a CD burner, a USB flash drive, T-shirts, bright dishtowels for his kitchen? Or because of our conversation which took him out of himself into another culture? A foreigner is always on unsure ground in Cuba. The usual rules of engagement do not exist because relationships are unequal — I don't mean the familiar inequality of rich and poor, class difference, educational disparity, but a systemic economic inequality between Cubans and tourists in a country that lives off tourism, dividing us into two distinct camps, held apart and at the same time thrown together in co-dependence by the dual economic system. Cubans are paid in *moneda nacional*, so they lack the choices we take for granted with our *convertibles* — to purchase imported goods, to travel, even to buy toothpaste or a beer — and must therefore rely on befriending us.

I don't really know how our friendship began. For me it was that instant recognition and feeling of familiarity in Erminda's kitchen during my second visit when Onaldo was so upset about the police coming to the house.

"Agh, it's nothing," Erminda had said. "They always harass couples until the relationship is established."

I had thought Onaldo was perhaps overreacting, remembering the boy who had drowned and how the police made him responsible for telling the parents. Anyway Teófilo had reassured me that summer, and our bond deepened after Pedro Iván's death as I struggled with the soap opera of my life in Baracoa. He stood on the sidelines of my dilemma, a wry observer, steadfast in his friendship, never judging me. Like his aunt Erminda, he encouraged me to go out and make the most of life in Baracoa. He took me dancing, though he did not dance himself, but by then I knew everyone and was on the dancefloor all night. I told Teófilo that I'd been a lesbian for a period of my life, until I'd met Onaldo, not that it was important for me to share this information — I'm as private as he — but one confidence deserves another, and I'd thought that it might encourage him.

"*Dios rompió el molde cuando Teófilo nació*" — God broke the mold when you were born — I told him. It was our joke, my way of telling him how much I valued him, but like all jokes it bore its own truth. Teófilo was indeed far from the patterned macho man. He was more like the gay men I'd spent my youth falling in love with, drawn by their difference from the boys who talked about themselves all evening and then thrust themselves upon me without warning, as though a monologue were foreplay. Teófilo was my rock as I once again walked an old battlefield, trying to decipher these new rules in another culture where everything might be different. A new language, another chance.

He took me to the beach on his motorbike, my arms around his waist, shouting all the way above the roar of the motor. As soon as we arrived we were stopped by *la policía*. We protested, reasoned, argued, Teófilo with the same wounded expression I'd seen when I'd asked him if he was gay, but the two young cops were stony-faced and Teo ended up with a fine for carrying a foreigner on his bike. It was only ten *convertibles* ($12 Canadian), nothing for me, but almost three weeks' salary for a Cuban. The cops knew that I would pay. We joked that it was the price of admission to Maguana, the golden, palm-fringed beach where we splashed into the ocean and let ourselves be carried out by the waves. Afterwards we lay in the sun talking about our lives and although I listened for clues to Teo's identity there were none, only that his father had died of a stomach ailment when Teo was a boy, and as an adolescent Teo had been knifed in the gut, under what circumstances he wouldn't say. A jagged scar snaked across his belly, narrowly missing his umbilicus.

Later we sat in the shade, our skin throbbing, and drank cold beer, still talking, an endless stream of words. My usual caution seemed not to exist with Teo. There was something about him that allowed me a rare freedom, both of us in some way fugitive, recognizing each other, respecting the boundaries of our captivity. I trusted him, something from my gut to his own wounded gut. There was no second guessing with Teo, he was the genuine article, despite his subterfuge.

We hiked up El Yunque, the long tabletop mountain that sits like the anvil it is named for 560 metres above Baracoa, and we talked all the way, gasping for words, breathless with the three-hour climb through thick rain forest ringing with the screech of wild parrots. We switched my camera to auto and posed beside the stone head of Antonio Maceo, a general in the Cuban war of independence against Spain. We look like lovers in those photos, he a gay man with two children, two ex-wives, and a grandson, and I a sometime lesbian juggling two Cuban men. On our descent, slithering down the red and ochre clay path, slick now with rain, we swam in the green water of a lagoon bounded by ferns and huge mossy rocks, the water reflecting overhanging branches of crabwood and myrtle.

A few days later, when my legs had recovered from the quivering descent, Teófilo took me to the cabaret at La Terraza. There was a comedian from Havana, a cross-dresser who made fun of *maricónes*, flaunting his fat belly, encased in a stretchy pink baby suit dangling a tiny penis. Teófilo laughed harder than anyone, and I laughed too.

A week before my April departure for Havana I dropped by the house. As soon as I entered I felt something wrong. When Teófilo greeted me I thought perhaps there'd been a death. His expression silenced me. I'd learned in Cuba not to react spontaneously or ask questions, but simply to wait patiently. In *La Lista de Espera*, a movie satire about a Cuban bus station, the passengers wait months for the bus to Havana, and life goes on as they wait. The situation would reveal itself.

Teo walked ahead of me onto the patio and introduced me to a Cuban woman lounging there with her Italian boyfriend.

They at least looked happy — they were in love. Teo slumped in a chair and I dragged another chair close to him, noticing a stack of empty rum bottles lined up against the wall and an overflowing ashtray on the arm of his chair.

"Where's your motorbike?" I asked. His big red bike was always parked in the front room by the altar to Elegguá.

"I took it to a friend's house," he said, lighting another cigarette, offering me a drink from his shot glass.

"You're a *borracho,* Teo!" I teased. "Look at all those bottles."

He laughed half-heartedly. "Some friends were over last night. And my uncle from Santiago. He likes to drink." He leaned forward and whispered. "I'm going to Santiago tomorrow." He jerked his head slightly and took my arm, guiding me into the kitchen, where he showed me all his movies — 750 of them — lined up inside cardboard-box lids. "I'm taking them to a friend's house. Have you heard what's happening in Baracoa?"

"The raid on Chucho's house?"

He nodded. "And Antonio's *paladar,* Benito's *casa particular . . .* "

"They won't come here, Teo. Everybody knows you have your *negocio.* They're looking for drug money."

He shook his head grimly, his mouth turning down at the corners. "When there's a crackdown in Baracoa no one is safe. I could lose everything. Look, *la policia* would walk in here, they'd see my DVDs, the work we did on the patio, the *sala* freshly painted, my computer, the bike . . . " He shook his head again and took a quick drag on his cigarette. "I'm leaving early in the morning, so we'd better say goodbye, Karina. I'll stay at my uncle's house for a couple of weeks."

I knew better than to argue. At first I had countered everything with my foreign alternatives, but I had learned, along with patience and silence, a course of non-intervention, walking sideways instead of charging forward with my dangerous ignorance. I wondered if Teófilo had a lover in Santiago, if he would feel safe enough there to indulge his secret desires, away from the goldfish bowl of Baracoa. Would it give an edge to an affair, the clandestine nature of it? Did it make the sex more intense to think that you were fooling everyone with a façade of marriages, girlfriends, 'normal' behaviour? Or was Teófilo only fooling himself? In a country steeped in eroticism, throbbing with it, Teo was an anomaly. Handsome and personable though he was, he lacked sexual vibration, as though he were denying an essential part of his identity.

He doesn't even *know* he's gay, I thought, because there's no context here for such knowledge, unless you want to be ridiculed. I remembered how quiet he'd been around Mario and how he laughed along with everyone else about the other 'out' gays in Baracoa — Osvaldo who gave salsa lessons at the Casa de la Cultura, Javiér who dressed like a woman and choreographed the cabaret at La Terraza, Lobo and Misha, two of his dancers, and Alfonso the hairdresser who travelled house to house with his comb and scissors, beloved of the señoras. None of them were taken seriously, and Teófilo, I knew, wanted very much to be taken seriously. He was proud. And he was vain. Before a photo he would comb his hair and fluff his collar up around his strong neck. I'd taken a photo of him and Felix with their arms around each other's shoulders and had given Teo a print, which pleased him greatly. He'd put it in the corner of the mirror next to the photo of the Italians.

"The love that has no name." When something is unnamed how can it exist? How could I really believe in the police raids, in the danger that was driving Teo from his home? When everything is received in whispers it can more easily be ignored, though the whispers continue echoing, governing silently even as we deny them.

And then I had a terrible thought — suppose Teo was having an affair and someone had denounced him. Was that why he was fleeing to Santiago, because he was afraid that the police knew he was gay? But I would not believe it. I couldn't bear to think of Teo in prison.

I helped him to parcel up his DVDs and we packed them into a battered suitcase that he pulled out of the closet where the kittens had been born. They were romping all over the house, jumping on each other, digging up the patio plants. Teo's clothes were laid out on the bed ready to be packed into his black shoulder bag with two pair of shoes standing neatly together, their toes under the bed.

"I'll miss you," I said, the words catching in my throat as tears welled, surprising me. I felt as though it were he who was going far away, his sudden move scooping my own imminent departure.

"I'll be here when you come back," he said. "Nothing changes in Baracoa."

There was defeat in that final phrase, after all our make-believe about another life for Teófilo, in Havana, in Europe with one of his tourist girlfriends, in Canada with the woman I was charged with finding for him. It was a game for me, but could I ever know what exactly it was for Teófilo?

"Don't forget to find me a girlfriend," he said as I climbed on my bike and leaned over to kiss him once more, "A very beautiful one!" he said in English with his heavy Cuban accent, and we both laughed.

～

Hard Guavas

THE DAY OF MY DEPARTURE LOOMED. I was due in Havana for another art opening on April 15th — Leila was coming from Canada with our drawings. But when I thought of leaving Baracoa panic gripped me.

I sat at the kitchen table with Erminda, staring at a bowl of hard guavas and a bunch of overripe bananas. Onaldo had been to the house while I was out and had left the fruit for me — another gift. We seemed in these last weeks to have missed each other at every turn, as though the stars were against us, an unfavourable configuration holding us apart. There had been a bag of tomatoes, then mandarins, a pumpkin, three potatoes, and a single hibiscus flower. Communications in Cuba are difficult at best. Nando and Erminda had been waiting ten years for a telephone, and whenever I called the Casa de la Cultura from a neighbour's house the phone rang and rang. Once in the night I'd woken with a distinct feeling of being watched, and had been convinced that Onaldo was there, outside my door. His absence was like a long held breath which left me dizzy and disoriented.

"That man doesn't know how to pick ripe fruit," Herminda quipped wickedly, thumping a hard guava on the table. "*Mira,* still hard."

"Did he say when he'd come again?"

"No, he didn't say nothing. He wouldn't even stay for a cup of coffee. He handed me the fruit, he asked about you, I said you were out. I thought he was going to ask where, but he didn't ask, so I said I don't know when she'll be back, then he left on his bicycle. The one you bought for him," she finished with a satisfied sniff. She picked up a dishtowel and flapped at the fruit flies clustered over the bananas. "*Come, come* — eat, eat, Karinita. These bananas won't last."

"I'm not hungry."

"Don't you worry about Onaldo. He'll come back. He's a *bandolero,*" she chuckled.

"But I'm leaving in a few days."

"You will return to Baracoa," she said cheerfully. "And you will stay in my house. Remember, Karinita, we Cubans have lots of patience."

How ironic that I had been in Yolanda's house, playing with Susana Rosa, helping her with her schoolwork. And he would think that I was with Felix. Yolanda had come home from work early and we'd all sat together, her and Susana Rosa and me.

"Come back soon, my sister," Yolanda had said. "We will miss you. When are you coming?"

I couldn't answer.

Susana had wrapped her arms around my neck and pouted, clinging to me. Then she'd whispered in my ear. "Karinita, come back soon and bring me some bracelets like yours."

There were many goodbyes in those final days, and all the time a bank of memories and sensations pressed into the white-hot absence of Onaldo. I rode past the Casa de la Cultura several times a day willing him to be standing out front. When I went in and asked for him the receptionist stared blankly at me and said, "He's not here. Try his house." But I wouldn't. I went to Yolanda's house where I knew I would be welcome, and to Teófilo's house, and to Alina and Clara and Evangelia. Then on my last day, returning to Erminda's, I saw him on the corner where he'd stood after Pedro Iván's death, waiting for me.

We went to Parque Colón and sat on a bench in the shade. I told him how I'd suffered his absence, how I'd refused to suffer and yet did, living over top of it, a double life. "I'm a stranger in your country; I need you here to help me. I don't understand this situation which holds us apart, this tangle of gossip and lies and contradictions, it drives me crazy."

It had all built up, everything somehow altered by the imminence of my departure. I had flashes of his point of view as I continued to speak with surprising clarity and honesty, almost like a dialogue written in my head and now finding voice in an alien language. I had to stand in his shoes. As Erminda had emphasized, Cubans must wait for us while we move freely in the world. All they have is patience.

Each time Onaldo spoke I cut in, parrying and thrusting, countering his habitual responses, insisting on honesty until finally he broke down and wept. It was so sudden that it shocked me and I held him and stroked his head, whispering, "*Mi amor, mi amor, calmate, estoy aquí.*" His sobbing was hoarse and noisy. His grizzled head was bent over his lap, arms rigid at his sides, hands gripping the bench as big tears rolled down his cheeks and dripped onto his trousers. I kissed his face, tasted the salt. He mumbled something and when I questioned him he repeated it angrily.

"I should have taken care of our love," he said, "I'll never find another woman like you."

It was like a tropical storm, sudden and intense, soon over. Then he was searching for his handkerchief, blowing his nose.

"Are my eyes red?" he asked. And with a sudden resolve, "I'm going to wait for you; we can erase everything that's happened in these four months."

As we walked in the midday heat back to Erminda's house, Onaldo said, "I've never in my life cried over a woman," and he seemed as surprised as I at what had happened.

He left me at the corner. I had an afternoon flight to Havana. I'd joked with Erminda that when I left Baracoa there would be a new river filled with my tears. But they were Onaldo's tears that had fallen, sweetening our river, taking the salt from my departure. There are no last words, and no endings.

Calle Enramada

A CROWD WAS GATHERED ON CALLE ENRAMADA. As he drew near Teófilo saw looks of amusement and fascination on people's faces. A young woman, holding the hand of a child, laughed and pointed as the little girl bobbed up and down trying to see, her *chancletas* slapping the sidewalk with each jump. Reluctant to push his way forward, Teófilo looked up at the sign which read *Enrique Estética: Canina y Felina*. He'd not noticed it before, though he came a couple of times a year to stay with *tío* Maurisio and *tía* Arisnilda. They lived in Reparto Mariana de la Torre, a half hour's ride from the centre of town, jostling cheek by buttock in the crowded bus, packed like cattle. But Teófilo liked the crowds of Santiago de Cuba. He had quickly learned to lose himself in them.

By the time he reached the front of the crowd the clipping was almost done. A poodle stood on the table ankle deep in white fluff, its pink skin shivering through a thin layer of remaining wool. A young woman with a determined chin, and a restraining arm tucked under the dog's belly, buzzed a final course over its rump. Teófilo watched, fascinated as the other voyeurs drifted away, bored now that the creature was shorn. Its owner, a handsome mulatto, waited to reclaim the dog. Teófilo stared at him and at the naked poodle, which continued to shiver and twitch nervously despite the heat of the afternoon. The mulatto picked it up and held it under one arm as he fished a five peso note from his back pocket, thrust it into the woman's hand, and stepped out onto Calle Enramada. Teófilo followed him. When they reached Parque Serrano at the corner of Calle Carniceria the tall mulatto turned suddenly and flashed a brilliant smile.

"Let me get rid of the dog first," he said, and Teófilo flushed with the shock of recognition.

"How . . . how did you know?"

"Eyes in my ass." His voice was smooth and husky, something fluid about the way he walked, with the poodle an anomaly in his muscular arms. "She lives at the corner of San Germán. Let's go."

His walk was subtle, not like the flamboyant *maricónes* who were stopped by the police all the time, forced to produce their identity cards simply for the sake of harassment. "I walk the dog for her every morning and once a month it's the parlour. She's out this afternoon. We can use her place."

He had spoken without looking at Teófilo. Perhaps he really did have eyes in his ass, the way he strode ahead, trusting that Teófilo was following.

"What's your name?"

He stopped then and turned, his green eyes startling Teófilo. "Rosendo," he said and turned again in one smooth movement, hips shifting side to side with his long stride.

Teófilo tried to keep up, dodging between people on the crowded street. It was like riding the bus, trying to force his way off as they approached his stop.

Rosendo entered a freshly painted yellow building opposite a church with a domed tower. Teófilo was just looking around to get his bearings when Rosendo hissed, without looking back, "*Pssst*," gesturing towards an ancient elevator.

The dog whimpered as they shuddered up to the third floor. Rosendo balanced it on his hip while he dug in his back pocket for the key. The dog was aquiver, squirming in his arms, and when it leapt and ran, yelping in a high-pitched scream, Teófilo ran after it and tackled it in the stairwell. He calmed the dog, stroking its nakedness with his free hand as he held it firmly under the belly. Rosendo was holding the door open, tapping his foot impatiently as Teófilo approached, hanging onto the dog, which had its nose buried in his armpit.

The apartment was filled with antiques — mahogany furniture from another era, every surface crowded with memories — Limoges vases, French figurines, filigreed photo frames — the walls hung with massive oil paintings darkened with age and grime. The dog leapt again, stumbling as it landed on the once-thick carpet, now threadbare in patches, and scurried into the bedroom and under the canopied bed, its bare pink ass wiggling as it disappeared.

"Want a beer?" Rosendo asked. Teófilo nodded, but Rosendo was already halfway down the corridor. Teófilo heard the refrigerator door open, cans popping, a fizz and the sound of swallowing. His mouth was dry, his palms sweating.

Rosendo walked straight up to him, a beer in each hand, and kissed him, thrusting his tongue into his mouth and grinding his genitals against him. Teófilo felt the hardness of his erection and laughed nervously as he grabbed his beer and gulped, the coolness of it coursing down his throat and into his stomach. Rosendo unzipped his pants, pushed Teófilo down on his knees and forced his cock into his mouth. He gripped his head with both hands and fucked with such force that Teófilo almost cried out. When Rosendo came Teófilo gagged on the jets of thick liquid. But he swallowed, then rose to his feet and kissed his lover.

"You want to fuck me? Fuck your way to freedom?" The mulatto rubbed the palm of his hand against the bulge in Teófilo's pants. "Some people want to risk it, floating to Miami in a rubber tire, food for the sharks. Me, I prefer to fuck." Rosendo dropped his pants, never taking his eyes off Teófilo as he turned, sticking his ass in the air. Then he spit in his hand and smeared his anus. "Come on Street Boy, fill me with your dreams."

As he entered Rosendo's body he heard the dog whimpering from the bedroom, then everything closed down and he heard nothing but the roaring of his own blood, the thundering of his heart as he pounded the darkness, muscles gripping his penis, grasping at it as he ploughed back and forth, sliding through spit and excrement. He wanted it to go on forever, that timeless place of loss that stank of blood and salt and death, then he came, whimpering and spurting, back to himself.

Immediately Rosendo was on him, spinning him around, thrusting into him with his wet cock, long and smooth, sliding home like a player in a game of *pelota*. Teófilo gave without protest, his body soft and malleable, open to the pain of pleasure, drawing him back to the depths as Rosendo's balls caressed his buttocks, almost tickling as his cock plumbed the darkness. Teófilo took his own cock in both hands and pumped it hard and when he spurted finally he didn't know if he rode the ocean or if he *was* the ocean, waves of loss washing over him as Rosendo ejaculated inside his body.

He came to with the dog licking his face.

"Come on, we have to get out of here," Rosendo said, "She'll be back soon."

"I never did this before," Teófilo said, pulling his pants up.

"What d'you mean?"

"Sex with a stranger."

"Hah, it's the best. But don't fall in love with me, *maricón*, we're not strangers anymore."

"Can't I see you again?"

Rosendo laughed, zipping up his pants, tight over his black ass. "I don't make plans. Haven't you noticed how things change all the time? We have to live minute by minute." He pulled Teófilo hard against him and kissed him on the mouth, a soft wet kiss, like a woman. "Bathroom's down the hall, first on the left," he said, jerking his head towards the corridor, releasing Teófilo slowly, his eyes still on him as he walked away.

Teófilo stared at himself in the mirror for almost a minute before he started to wash his hands, splashing his face and rinsing his mouth with the sluggish water. The towel was pink and fluffy, but it smelled of aftershave. On the shelf was a bottle of *Adonis*. Teófilo shrugged and opened the bottle, dabbing a bit on each cheek. He looked in the mirror again and grinned.

"Hey c'mon, we gotta go!" Rosendo called from the *sala*.

He hurried back, still grinning and placed his hands casually on Rosendo's shoulders. "Where do you live?"

"Everywhere. I move around." His head to one side, a half smile, a quizzical expression.

"Is there a telephone number?"

"You want to waste your pesos trying to track me down?" He laughed, his teeth strong and dazzling white, his mouth twisted. "Come on, Street Boy, you're a good dreamer, but wake up now." He slapped Teófilo's ass and yanked him out the door.

The elevator gate was still open. Rosendo pushed Teófilo in and slammed the metal grille, barely missing his fingers.

"Rosendo!"

Already he could hear him running down the marble stairs. By the time the elevator reached the ground floor the mulatto was gone, swallowed by the streets of Santiago.

⌖

Ololo

April 2008

I COULD NOT HAVE IMAGINED WHEN I left Toronto in mid-December what lay ahead of me. I flew from Baracoa on April 10th, Onaldo's words echoing — "I'm going to wait for you, we can erase everything that's happened in these four months."

When I walked into Cíntia Rodriguez' *casa* I found Leila in our old room, just arrived from Toronto with our drawings. They were curled inside their tube, balanced against the wall. Leila had wrapped the tube in orange plastic with a swaddling of duct tape. I hardly remembered those pencil marks on paper after all that had passed. I didn't even open the tube to look at them. I somehow expected them to have faded, the graphite eaten by the creamy paper ravening for more tooth. I turned to Leila, full of questions, but she was so excited to be back in Havana she could talk of nothing else — our gallery friends, plans for the evening, those first vivid impressions before the senses accustom and settle.

The next day we carried our drawings to the gallery, taking turns in cradling their unwieldy length. Anamaría and the staff helped us to carry them into the gallery and hang them, the figures again so familiar as they unfurled and took their place on the far wall. Leila and I stood before them and read that cryptic language of desire scrolling from their mouths, interrupted by the deflector flaps of the satellite which bounced their cries down into the giant mouth of a dish anchored on the Yorkshire moors. The satellite is part of a global surveillance system, code name Echelon, developed by the US and Britain after World War II. It captures telephonic and electronic messages and directs them to listening posts around the world, where code words or phrases are flagged by computers. What would they make of it in northern England, the sheep grazing on those blustery hills . . . *Ololo oimololo . . . amabo lolima . . . panololo anhelando wola oonolei?*

Nobody questioned us about the meaning of our exhibit. Cubans understand surveillance in a very personal way. When Anamaría entered the gallery, I watched her eyes and saw her observe everything from the corners of them, taking it in almost surreptitiously, the smoothness of her, the softness of her mouth belying that hidden edge. As we hung the huge figures, aligning them on the uneven wall, Anamaría and Florissa, the gallery director, talked about their lives, making jokes of the difficulties, giving us clues to the turmoil beneath their elegance — their smart clothing and jewellery, their painted nails and immaculately groomed hair.

Florissa asked me about my life in Baracoa, her eyes flashing flirtatiously. But before I could answer she said, "*Mira,* my daughter Paloma, and my two older children," showing me their photo on the office computer. "Now that Paloma is ten we don't get free milk for her any more. She drinks a lot of milk. How am I going to buy it on my salary? This is a good day for me; you see how happy I am? Today you invited us for lunch and we sat in the sun and ate fish and drank beer. This is illegal! Because we work with you we're not allowed to accept your invitation, but we did it. We take risks all the time. Oh yes, and that fish was illegal. Like beef and shrimps, red snapper is illegal. I cannot buy this fish and eat it in my house. It's for tourists to eat in their hotels and restaurants. And now our new president says we can stay in tourist hotels and eat there. But we must pay in tourist money, not our own Cuban pesos!" She threw up her hands and laughed in exasperation. "This is a good day for me, Karina, because I'm at work. Tomorrow the weekend begins and I must clean the house, wash the clothes, shop for groceries, try to find the lowest prices, then cook a meal for my family and try to relax a little, but there's no time. And my husband works hard too; we're doing all this together. Our children help as much as they can, but they have their school work. Paloma practices violin every day for two hours. *Ella es muy talentosa.*"

The satellite camera was behind her, a paper tiger stalking through the door she had finally opened, a door that had been closed fourteen months earlier when we'd constructed our *cimarrón* and left him in the corner of her office. The veils had fallen in Baracoa and now they were falling in Havana, revealing to me a nation of people sick to death of their bloody Revolution.

Anamaría smiled at me. "Come," she said, reaching for my hand. "I'll take you and Leila to the studio to meet the dancers who will perform at your opening. They'll be waiting for us."

"What's that?" I asked, touching a tiny circle of transparent plastic stuck to her earlobe. She laughed, hesitated a moment, then pulled down the waistband of her skirt. I saw the pale scar of the hysterectomy I knew had almost killed her. She'd been two months in the Baracoa hospital, close to her mother's home in Imías. It's a Dickensian institution with no facilities of any kind despite excellent surgical treatment. My friend Léster had operated on her and, she said, had saved her life. I saw the plastic tabs circling her stomach, crossing the pale pink scar. I looked up into her eyes, questioning.

"For my pain," she said, a bitter smile playing on her lips. "To mark the acupuncture points and hold the treatment. They help to release my pain."

Yoandris came from the radio station next day and greeted us warmly.

"I remember your *cimarrón* and the red dog from last year," she said, tilting her head with a sidelong glance at our drawings, as though a direct look might endanger her.

She questioned us in her soft voice, holding the microphone to our mouths, the tape recorder resting on the table between us as she asked about the process of our work together, the materials we use, about our map-making — the rivers and highways that mirror the veins and arteries of the body. Yoandris came back to the gallery two days later with a television crew — two elegantly dressed women with flowing hair and casually worn makeup, their words punctuated by elaborate gestures, while the men accompanying them busied themselves with camera and sound boom.

Felix was supposed to join me in Havana but he never turned up. I received a telephone message at Cíntia's *casa* — some story about a robbery in the Camagüey bus station, losing his clothes, his money, having to return home, when in fact he'd never left Baracoa, it turned out later, because Anilbis had confiscated his *carne de identidad*. No matter. It was Onaldo I was thinking of, watching for him on the Havana streets as though he might magically appear and take me in his arms. I feed on absence — it is my way — the lifelong absence of my father into which many elusive men have stepped temporarily.

Three dancers came to perform at our opening. A dark-haired woman in trench coat and sunglasses crouched on a high sill, hidden behind a tabloid newspaper easily recognizable as *Granma,* the official voice of the government, which has carried almost fifty years of Fidel's speeches and now publishes Raúl's proposed reforms. The other two dancers, the lovers, circled each other in front of the wall where our figures hung with their vital organs exposed to surveillance, words of desire swirling towards the satellite like defiant banners while their landscape telescoped beneath them as though they travelled eternally towards each other in planes which had disintegrated, leaving them stranded in the sky.

The man and his lover, her red hair pulled back into a ponytail, reached towards each other, pushing and pulling against invisible forces. The detective slid from her sill scattering papers in the air. She moved briskly back and forth, stopping, head swaying from side to side like a cobra about to strike then, finger and thumb to her glasses, observing the couple. The girl was lifted in the air, her hair flying as her lover's hands held her firmly, imprinting her as their words were swallowed — incoherent utterings echoing with the urgency of primitive sound evolving into sense . . .

Ololo oimolulu amabo lolima
mandando no llegando
mandando anhelando
desolado no llegando
anhelando interceptado
cuídalo ololo

With hands and eyes, and necks angling, they danced their desire for each other, for something other. And the depth of that desire, communicated silently, began to touch us all as we watched them, upstaged by the trench-coated stalker.

Finally, defeated by the impossibility of their dance, they limped together down the centre of the gallery, her arm around him, then he wrapping his arm, a broken wing, around her. We parted to allow their wounded passage and began our applause, not knowing what else to do. We are collective creatures. We must gather in witness to the ritual of crisis and become part of it to be carried forward as a society of souls. Personal knowledge is not enough.

⌁

Caridad and the Magic Maleta

AFTER THE OPENING OF *OLOLO* LEILA WENT to the colonial city of Trinidad to meet up with her partner for a few days' vacation, but I stayed on at Cíntia Rodriguez' *casa particular* and began to gather myself for the return to Canada.

Stored in the cupboard of my room was the suitcase I'd brought to Havana more than a year ago, filled with art materials to create our *cimarrón*, his colonial mistress, and the red dog. The suitcase had been in Christopher's apartment in Toronto when we'd cleared it out, my sisters, my mother and I, in an efficient daze of disbelief. I had taken it at the last minute with a few other keepsakes — scraps of paper with poetic fragments and enigmatic messages — *Still not over it yet, Never taken me so long to get over it before; I lay beside you through the night, my toes curled with pleasure* — notebooks filled with his sloping hand, his address book, some classical cassettes — *Kol Nidri, Misa Criolla,* Tchaikovsky's *Sleeping Beauty,* Pergolesi's *Stabat Mater.*

I opened the case. It was battered and old, the smoky aroma gone finally, obliterated by the ubiquitous smell of mold that lurked in Cíntia's closet. What could I do with it? In Cuba nothing gets thrown away. Necessity is the mother of recycling. That morning over breakfast Caridad, Cíntia's cook, had told me of her search for a *maleta*. I wasn't sure if this signified a suitcase or a shoulder bag and had thought to look it up in my dictionary — *maleta, maletín* — I always confused the two words.

Caridad served a magnificent breakfast of guava, papaya, pineapple and watermelon, followed by scrambled eggs with sliced ham, a long loaf of crusty bread with butter and honey, a plate of sliced cheese, and delicious Cuban coffee with hot milk. She was a small plump woman, thirty-seven years old, with a glory of black curly hair which she wore tightly pulled back, and sometimes piled on top of her head. Her hands moved constantly, passing plates, gesturing, rings flashing on every finger and even on her thumbs as she spoke with mind-numbing rapidity. I wondered how she preserved her long and perfectly polished nails through all that chopping of fruits and vegetables and meat.

One morning she told us her story — Leila and I — and I had seen it then, a transparent plastic slice resting behind her left ear. Until then I had thought my Spanish so bad that she perhaps didn't understand me. Her husband had beaten her and boxed her ears until they'd bled. Her sons were little then — she couldn't leave despite the ringing in her ears which got louder and louder, blocking out the sound of her children's laughter and the warning voice of her mother. She'd left him eventually and started working for Cíntia, but she had to travel an hour, sometimes two, between Centro Havana and La Palma where she lived with her boys. One was grown now, studying computer science, but the other was still in school.

"My boys are so smart," she said. "They will have a better life than me."

I always took care with Caridad after that morning, touching her shoulder gently as I entered the kitchen, looking her in the eye as I spoke.

"I've never been outside Havana," she'd told me. "It's impossible for us to travel in Cuba unless we have friends or family to stay with."

Caridad's weekly salary was ten pesos, less than what I paid for two hours on the internet at the Hotel Inglaterra. And yet she was earning almost three times the average Cuban salary because she worked for Cíntia and was paid in convertible currency.

I spent the day saying my goodbyes, e-mailing Vida to pick me up at the airport in Toronto, everything focused on my departure from *El Caimán*. Havana sits on the tail of the reptile and I felt the difference after living four months dangerously close to his snout. With one casual swish of his tail he could flip us all to Miami.

I missed Leila. I missed Erminda, Yolanda, Felix, Calixto, but mostly I missed Onaldo. Not missed exactly, because despite everything that had passed between us he still lived in my exultant heart circled with candles burning brightly, an enduring presence. The Spanish expression, *hace falta,* was a more accurate description of my feeling. I felt the lack of him, of his physical being, so intimate and immediate — a visceral response.

Language shapes our thinking and feeling, so there is a part of me now that finds expression only in Cuba. With English-speaking friends in Havana I had searched for our own words to exactly express my meaning and had fallen back on the now habitual Spanish. Yet when I recalled our conversations, mine and Onaldo's, I couldn't believe that they had not been spoken in English. Surely I was not yet capable of such intimacy in Spanish, the depth of our understanding gleaned from those risky and intuitive sounds? Another mystery, the reach of desire beyond language, learned under the kitchen table and long forgotten.

I remembered the spurt of English words that would rise in me as I woke from a dream in his room in Baracoa when we'd first met, his body joined to mine as though we had always been there, one flesh. How I would catch myself and laugh, still rising from my dream world into an easy translation. I would write him a letter and mail it early in the morning before I went to the airport.

Caridad cooked chicken on that last night. There was rice mixed with onions and red pepper, beet salad and fried platanos, and she was cheerful as ever as we talked through the meal until it was time for me to pack. I'd given away most of my clothing, but there were a few last-minute things — soap, a half bottle of shampoo, a pair of blue beaded earrings, and of course the musty suitcase from which our *cimarrón* had emerged. I felt hesitant about offering it to Caridad. Would she want it? Perhaps I should just leave it in my room for whoever might need it.

I caught her eye through the open door as she carried an armful of laundry across the courtyard. "Do you want this, Cari?" I held up the suitcase and she stared at me a moment, her eyes round with wonder. I began to explain about the suitcase, feeling embarrassed as I made excuses for its battered state, but she dropped the bed linens and took the case in her arms.

"*Maleta!*" she exclaimed, "*Maleta, maleta!*" and she danced around the courtyard clutching it to her breast. "I've wanted a *maleta* for such a long time," she crooned. "I went to look for one in the store but it was too expensive. Oh, *maleta, maleta!*"

Caridad's eyes disappeared with the force of her joy, her shoulders hunched to her deaf ears as she embraced the suitcase.

Later that night, as I packed my few remaining belongings (everyone arrives in Cuba laden and leaves light, there is such need), I imagined Caridad travelling home to La Palma with her magic *maleta*. Perhaps she would stand in the crowded bus clutching it, wedged in by the press of bodies swaying and shuddering with the movement of *el camello*, imagining herself on a long journey to a place she had never been before. Not to the familiar broken building on Calzada de Managua with the dingy kitchen and two tiny rooms she shared with her sons, but to Vedado where the streets are wide and leafy, lined with embassy buildings, or to Pinar del Rio where the earth is rich and red with tobacco growing beneath a hot blue sky. Or to Santa Clara to see the statue of Che, to Trinidad, the coastal colonial town featured on all the travel posters, to Santiago de Cuba, cradle of the Revolution, where she might sit in Parque Cespedes in the evening and listen to the birds singing. And finally, with her *maleta* full of offerings, to the altar of *La Virgen de la Caridad del Cobre*.

When I woke the next day my path was clear. I renewed my visa, changed the date of my plane ticket, e-mailed Vida again, and took a taxi to the bus station. Something was compelling me to return to Baracoa.

The Whales were Trying to Tell Us

EVERY MORNING THE PEOPLE OF BARACOA OPEN their front doors or climb the stairs to their rooftops to look at the ocean. Yemayá in all her aspects — deep blue, or white-flecked turquoise, sometimes a stormy blue-grey. And on a moonless night the oily darkness of the water, breathing like an invisible and uncontainable creature.

Many people saw them. Some said they were blue and white, rising out of the ocean. Others said they were grey or black, glinting in the sun with a pearly iridescence as they breached. The first sighting was at Club Nautica in Reparto Turey where the beach is strewn with coconut shells, and on Sundays old men scuff through the débris picking up bits of plastic and metal, stuffing them into frayed sacks.

Two whales entered the bay at Turey. It had never happened before. Word spread fast and by the time they had circled the bay and swum out into the open water everyone was watching from rooftops and balconies, and from atop the seawall that separates the Malecón from the brutal rocks that buffer the waves. After the disaster there were many who said the whales had been a sign of what was to come.

"Never before, never in my lifetime nor in my father's," a shocked man reported to the television camera, but it was not the whales he spoke of.

It had been too late to get a seat on the plane without bumping a Cuban, so I'd taken the overnight bus as on my first visit, changing in Santiago de Cuba, winding across the dizzying heights of La Farola, arriving finally, feeling nauseous and exultant as we rumbled along the Malecón past all the familiar sights. It begins at Parque Colón, where the monstrous figure of Cristóbal Colón looms, and arcs the length of the waterfront. There was La Rusa in the distance, the ochre walls of the famous hotel dwarfed by the infinity of water it faces. Beyond La Rusa lies Parque Infantíl, then the La Punta school and a pair of dilapidated Russian-built apartment blocks eaten away by the salty air, and finally the bus terminal on the corner of the Plaza de la Revolución. Behind the Plaza is the mouth of Bahía de Baracoa, with Hotel Porto Santo perched on the cliff, and beyond it the Gustavo Rizo airport where twice a week the plane swoops in from Havana, so close to the ocean in the final seconds that the passengers hold their breath for the purchase of land beneath the wheels. And where a traffic controller, (the brother of Erminda's neighbour, Damaris, the one with a telephone), was sliced by the propellers in a moment of distraction.

Parque Infantíl is enclosed by a concrete fence covered with animals in painted relief — elephants, giraffe, tigers, monkeys, a bull — all fading to pastel as their colours are consumed by the sun. There's a cafeteria at one end next to a bush of flowering hibiscus. I saw Onaldo in the distance, approaching between the swings and teeter-totters with his distinctive gait — head up, chin leading, body swaying slightly. When he saw me he raised his hand, waving, and I watched him come until he stood before me.

"Forgive me. The meeting ended just now."

He sat beside me on the bench, leaned to kiss my cheek, his hand on my shoulder, hesitant. His proximity disarmed me. Everything felt normal again, and my body relaxed into the luxury of his physical presence, secure, unquestioning. Even if our bodies suddenly vaporized that feeling would still exist in this place and I could always return to recapture it. The old desire arose with its open mouth, refusing to back down despite the confusion of lies and gossip echoing in my head, and a flame of anger that burned in me yet, trying to consume my desire.

I said nothing at first. Onaldo seemed reassured by my presence as he spoke enthusiastically about the changes that had been announced since Raúl had been officially elected President. He knew what interested me. He talked about the promised restructuring of government, the easing of restrictions, a possible merging of currencies, support for private enterprise, increased freedom . . .

"What freedom?" I asked, wanting more than rhetoric.

"To stay in tourist hotels and eat in restaurants, to travel abroad . . . You know, Karina, all the things we planned for our life together."

"But with *convertibles*, not *moneda nacional*. This isn't about a lifting of restrictions, Onaldo. It's about boosting the economy with the tourist peso. No Cuban could afford to stay in a tourist hotel."

"You can invite me to Porto Santo tonight," he grinned.

"It's too late for that," I laughed. Was he playing with me, trying to reel me in again, the big Canadian fish? Or was it just a bitter joke?

"Not too late for me, Karinita. All that we've lost . . . " He touched my arm with the old urgency. "We can erase the past, start afresh. You cannot imagine how I suffer."

I watched a small boy circling the park in the darkness on a bike too big for him, and I was afraid that he would injure himself on the crossbar. I was no longer listening to Onaldo's words, though I heard his deep voice, his warm and persuasive tone, something about Migdalia and the grandchild, Yarisel, the increasingly rapid rhythm of his words. He always talked faster when he spoke, finally, of his emotions. The wind had picked up and a gibbous moon slid out from behind the clouds illuminating El Castillo, the hotel on the hill above Baracoa. Onaldo had told me that in the Batista days it had been the police headquarters where dissidents were taken to be tortured. He had been able to see El Castillo from his front balcony before it collapsed under the weight of the building materials he had bought with my money.

"When you went to Havana for your exhibit I didn't think you would come back."

"Neither did I."

Our eyes met for a moment and we collapsed with laughter. When I looked up Onaldo was bent double, his shoulders shaking, then he sat up and slapped his knee in that disarming way, full of a surprising mirth.

I don't know where the conflict came from — it was not in us. I felt myself being pulled by thick weeds wrapping around my legs, holding me under.

"How could the two currencies merge?" I asked, grasping for something concrete. "Salaries would need to multiply by twenty-four in order to be on par with the tourist peso."

I thought he would give me his usual shrug, that gesture of acquiescence, but his body was filled with purpose as he spoke, leaning towards me, eager as a young man with his whole life ahead of him.

"Karina, we could go to Santiago for a few days, get away from Baracoa — *una luna de miel.*" He caught my hair where the wind was blowing it across my face and looped it behind my ear, smoothing my cheek with his soft fingers, tracing my upper lip.

"Onaldo, I agreed to meet you here for old time's sake," I said, catching his hand in mine, though I didn't move, not yet.

"If that's what you want?" He was half smiling.

"You opened a door on Cuba for me. I'll always be grateful for that. And you had your first trip outside . . . "

"Do you think there's a chance for me to make another trip to Toronto? *Ay, Cumbembé* will be published in September."

"It's too soon."

"I know if we got away from Baracoa things would be different, away from the gossip, the lies . . . "

"The University needs to give a chance to other visiting speakers."

I let go of him then, and he nodded almost imperceptibly and stared ahead at the boy speeding by in the darkness. How easily he accepts, I thought, the equilibrium we struggle for. But is it real? What's going on inside him?

Although his visit to Toronto had been a success, with students flocking to his lecture on Afro-Cuban culture, most of their questions had been about Cuban politics — about the effects of the embargo, about Fidel and the future of Cuba — Onaldo had soon become bored with their tedious inquiries.

"The story of Cuba is in the experience of daily life," he'd told me. "It's not about a week in Varadero or a few conversations with tour guides."

He'd found himself for the first time an exotic figure — a not entirely comfortable experience, although he had taken it in his stride. An image flashed into my mind of Onaldo looking up at the CN tower rising above the 'towers of capitalism' as he playfully called the downtown office towers. I had photographed him bundled up in a borrowed winter jacket, those towers behind him, grinning with the adventure of it all as he looked past me into the light reflected off Lake Ontario. Leila and I had taken him to the Muskokas, where we canoed to the centre of the lake and sat in a blaze of fall colour, Onaldo's bright orange lifejacket emboldening him as he wrestled with his paddle.

"Don't you think it's a bad joke for Raúl to drop restrictions when he knows no one has divisa?"

"There are rich Cubans in Havana — people who have cell phones, computers, money to travel."

"You mean people with relatives in Miami, or with foreign lovers who find themselves providing for the whole family?"

His eyes flashed. "*Poco a poco,* little by little," his forefinger stabbed the darkness, "We find the way to survive with our own *negocios* . . . you know how hard we work."

There it was, the 'we,' excluding me as he stared directly into my eyes and the darkness closed in, enfolding us.

The young cyclist braked on an arc, spraying dust as an older boy slouched towards him, calling his name. "¡Papito, Papito! *Ven a la casa. Mami preguntaba por tí.*" The child almost fell, tumbling off the bike, hopping on one leg, then the older boy jumped on and lifted his little brother, sitting him side saddle like a girl.

I knew that Onaldo's loyalty lay with Migdalia and that, no matter how intimate we were there would always be a part of him I could never share because I'm not Cuban, I haven't lived through it.

He shifted, stretching his long legs, the familiar knobbly knees jutting through his pants. He threw one arm across the back of the bench and I felt the hairs on his skin barely touching my neck.

"Some people think the lifting of restrictions is a trap, to catch the ones with money. The fact is, Karina," he leaned closer to me, lowering his voice, "Everyone is engaged in private enterprise, one way or another, we can't survive without it, but it's all illegal. *Doble cara . . .*"

The exact words I had used when our trouble started. I'd called him a two-faced hypocrite and it had cut him to the quick. I regretted it now, thinking of all that we had lost, casualties of those prohibitions that ironically Raúl now promised to ease. And I wondered if we really had lost everything, and if it was too late, or if I simply had to brave it out and let it all wash over me.

I looked up over the rooftops and saw a tumult of stars. I was trying to return to some long-forgotten place, somewhere I had no name for. Where was that feeling of perfect security I'd had when Onaldo arrived and sat with me? If I lived in that place I would be indestructible. I wanted so badly to go home, like my old mother sitting in her own house after Chris's death weeping to go home. It didn't make sense, but I knew that if I could reach that elusive place all our conflicts would dissolve, ice in warm water. I could only glimpse that condition of bliss for a moment and then I would forget, until the next time, all the moments accumulating in me into a greater desire for freedom. Onaldo was my portal to a world from long ago, extraordinary man that he was, housing his own bundle of lies and contradictions.

"There's been a change in the laws on ownership too. It may be possible very soon for Cubans to buy and sell houses . . . "

He trailed off suggestively as I turned to look at him.

"What?"

"A house," he said. "You could buy a house in my name, in Erminda's name, it doesn't matter. I could look after it for you, arrange rentals to tourists . . . "

"And go on living in Migdalia's house?"

"*Mi amor, tu sabes la lucha.* We help each other, nothing more. Won't you give me another chance?"

"*La lucha, la lucha!* The national dance of Cuba! Someone should write the song. Everyone's singing it."

His mouth turned down at the corners. "You used to be more sensitive."

"Onaldo, all your stories — I don't know what's true and what isn't. Your return to Migdalia's house, the robbery in Havana, the building materials . . . "

"*Mi amor!*" he protested, but I cut him short.

"It doesn't matter. For me, the struggle is emotional, because my material needs are taken care of. That's how it is in my culture; we suffer because we're unhappy, not because we're hungry."

"We're not hungry in Cuba! We just don't have a choice of what to eat."

I could tell he was angry which frightened me. Onaldo could absorb a lot but when he reached his limit he would burst into flames. I'd been burnt more than once.

I gestured impatiently, searching for the right words. "*Mi amor,* one of the problems for us has been this . . . cultural clash. I feel like I'm dragging you into a world of emotions that you're not used to dealing with. I understand how you've had to swallow everything because of the political climate, so you're not accustomed to processing your feelings. How do most couples live in Baracoa? They work all week and on Sunday the men get drunk while the women clean house and do the laundry, then they go to church. Family is everything, getting food on the table, struggling to meet everyone's needs."

THE WHALES WERE TRYING TO TELL US

"Your needs are created by capitalism with televised propaganda and huge billboards like the ones I saw in Toronto," he countered.

"Yes, everybody shops," I laughed, "Even here. Walk down Jose Martí any day and you'll see crowds of people lined up outside Novedades. You know the old joke? Why do Cubans have flat noses? From staring into shop windows. You don't need ads; you have tourists walking your streets. You see our cameras, our watches and backpacks. We're walking billboards." I sighed. "At least Fidel has a sense of humour. On the road from Havana airport there's a billboard of the American president with the caption, *Bush, number one terrorist!*"

I have to give him credit for his opportunism. He seized that moment as we laughed together, and somehow he entered, fusing with me in an old familiar dance. He is the most seductive man. And when you laugh with someone like that, laughing and laughing beyond whatever sparked it, you become like children with no need for words. Onaldo embraced me then, his arms secure around my body, and his hands came up to hold my face as he kissed me. He has a beautiful mouth with a distinct cupid's bow outlining his upper lip. He had shaved for our meeting. I felt the smoothness of his skin and smelled the white musk I had given him.

"I came back to say goodbye to you, Onaldo, some final words . . . "

"There are no final words," he replied with certainty. "There are no beginnings and no endings. We belong together."

We sat in silence, balanced on either end of our teeter-totter, although we were in reality pressed close. I held my breath, unable to speak for fear of falling again under the spell of the night, into the warmth of his embrace.

Finally Onaldo spoke.

"Rosana has predicted that something is going to happen."

Rosana was a blind poet-seer who lived in Baracoa with her partially blind husband. A tiny woman with braided hair, she wandered all over Baracoa, reaching with her long white cane, her face to the sky, guided by her husband with his rolling white eyes. She had predicted Onaldo's trip to Canada before he'd even met me.

"She says something is going to happen in Baracoa, a force of energy coming from the north."

"A storm?"

He shrugged. "She's a poet. She speaks in metaphors."

Walking home along the Malecón I realized that we had not spoken of Felix. It was as though he didn't exist. The bubble I shared with Onaldo had a very specific landscape into which filtered only what fit. When I was with him everything looked different. It drove me crazy that I could live in different worlds, like a chameleon. The only time I could trust myself was when I was alone in my place of infinite possibility.

I stood on the seawall and looked out into the darkness. It had been a rare calm day and now the wind had come up and was blowing stronger every minute. I saw the blurred shape of the land rising at the end of Playa Caribe where the bay curves, and I thought of the boy who had drowned there fifteen yards from his home, taken by the familiar ocean, sucked under and swept away. I thought of my bloated dog-pig buffeted by the waves and pulled out to sea — how Yemayá grasps and takes what she wants. The wind blew a lock of hair across my face again and I turned into it, into that gathering of energy awaiting its moment.

The wind continued to blow for three days, until everyone felt uneasy with the persistence of it. By Wednesday night, two days before the full moon, the waves were rolling in fast, splashing over the parapet onto the Malecón. Erminda and I went to Irma's house and stood on her rooftop terrace in the moonlight. We felt the spray on our faces, and Erminda screamed from the corner of the balcony as a wave broke on the roof of the adjoining house. All the houses on the Malecón are joined, except where the streets run down from the cemetery on the hill, dividing them into blocks.

"*¡Dios mío!*" Erminda exclaimed as we scuttled down the narrow stairs to the ground floor. Already people were running to help their waterfront neighbours move their valuables to the upper floor, where one existed, or to someone else's house.

The ocean pounded the town all night and as I joined Erminda on the front steps on Thursday morning and looked down the street I saw the waves rising higher and higher, leaping over the parapet onto the Malecón which was now a river running southwest with the force of the wind behind it.

All morning the wind gusted as hundreds of people were evacuated from their homes. Helmeted firemen rescued those stranded on upper floors with nothing between them and the ground but broken stairways. The force of the water had taken everything and still it raged. Refrigerators and mattresses were tossing in the waves; sections of the side streets had been lifted and lay scattered in broken lumps of concrete. Teenage boys waded in the river, snatching at chair legs, plastic roses, a table floating upside down like a life raft. They were deaf to the people screaming at them as the waves gathered and swept in relentlessly, crashing against whatever was in their path with a force that drove the spume fifteen metres into the air.

Erminda would not leave her house. She was washing the bed linen in her new washing machine, still entranced with the novelty of its accompanying spin dryer. "With all this wind," she said, "the sheets will dry quickly."

I went out with my camera and walked to Parque Colón where I saw the entire bay of Playa Caribe awash with sweep after sweep of surging, sucking foam. Sections of the seawall had been broken and the Malecón was impassable. People stood solemnly watching the assault of an ocean risen beyond its limits for the first time in human memory.

"Nothing," an old man said, turning his cloudy eyes on me, "Nothing has been as bad as this, not the hurricanes, nor the tornadoes, nothing. It was unimaginable and here it is before my eyes. The whales were trying to tell us."

But this was only the beginning of what was to come.

I started walking east, one block above the flooded Malecón, and as I captured the jubilant spume with the eye of my camera, I was soon coated in a fine spray of salt. A small man in a ragged red shirt danced on the edge of the newly created river, elated by the energy of the waves, then came another wave exploding and everyone screamed and ran back up the street, the swirling water pursuing them, swallowing everything in its path. A group of people had clustered high on the cornice of a crumbling building. I watched them, imagining a wave lifting them, carrying them out with its irresistible suction. But no-one was taken, no-one drowned — only the material accumulation of their difficult lives floated senselessly out to sea.

When I reached La Rusa I saw the street all broken where Onaldo and I had stood on the day of Pedro Iván's death, before we knew. The waves that had tossed the bloated dog-pig had seemed turbulent, but were dwarfed now by all that had happened. I couldn't believe it had been only four months. Those months had passed with the fullness of years.

A uniformed woman was sweeping water from the doorway of La Rusa. I saw the emptiness inside the bar where we'd sat, the furniture gone, the television, the bottles. People stood silently outside on the broken sidewalk, blank expressions on their faces. Some would appear on the television that night, on a special programme devoted to coverage of the national emergency, with helicopter footage of boys braving the river and a vortex swirling above an invisible drain sucking everything under.

I took Calle Máximo Gómez, the street behind La Rusa, and walked towards Parque Infantíl, past women standing in the wet rubble of their balconies, unusually silent, their hair rollers covered by little scarves. The only sound was from the children, screaming and splashing each other.

The park was completely destroyed — the swings and teeter-totters had become columns of twisted metal, the cafeteria and hibiscus bushes were gone, the walls were strewn along the flooded sidewalk, piles of broken concrete with here and there a fragment of painted elephant trunk, a monkey's ear, tiger's paws. The only section of the wall left standing had three animals on it — a bull, a donkey, and a duck.

Beyond the park the La Punta school was an evacuated shell, and the local market building was destroyed, its wooden stalls in splinters. On market days when the big trucks had rolled in from the countryside those stalls had been piled with tomatoes, cabbages, malanga, boniato, cucumbers, with braids of garlic and golden onions hanging from the awnings. All destroyed. The gardens of Cabacú would be flooded with salt water. They would have to bring in many truckloads of earth before they could replant.

I turned back towards Parque Infantíl and walked through thick red mud, congealing like blood, looking for our bench. But when I found the place it was gone, all gone. I stood there listening to the echo of Onaldo's voice — *There are no final words — no beginnings and no endings*... I turned once more to watch the water, ephemeral in its constant motion, like a playful animal, mindless of its power. And I knew he was right.

↤

Epilogue – Day of the Tsunami

January 2010

HAITI IS ONLY EIGHTY KILOMETRES SOUTHEAST OF Baracoa so when Port-au-Prince was struck by a devastating earthquake a tsunami alert was immediately broadcast by helicopters over the town of Baracoa. It was around six in the evening, already dark, people just home from work, cooking their dinner. After the helicopters came trumpeting their message over the rooftops 30,000 people were evacuated from their homes in more or less twenty minutes, not to mention people up and down the coast, from Maisí to Boquerón and beyond.

In small places large events become apocryphal. Stories sprout from tiny seeds, spreading their roots underground, and after they've flowered and gone to seed again the wind of *chisme* comes and carries the tales all over town until they become the realities of daily discourse which govern lives and provide the markers that are required to hold a people together.

The tsunami is spoken of daily in Baracoa. Aches and pains are blamed on it. Events are measured by it. Dogs were lost in the confusion, muscles were strained, houses were abandoned and things lost, although no actual robberies were reported.

Pausing only to pick up Loli and tuck her under his arm, Onaldo ran for the high ground of El Castillo. Yolanda and her family ran from their house in La Playa, clinging together in the crowds, climbing through the mountains in the darkness with no flashlights, no boots, sloshing and slipping barefoot through the mud — it had been raining for days. People in the centre of town and in La Punta headed directly north to El Castillo with Onaldo and Loli, while on the other side of town Erminda and Nando climbed with their neighbours up the steep hill towards the archeological museum of El Paraíso.

"Nothing, we took nothing," Erminda says as I stand in the doorway of her kitchen, watching her heat oil in a frying pan. "And there was no panic, Karina. We were calm and orderly, as Raúl told us to be."

A woman's voice calls from the front porch, "Erminda, it's me! I have platanos from my garden!"

"Come in, come in!" Erminda shouts, and turning to me, "It's Mirian Zelda, remember? From the *casa* next door to *la funeraria*."

She abandons the egg she's frying and hurries to the front *sala* to talk with her friend. Low voices, urgent discussion, the tone belying the content.

"*El día del tsunami . . .* " Erminda begins, preface to yet another account of her aching back. The doctor has told her that she has muscle contractions caused by running up the hill to safety. There were people in wheelchairs, she says, old folk with canes, Evangelia with her painful legs, supported on either side by her sons, and people all around looking for their children, their dogs . . .

"The Serrano family struggled up the hill with their mother's coffin," Mirian Zelda says as she rocks back and forth in Erminda's kitchen chair, "But there were two funerals on that day, and the Penalba family abandoned their *abuela* and ran for their lives."

"*Chica*, she was already dead," Erminda says. "What more could God do to her?"

At the hospital Léster, in the midst of a surgery, had sewn up his patient rapidly, making sure to remove all swabs and clamps from the man's gut, and had run for his own life with the nurses and interns. Those who were mobile were helped to safety while the others were left to fend for themselves, be they on intravenous, drugged, or anesthetized. The day of the tsunami had all the makings of a *tele-novela*, but it was even better because it had really happened and everyone had lived through it, survived it, shared it, and bore the scars to prove it. They had been spared, *Gracias a Dios*. To many this was a miracle of divine intervention, causing church attendance to swell, while others knew that there was a natural explanation — it had been a horizontal and not a vertical earthquake.

Erminda confides to Mirian Zelda over her congealed egg that the doctor could have been wrong, because in fact she had not rushed up the hill. She had walked slowly, taking her time with old Nando, so how could she have strained a muscle? No, it was something else, the pain was directly behind her heart.

Irma arrives with her stethoscope and she cuffs Erminda's arm and inflates it to measure her blood pressure. This is their daily ritual, part of a code that Cubans use to communicate the stresses and strains of their difficult lives, a code which masks the larger issues that hold the personal in their massive grasp, and over which ordinary people have no control.

After it is done and her high blood pressure confirmed once more, Erminda tells her joke about an island full of people with *presión alta* — about the explosion of her pressure cooker, parachuting everyone to Miami, Canada, Spain. *"Me voy a Canadá!"* she chirps, winking at me and thumping a bunched fist into her palm in that familiar Cuban gesture.

Three years in a row Baracoa is hit — first with the storm that floods the Malecón and destroys Parque Infantíl — just a beginning — then with a series of hurricanes, the third one, Hurricane Ike, touching down in Baracoa, flooding the town for three blocks, destroying homes, driving people to higher ground. (Teófilo names one of his new kittens Ike). The evacuated families take refuge with their relatives, crowding together, filling narrow spaces while they wait for new homes that could take years to build, like the house Alicia was promised when the hurricane of '97 destroyed her mango house. She moved into her daughter's apartment for emergency refuge, hardly expecting to die there twelve years later, just as Fidel perhaps did not expect tourism, adopted as an emergency measure, to become the dominant agent of change in his country. But life in Cuba is a long emergency.

The government has plans to build on higher ground above the town of Baracoa, but the Malecón dwellers want to stay near the ocean. It is inside them. They walk back to their devastated homes and begin to piece them together, refusing to relocate.

With each storm warning Lorenzo collects more plastic to cover his clothing and shoes. He hunkers down and watches the huge waves from his refuge in the bay at El Turey. He would rather drown with his German mementos than leave the water's edge.

And then, on January 12th of 2010 the tsunami hits, truly apocryphal since it never manifests, but has consequences nevertheless. The threatened tsunami gathers and focuses the people of Baracoa in yet another triumph over adversity, echoing down through their difficult history.

Lorenzo climbs the steep hill to Hotel Porto Santo which sits between the airport and the bay with a sweeping view over the town. On the cliff top, above a tiny beach where newly married Cubans go to be photographed, (the groom plunging into the waves with his bride in his arms and her dress trailing in the salt water), stands a facsimile of the wooden cross reportedly staked by Columbus in 1492. Many people are clustered there watching the ocean anxiously, as the Taíno watched in wonder when Columbus approached in his white-sailed galleon.

The angel in the cemetery high above Baracoa watches the ocean for a sign — another sighting of whales in the bay, another swollen dog-pig swirling, another creature rising from the deep.

The stone head of Antonio Maceo watches from the summit of El Yunque. Each year on April 1st he sees the procession from the Obelisco, which marks the spot at Playa Duaba where he disembarked during the war of independence against the Spanish. On that day the streets are full of vendors and revellers and there is free beer, weak and watery, flowing in the streets.

Disembodied souls hover briefly over the house of Mirian Zelda but then, like humming birds, they dart away, searching for the bloody hibiscus. Only they know the answer to the mysterious disappearance of Marek Svoboda.

After centuries of stillness El Caimán lifts his lazy snout a mere centimeter as a camera drifts by and is then sucked under by a wave. After the hurricane Onaldo had been snapping pictures of the flooded streets when a wave snatched the camera from his hands, leaving his face shocked, his throat raw, as though the water were a living thing with a grip and slap as firm as flesh. Or perhaps he merely sold the camera — who can say? Life must be embellished, stories told, or we would die of boredom. Imagine his *memoria flash* taken by a thieving ocean, his story of the Havana robbery floating like a message in a bottle, desperate for a reader, a listener, some response — like the farmer standing in his parched fields being interviewed by a foreign journalist, agreeing with Fidel's numbing statistics about the harvest, saying all the right things until the very last question.

"Do you have a message for our worldwide listeners?"

"*Help!*"

El Caimán begins to stir in his long dreamtime. His tail twitches. His snout quivers. He dreams of opening his great jaw, snapping at the air with a hunger so voracious that he could twist his body and consume himself then rest again, regenerating in the salty, stinking embrace of the primordial ocean. As he wakes, his golden-red eyes opening and blinking lazily, he realizes that his dream is not indeed a dream. He tastes his own blood, chews on his flesh, tender beneath the scaly skin, and he is intoxicated, his pain subsumed by the satisfaction finally of his hunger. How can you love and betray at the same time? This is how.

All around the snout of *El Caimán* the ocean turns red, a skirt wavering and disappearing along the fragile coastline as the land is slowly submerged.

⤚⚬⤙

ACKNOWLEDGEMENTS

THESE STORIES SEEK TO EXPRESS THE LOVE, admiration and deep commitment I hold for my Cuban friends — people who have inspired in me a passionate curiosity and a desire to understand them in their many and fascinating complexities, their contradictions and infuriatingly evasive ways.

Thanks to Tomás Aquilino Lopez for the title of this book and for being my Cuban reader, adviser, and a trusted friend; to Susan Barker, Joy Gugeler, Aija Mara, Anne Milligan, and Susan Hurlich for reading and giving valuable critiques; to Susan Barker for the Valentine's Day anecdote; to Wolf Borenstein for his generosity and inspiration; to Viv Moore for her longstanding friendship; and to David Cupper who primed me for my first visit to Cuba.

Thanks as always to the sterling people of Thistledown Press, and to Seán Virgo for his editorial expertise.

Thanks to Miguel Maury, a true friend in Havana; to Steve Paulsson for his love, support, and generosity with his copy-editing skills; and a huge thank you to Lynn Hutchinson who first suggested Cuba to me, who was an early reader and sensitive critic of these stories, and whose friendship and understanding have been essential during this process.

∾

"The Death of Pedro Iván" won the Prism International Creative Non-Fiction award in 2008 and was published in Vol 47:2 of *Prism International.*

"Her New Red Dress" was published as "Linancia", 2007, Vol 30:4 of *Room Magazine*

"The Barbacoa" and "La Terraza" were published as "The Barbacoa", 2009 in Vol 31:4 of *Room Magazine*

"Señora Amable Ponce" was a finalist for the *Malahat Review* 2009 Creative Non-Fiction award.

The "Ololo" poem was written by Lynn Hutchinson and Amanda Hale.

CURRENCY NOTES

CUBA'S DUAL ECONOMY DATES BACK TO AUGUST 1961 when a boat carrying seven tons of new currency, printed in Czechoslovakia and bearing the signature of Minister of Finance Che Guevara, anchored in the harbour of Santiago de Cuba. The old Cuban peso, pegged to the US dollar, had been replaced by new currency, worthless outside Cuba, as a solution to the private stockpiling of cash that was financing counter-revolutionary activities.

With the collapse of the Soviet Union in August 1991 Cuba went into financial crisis as it faced the US trade embargo without the aid of its post-revolutionary benefactor. In 1993 the US dollar became legal tender, encouraging hard currency to enter the economy. A year later the convertible peso was introduced at par with the dollar.

In 2004, once again in crisis due to hoarding, the government withdrew the US dollar from circulation. The result is a two-tiered economy consisting of the Cuban peso (*moneda nacional*) and the convertible peso (*convertibles* or *divisa*), used by foreigners in exchange for their own national currency, and worth twenty-four times the value of the Cuban peso.

AMANDA HALE has published three novels. *Sounding the Blood* was a Fiction finalist for the BC Relit Awards; *The Reddening Path* has been translated into Spanish, and is available in English as an audiobook; *My Sweet Curiosity* was long-listed for the Relit Awards. Hale divides her time between Toronto, Hornby Island, BC, and Cuba.